IMAGES
of America

WARRINGTON REVISITED

The Warrington Historical Society, formed in 2007, is a 501(C)(3) nonprofit corporation. The seal of the society consists of a rendering of the County Line School House located at 10 Folly Road; the year 1734, recognizing the founding of the township; and the year 2007, representing the establishment of the historical society. (Courtesy of the Warrington Historical Society.)

On the Cover: Joseph H. Penrose Sr. and a farmhand harvest the farm's crop with the help of two strong horses. Being pulled behind the wagon is a loader, which was used to lift the crop up and over the back of the wagon. The men in the wagon would use three-tined pitchforks to fill it until no more could be loaded. (Courtesy of the Penrose family.)

IMAGES
of America

WARRINGTON REVISITED

Mary Doyle Roth and Kenneth Samen
for the Warrington Historical Society

ARCADIA
PUBLISHING

ISBN 978-1-4671-2247-4

Published by Arcadia Publishing
Charleston, South Carolina

Printed in the United States of America

Library of Congress Control Number: 2014935711

For all general information, please contact Arcadia Publishing:
Telephone 843-853-2070
Fax 843-853-0044
E-mail sales@arcadiapublishing.com
For customer service and orders:
Toll-Free 1-888-313-2665

Visit us on the Internet at www.arcadiapublishing.com

This book is dedicated to past residents who invested in the township's future and current/future residents who take interest in the township's past.

Contents

ACKNOWLEDGMENTS

On behalf of the Warrington Historical Society, I would like to recognize our vice president, Kenneth Samen. He initiated this project and committed to an earlier submission date so the book could be received before the important holiday sales season. In order to present a more well-rounded history of the township, he sought out interesting images. Ken completed the draft by selecting and formatting the pictures and documenting the descriptions. He also recruited his wife, Melissa Samen, to be our volunteer editor. She spent many days recommending better wording after every revision. Gwyn Walton also edited and reviewed, and she made some great revisions. The society thanks them for their hard work producing *Warrington Revisited.*

With this book, email and social media were important tools for us. We were able to reach out to more people and received their information and images quickly. We gratefully acknowledge all of the people who dug through their family archives to find us interesting pictures and facts. The individuals are too numerous to be listed here, but without their contributions, this book would not be possible. I hope they are pleased with our presentation of their recorded histories. Although we could not fit all of their stories and pictures into this work, we do plan to make them part of our newsletters.

We extend special thanks to those who have been involved in the conservation of Warrington Township's history. Those recently active include Connie Ace, Stuart Cohen, Greg Ford, Kathy Newcomb, Mary Doyle Roth, Ken Samen, Donna Sempowski, Sean Stetler, Carol Lee Vosteen, Gwyn Walton, Shirley Yannich, and Scott Yates. Those previously active include Dotsie Dillingham, Jane Henderson, Jayne Lester, Tom Mackin, Krista McDemus, Sarah Murphy, Don Riley, Sue Sowden, and Joe Wright. Former township historians Bill Lueckel and Dolores Deabler Capone deserve special recognition since they were the originators of many of the images and documentation we rely on today.

The best part about working on a book like this is reliving all of the great Warrington stories and memories. It was a wonderful place to grow up!

Unless otherwise noted, all images appear courtesy of the Warrington Historical Society.

—Mary Doyle Roth
President, Warrington Historical Society

INTRODUCTION

A 1684 map created by Thomas Holme (William Penn's surveyor) is the earliest known documentation that makes reference to the area now known as Warrington Township. This map confirms to historians that there were five landowners in the Warrington vicinity—Samuel Carpenter, Charles Jones, Robert Vickers, Richard Sneed, and Richard Ingels—none of whom lived on the land that they owned. During this time, the area consisted of unbroken wilderness and was populated by a few small traveling villages of Native Americans called the Unami ("people down the river") of the Lenni-Lenape tribe ("original people," "men among men"). Artifacts found years ago by farmers plowing their fields show that one of these villages was located at the western boundary of the township on the slopes above the Neshaminy Creek, where Park Creek and Little Neshaminy Creek meet. Another village was located on the eastern boundary of the township, close to Little Neshaminy Creek, where the Palomino Farms Development is today.

Several historical writings from over 125 years ago on the subject of Warrington Township begin with a quote taken from the record of the October 1734 General Court of Quarter Session: "Ordered that the land above and adjoining to Warminster Township shall be a township, and shall be called Warrington." At the time of Warrington Township's organization, documented landowners were William Allen, John Jones, Andrew Long, Mathias Lukens, Robert Miller, John/Robert Nailor, Joseph Paul, Daniel Pritchard, Charles Tennent, the London Company, and the proprietaries. As time went on, the population grew, as noted in United States decennial censuses: 1790—NA (census data lost), 1800—NA (census data lost), 1810—429; 1820—515; 1830—512; 1840—637; 1850—761; 1860—1,007 (this increase due in part to the expansion of township borders); 1870—949; 1880—NA (almost all of the 1880 census data was destroyed in a fire in 1921); 1890—820; 1900—883; 1910—822; 1920—822; 1930—1,139 (Joseph Barness built his first house in 1925); 1940—1,307; 1950—2,336; 1960—4,148; 1970—7,550; 1980—10,704; 1990—12,169; 2000—17,580; 2010—23,418. The data from the census clearly shows the progression of Warrington's growth from a sparsely populated agricultural community, consisting of open land and farms, to a community of housing developments, industry, and shopping centers.

Below is text of the earliest (and largely unknown) documented history of Warrington Township from the *Business Directory and Gazetteer of Bucks County, Pennsylvania*. It was written by S. Hershey in 1871.

> Warrington is one of the western border line Townships of the County. With the exception of the Northeastern line, which is somewhat irregular, the Township is in shape a parallelogram. It is bounded on the Northwest by New Britain; on the Northeast by Doylestown and Warwick; on the Southeast by Warminster and on the Southwest by Montgomery County. The Township is 4 miles in length, and 2 1/2 miles in width, containing an area of 5,397 square acres. The surface is generally undulating, and inclined to be hilly. Agriculture is the principal pursuit of the inhabitants. Most of the Township is well adapted to Agriculture,

but some portions of it having a thin marshy soil, is better adapted to grazing and dairying. Several of the most prominent public roads in the County intersect the Township, and the tributaries of the Neshaminy drain all parts of it.

Early History: Amongst the early purchasers of land were Samuel Carpenter, Charles Jones, Robert Vickers, Richard Sneed, and Richard Ingels. Nothing is left on record to show that any of the persons named were actual settlers in the Township. The Governor of the province, Sir William Keith, in 1721 purchased a tract of land of 800 acres, partly in Horsham Township, Montgomery County, and partly in Warrington Township, Bucks County. He caused roads to be laid out to connect with Philadelphia. The greater part of one of these roads is now the Doylestown and Willow Grove turnpike. Owing to the contiguity of the Western line Townships to Philadelphia; they were often overrun by British soldiers, during the occupancy of that city by the British army. General Lacey, a General in the American army, and a native of Bucks County, was intrusted [sic] with the command of a detachment of American soldiers, and sent to protect these regions from pillage. Many sanguinary conflicts took place in Warrington and Warminster, with varying fortunes, until the British were forced to evacuate Philadelphia, when the incursions ceased, to the great relief of the inhabitants.

Creeks: Little Neshaminy—this is the largest stream of water in the Township and runs obliquely across the Southern part of the Township, from Montgomery County, and after leaving Warrington enters into the Northern corner of Warminster.

Neshaminy Creek—though this stream does not touch the Township, several of its tributaries have their source in the Northern and Middle portions of the Township.

Towns: Eureka—formerly called Pleasantville, is on the line, between Bucks and Montgomery Counties. It contains a store, hotel, German Reformed Church, and about 8 dwelling houses. The Post Office called "Eureka," that is on the Montgomery County side, has but recently been established.

Warrington Square—but more often called Neshaminy, is situated on the Doylestown and Willow Grove turnpike road. It contains a store, hotel, coach, and other shops, and about 10 or 12 dwelling houses.

Warringtonville—is a business little village, situated on the Doylestown and Willow Grove turnpike road, in the Northeastern part of the Township. It contains a store, hotel, large coach and smith shops, and about 15 dwelling houses.

In celebration of Warrington Township's 280th anniversary in 2014, the Warrington Historical Society proudly presents *Warrington Revisited*. The journey of the township from past to present will leave readers with a sense of pride for what has come before them and what will take place in the future.

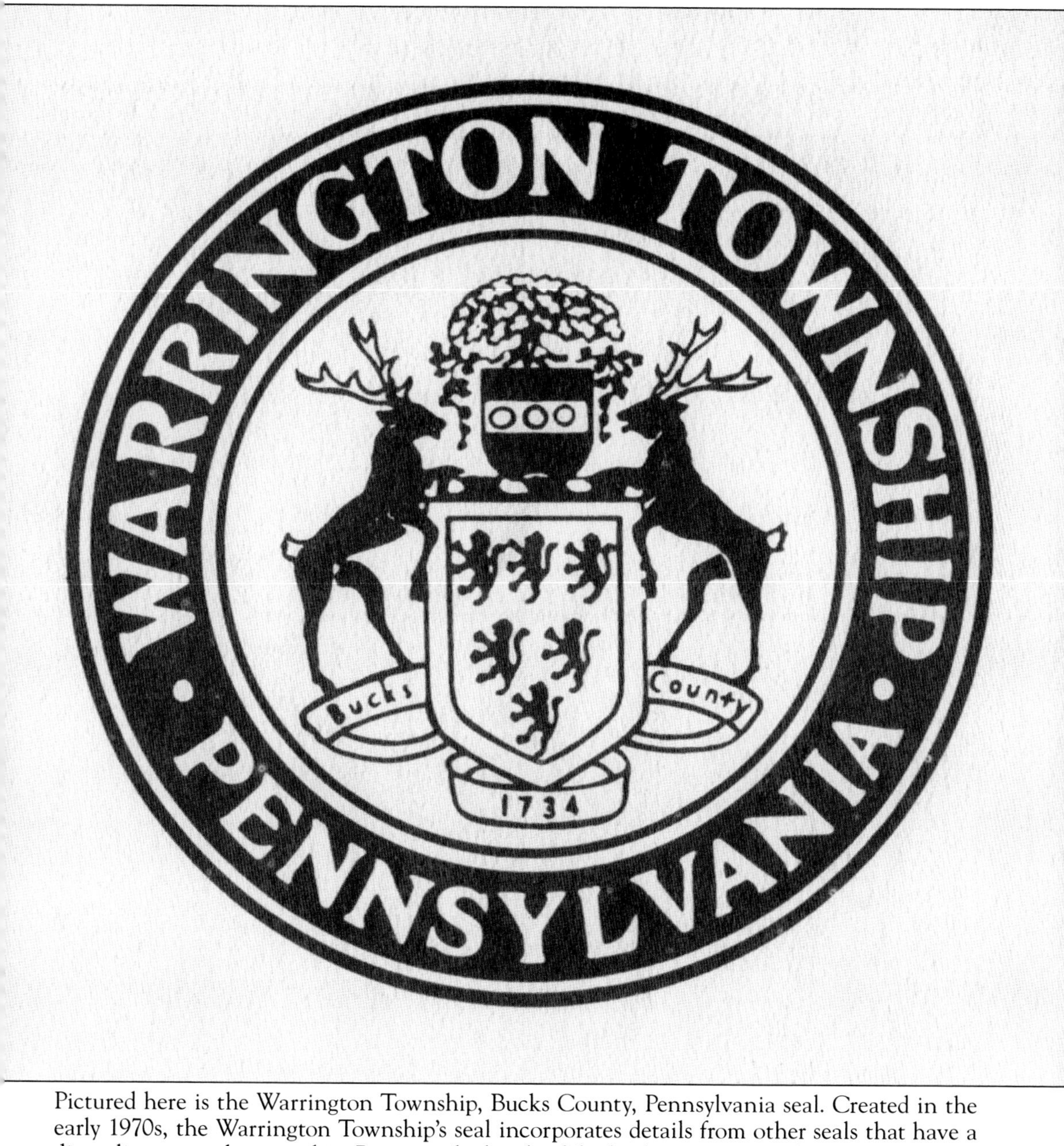

Pictured here is the Warrington Township, Bucks County, Pennsylvania seal. Created in the early 1970s, the Warrington Township's seal incorporates details from other seals that have a direct lineage to the township. Between the heads of the bucks are a tree and vine. These items were inspired by the Bucks County seal and were originally directed for use by Penn's Council in 1683. Under the tree, to honor a portion of the William Penn family crest, is a small shield with three circles. The two bucks also frame a large shield bearing six standing lioncels. This portion of the township seal replicates part of the crest of the Warrington Borough Council, located in England, and symbolizes the family of the first Lord of Warrington, Paganus de Vilars. The lioncels traditionally symbolize bravery, valor, strength, and royalty. Finally, the stated year of 1734, at the bottom of the seal, represents the year Warrington Township was formed.

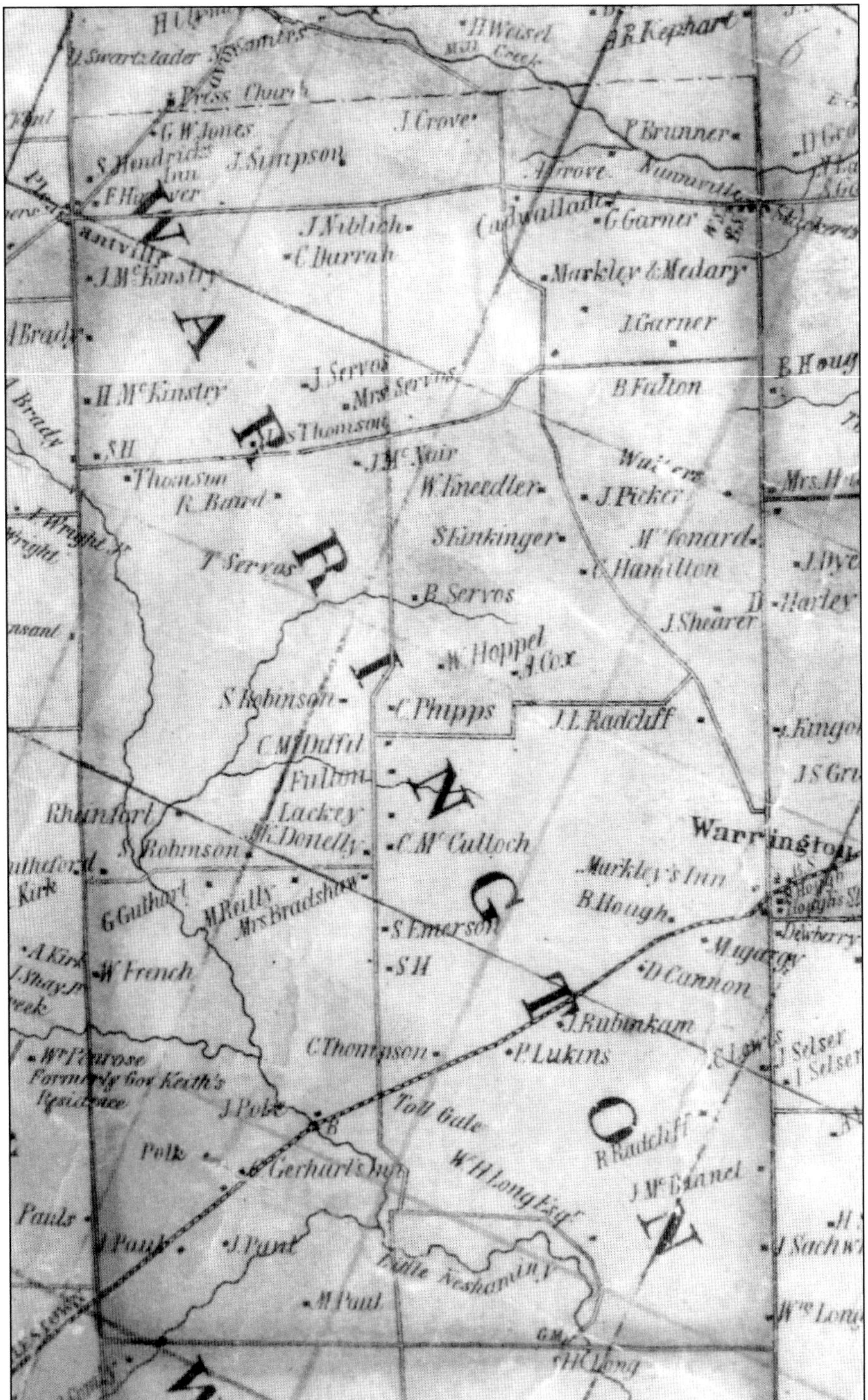

This map, produced by W.E. Morris, depicts Warrington Township at its original (and smallest) size. The borders of the township encompassed the area situated just north of Lower State Road, Bristol Road, Valley Road, and County Line Road, consisting of 5,397 acres, or 8.43 square miles. The township soon expanded its borders in February and September 1850.

One

Lost Structures

Many noteworthy events have taken place within Warrington Township's borders during its 280 years of existence. Numerous individuals and families of great significance were born, lived, and died on this land, and many important structures were built and razed along its lanes, roads, and highways. The following images represent just a few pieces of Warrington Township's history that have been lost to time, development, and modernization.

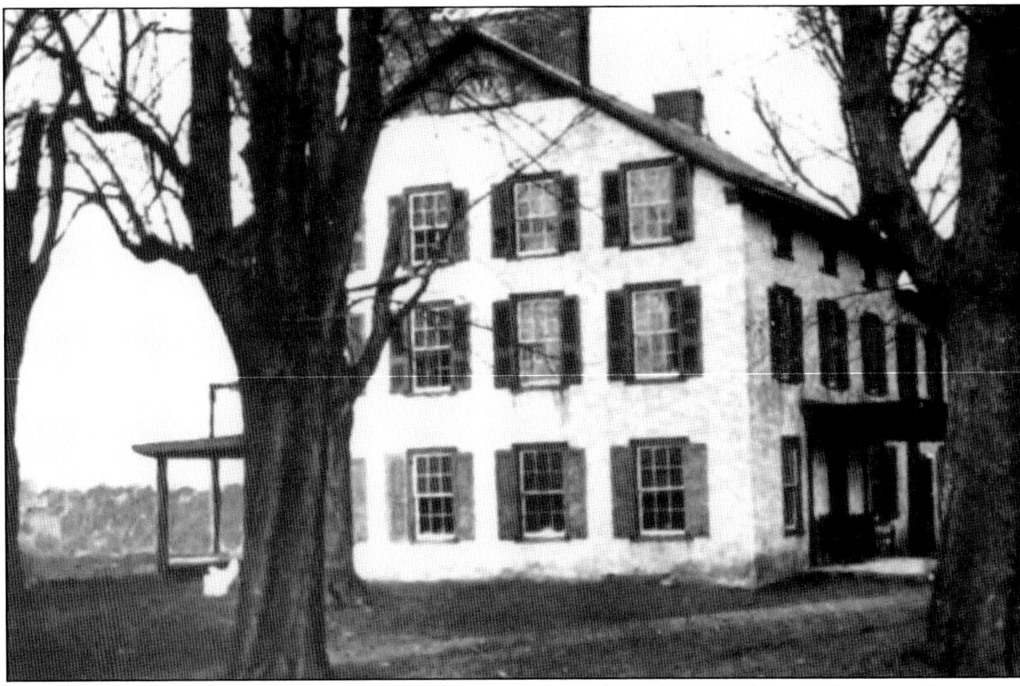

On November 2, 1727, Joseph and Elizabeth Paul purchased more than 300 acres of property in what would later become Warrington. Their son James married Mary Worth, and in 1749, James and Mary built the original homestead that was located at 213 Easton Road. Pictured is the house as it stood in the late 1920s. Later, the Penrose name would be linked to the property through marriage.

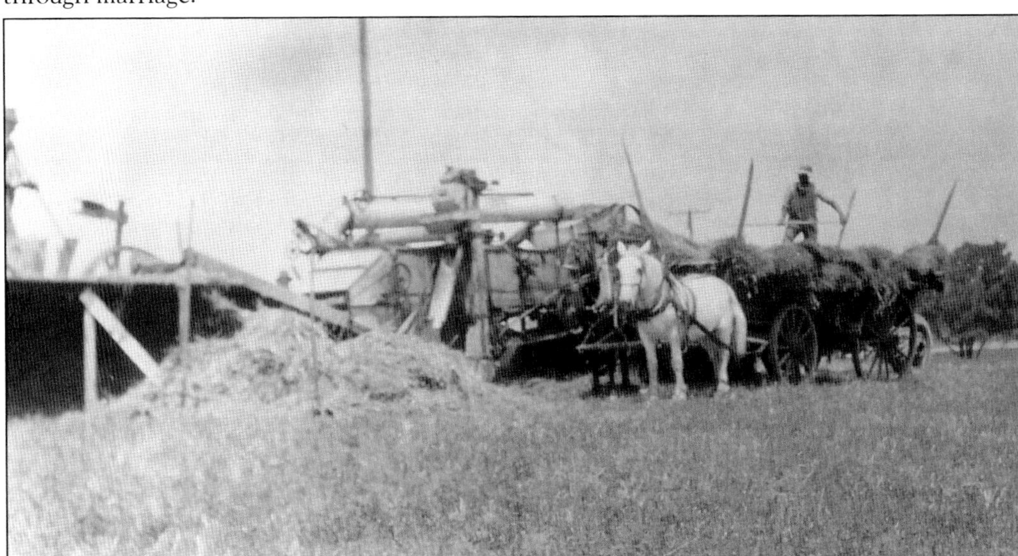

The William Penrose farm was described by W.W.H. Davis in 1905 as "one of the extensive and valuable farms of Warrington Township, comprising 300 acres, upon that are three sets of farm buildings, houses, barns and outbuildings. It is surrounded by a fine stone fence, the gates being formed by heavy pillars, and beautiful forest and evergreen trees adorn the land, while in the rear are many fine fruit trees."

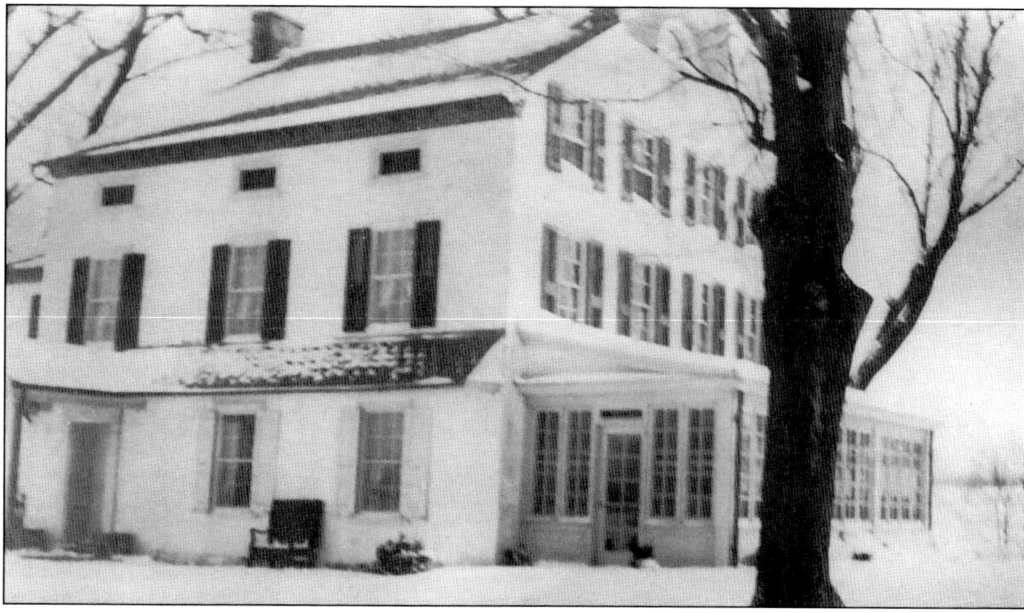

For a period of time, the house at 213 Easton Road was used as a tenant house, with the Penrose family living in a more accommodating home across Easton Road. This house was greatly "modernized" in 1929 when the Penrose family decided to once again occupy it. The remodeling included a new back vestibule and the addition of a single-story porch/sunroom to the side of the dwelling.

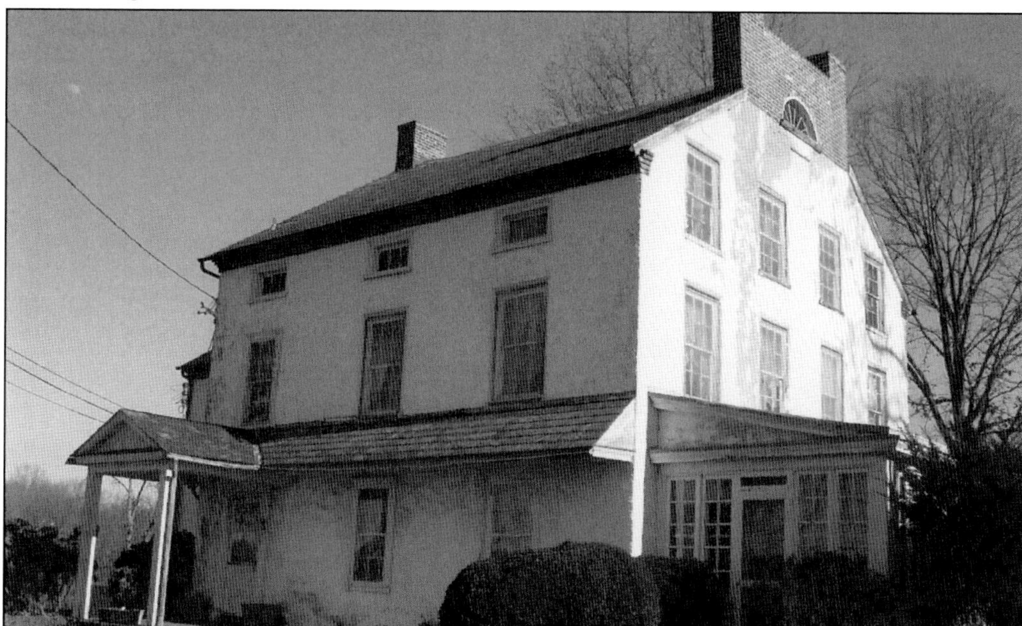

In early 2011, the remaining 69 acres of Penrose land were put on the fast track for development. The house that had stood on the property since 1749 and other farm buildings were eliminated from the development plan. On May 20, 2011, the house was destroyed by the developer. Date stones and a few other artifacts were to be preserved, but these were lost during the demolition process.

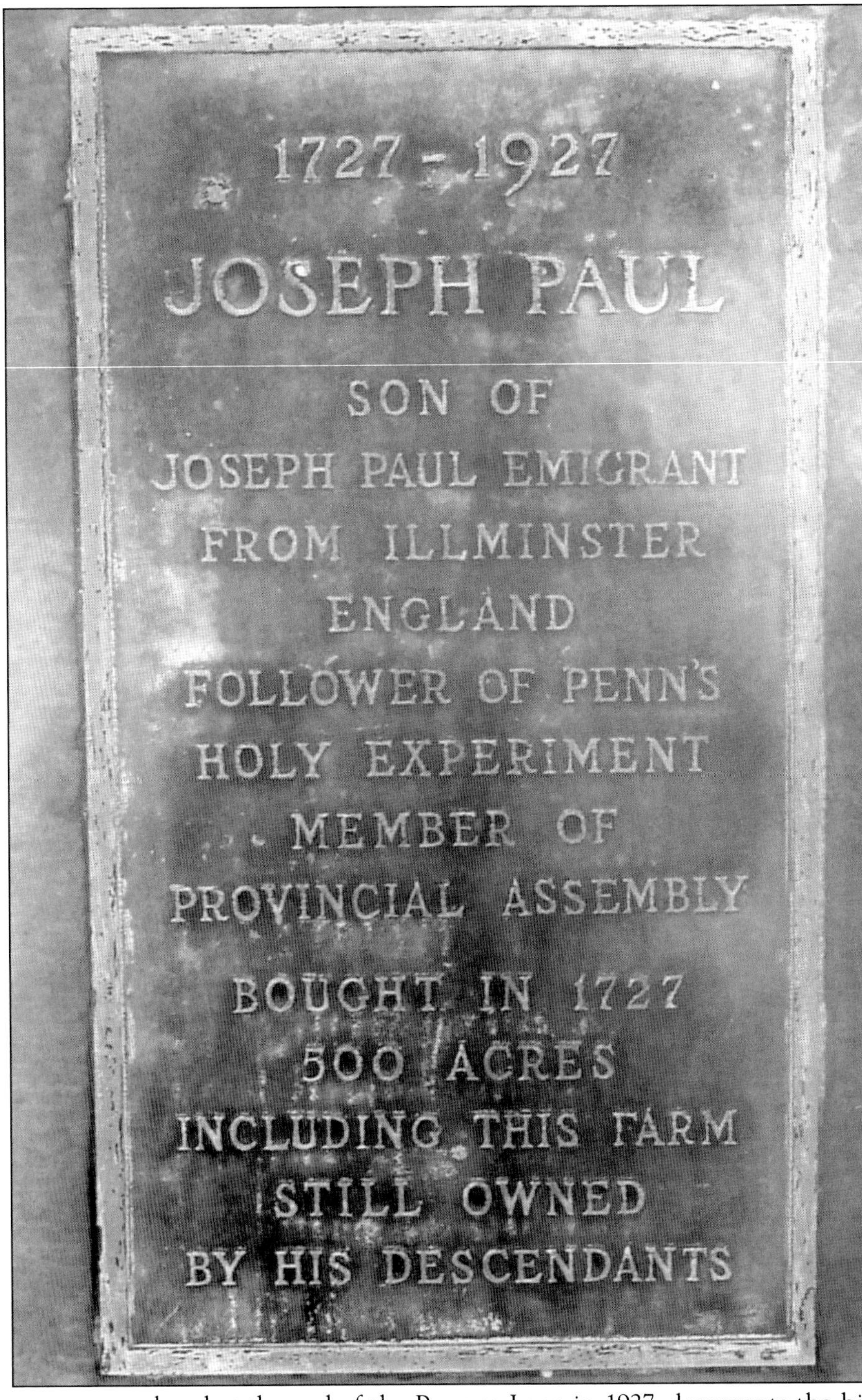

This monument, placed at the end of the Penrose Lane in 1927, documents the historical ownership of the property that was located at 213 Easton Road. In July 2009, the property was sold for development, thus ending 282 years of ownership by the descendants of Joseph Paul. This monument was to be preserved, but it was lost during the demolition process.

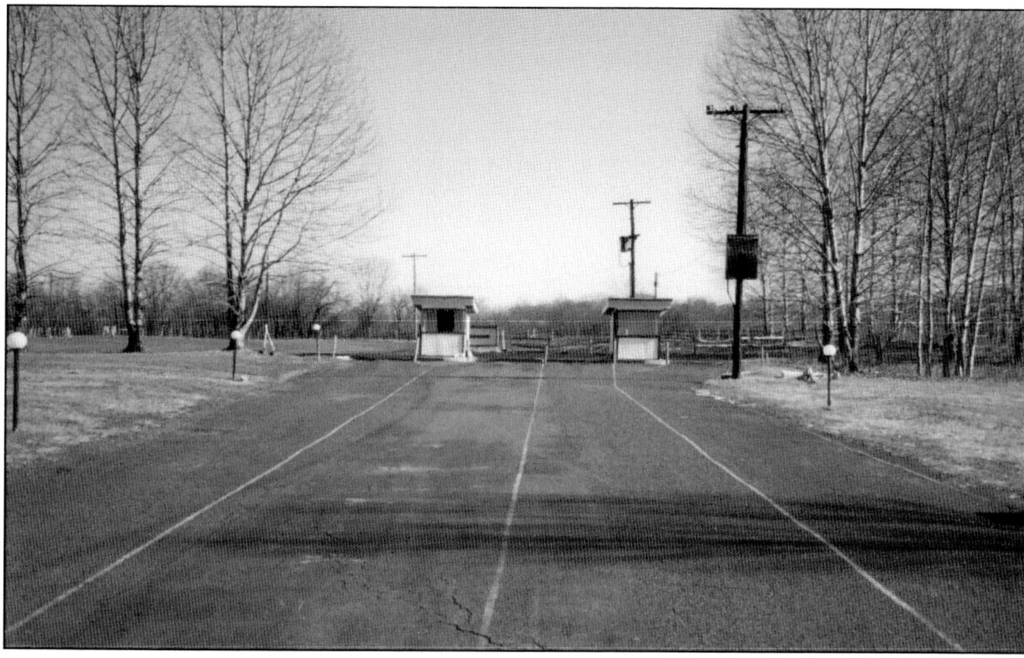

In 1951, Joseph Penrose Sr. opened a drive-in movie theater at 401 Easton Road. The Bucks County Drive-In originally had one screen and no snack bar. This was the first drive-in in the area to install in-car air-conditioning. Later, the drive-in housed two screens, a snack bar, bathrooms, and a playground. (Courtesy of Robin Anderson.)

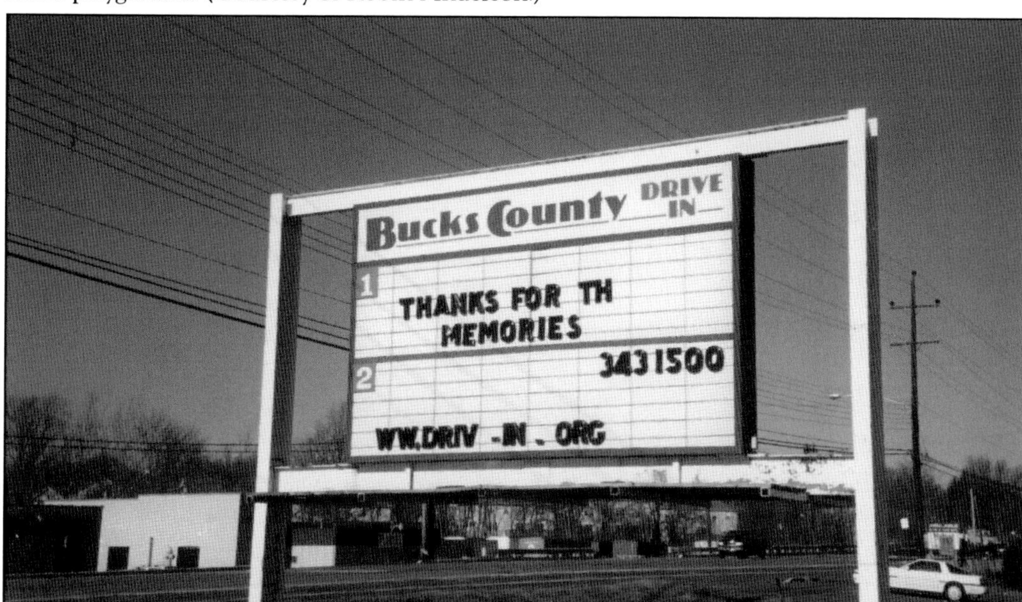

Once the second screen was added, the drive-in was known as the Bucks County Twin Drive-In and could park over 750 cars. It was forced to close in 1999 when the property was sold to developers. The Bucks County Twin Drive-in in Warrington Township was the last survivor of the outdoor movie experience in the area. (Courtesy of Robin Anderson.)

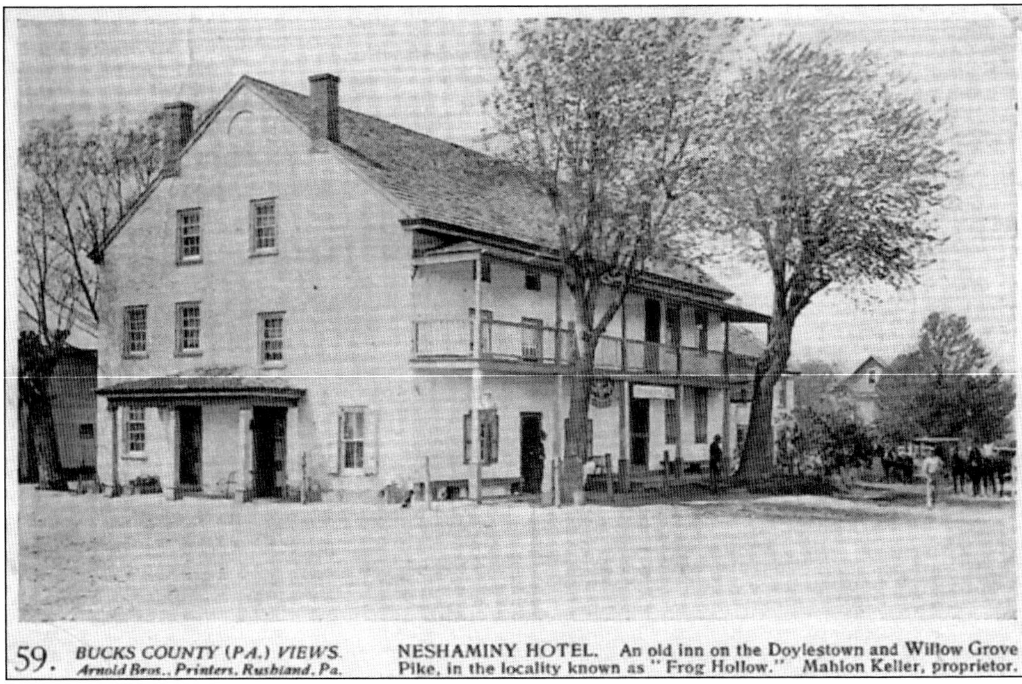

In 1876, Mahlon Keller bought and maintained the inn (seen here around 1910). For many years, the inn served as the location for Warrington residents to vote and as an assembly place for township organizations, including the school board, township supervisors, and fire department, to meet. (Postcard published by Arnold Brothers; courtesy of Peter Brunner.)

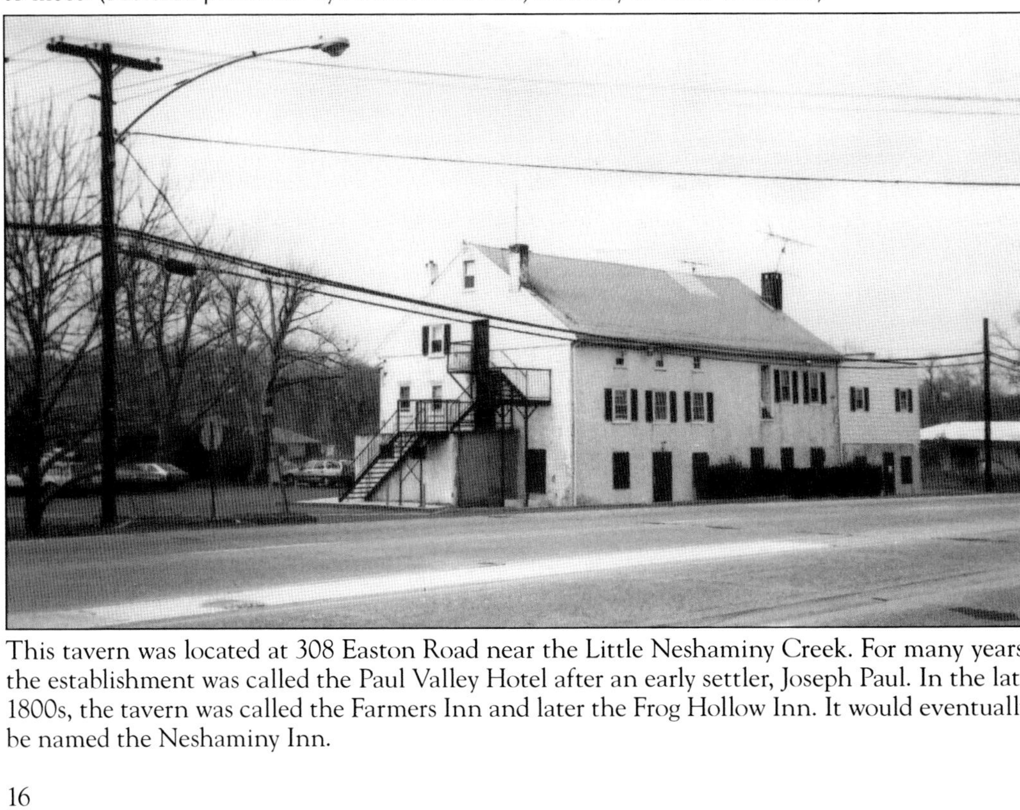

This tavern was located at 308 Easton Road near the Little Neshaminy Creek. For many years, the establishment was called the Paul Valley Hotel after an early settler, Joseph Paul. In the late 1800s, the tavern was called the Farmers Inn and later the Frog Hollow Inn. It would eventually be named the Neshaminy Inn.

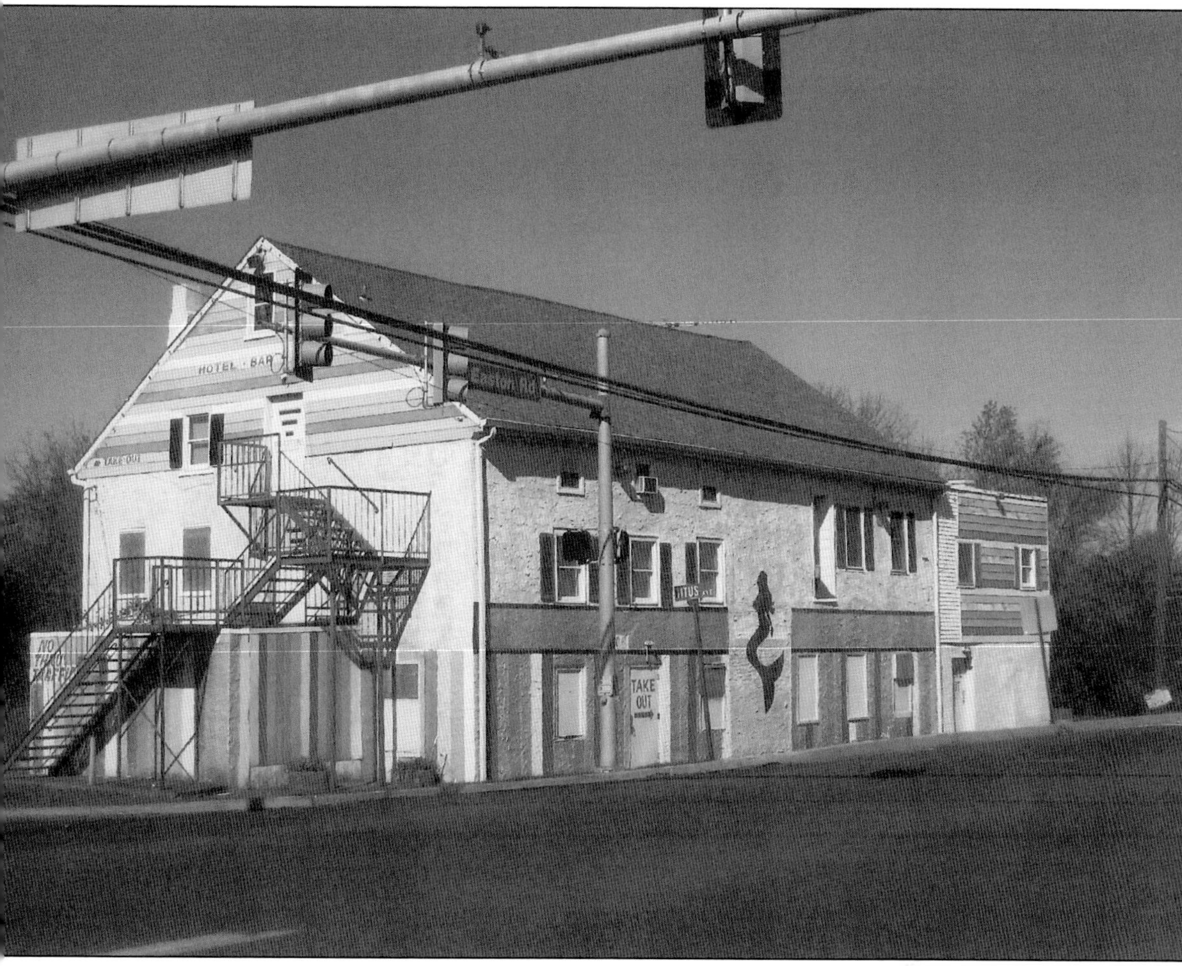

As Easton Road became more traveled, the need to widen it was inevitable. First, the trees that shaded the front of the inn were removed. Then, the overhangs and porches fell victim to the need to keep traffic moving. Later, the roadbed of the intersection that used to be level with the door entrances was raised about three feet. Joseph Hirsch bought the building in 1964 and renamed it the Old Time Hotel. He purchased an adjoining parcel in 1965 for around $25,000 and opened the establishment as a go-go bar. In the early 1990s, Hirsch painted the building a series of brightly colored stripes in response to the supervisors' attempt to ban signs that depicted nudity. The inn was razed in July 2013. The building constructed to replace the inn houses a mural that tells the rich story of the Neshaminy Village's past.

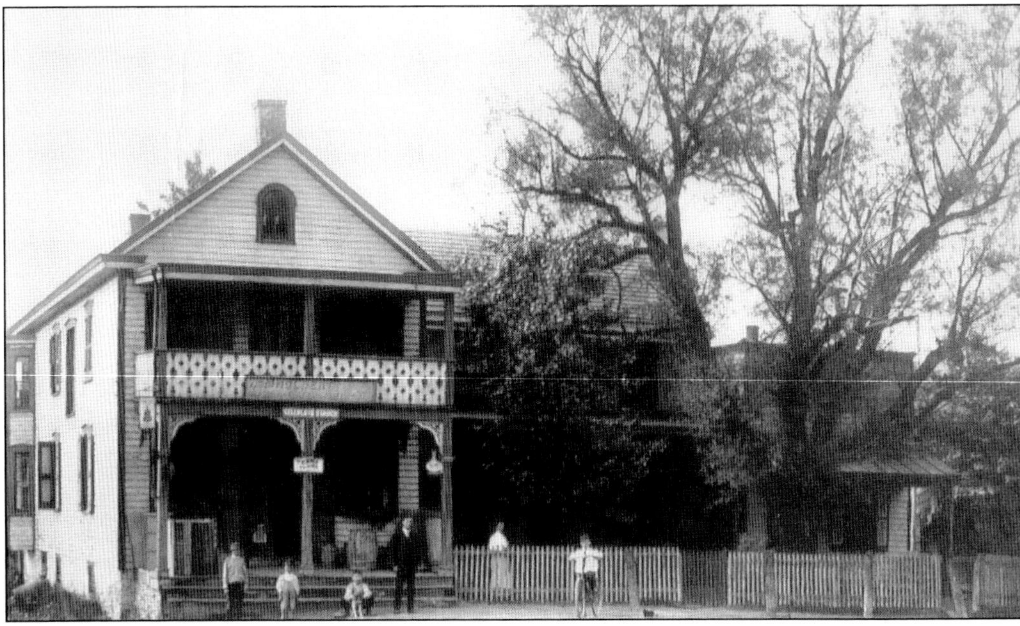

Long before Wegmans, Walgreens, Lowe's, and Home Depot, there were general stores. Frances Gurney Lukens, William Holbert, Norman Cornell, and Ervin Mayer were all past keepers of this general store and post office located at the corner of Bristol and Easton Roads. Today, this is the location of a gas station. (Courtesy of the Holbert family.)

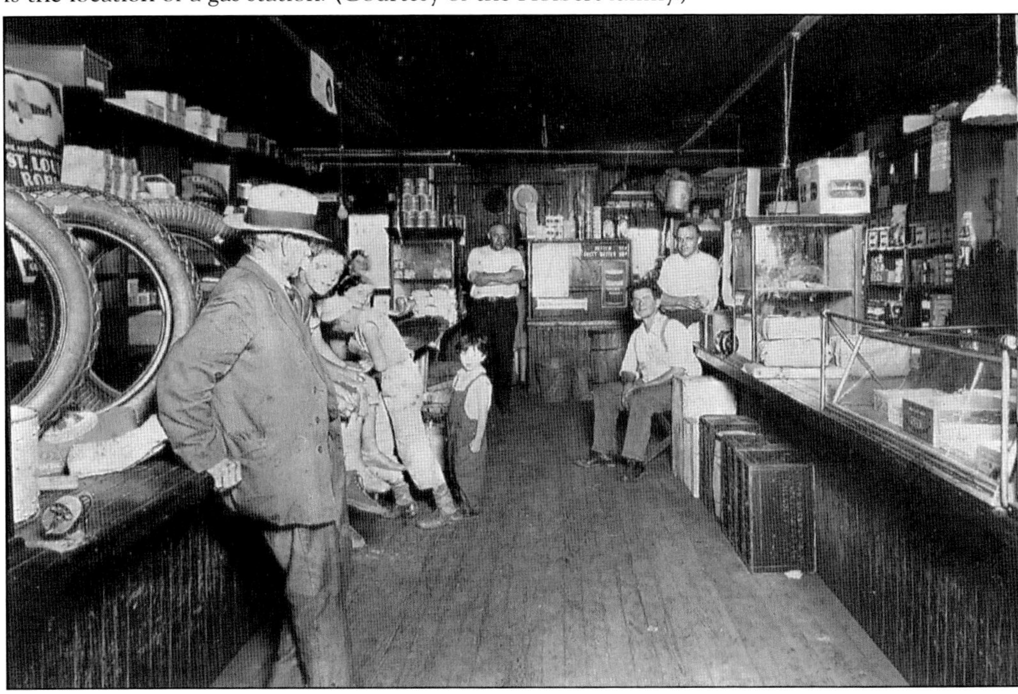

This photograph from the 1930s shows the inside of Holbert's General Store and the type of merchandise that was available under their ownership. General merchandise was located on the main floor, while linens and clothing were displayed on the second floor. The village's mailboxes can be seen on the far right. (Courtesy of the Holbert family.)

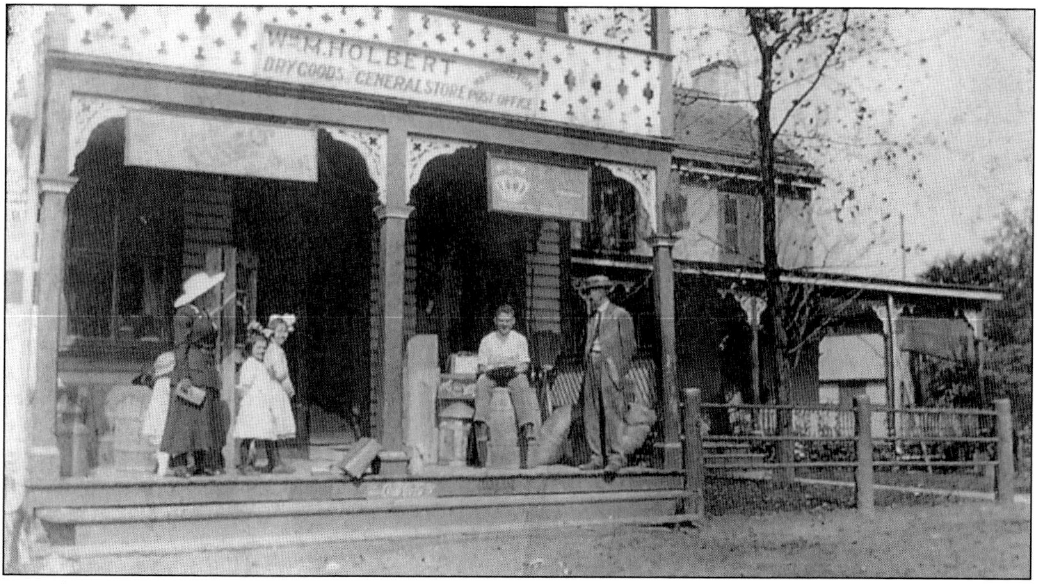

Seen here is a close-up view of the porch at Holbert's General Store, taken around 1925. Norman Cornell bought the general store from William Holbert in 1929 and owned it until 1944. Holbert went on to run a hardware store next door that his son Howard would one day manage. (Courtesy of the Holbert family.)

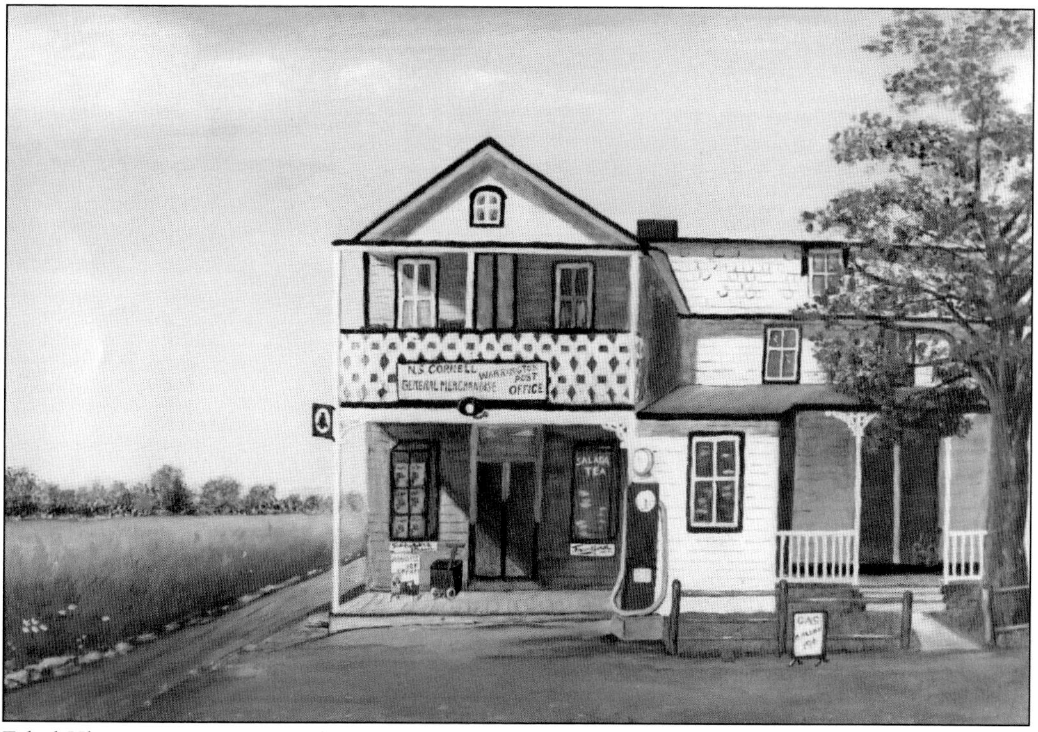

Ethel Klein, a community volunteer and avid painter, painted many views of Warrington. Her painting of the Cornell general store hangs in the large meeting room of the township building. Walt Burger purchased the store a year before the building was taken by the state for the widening of Easton Road.

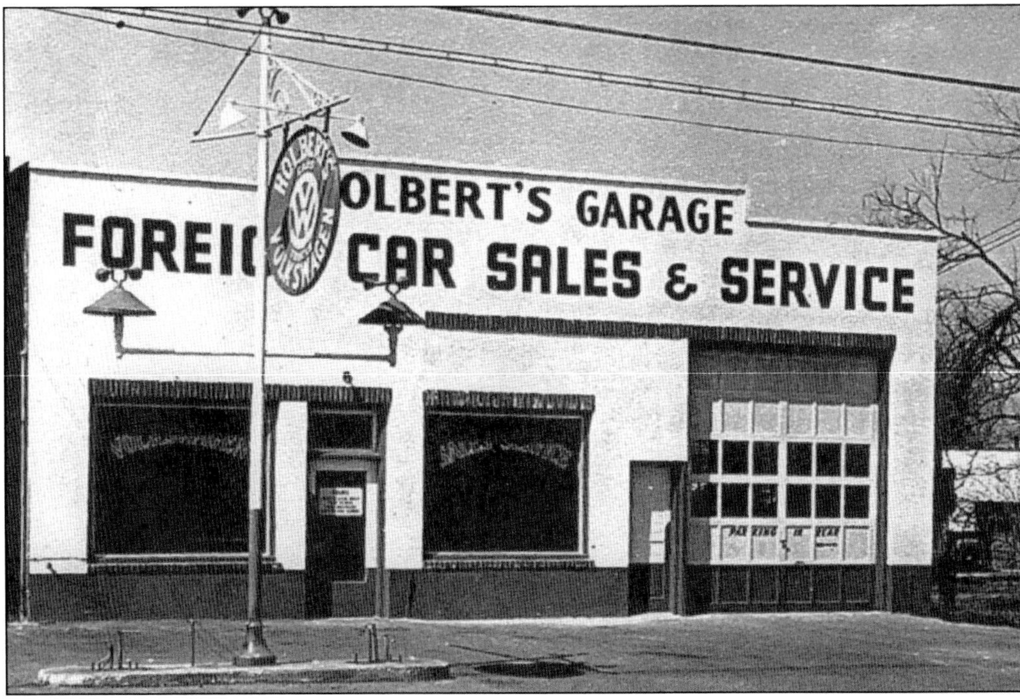

In 1951, Bob Holbert (Howard's son) started a repair-and-parts business specializing in foreign and sports cars. It was appropriately named Holbert's Garage and Foreign Car Sales & Service. In 1954, Holbert's Garage became one of the first authorized Porsche dealers in the country. In 1955, Volkswagen was added to the inventory. (Courtesy of the Holbert family.)

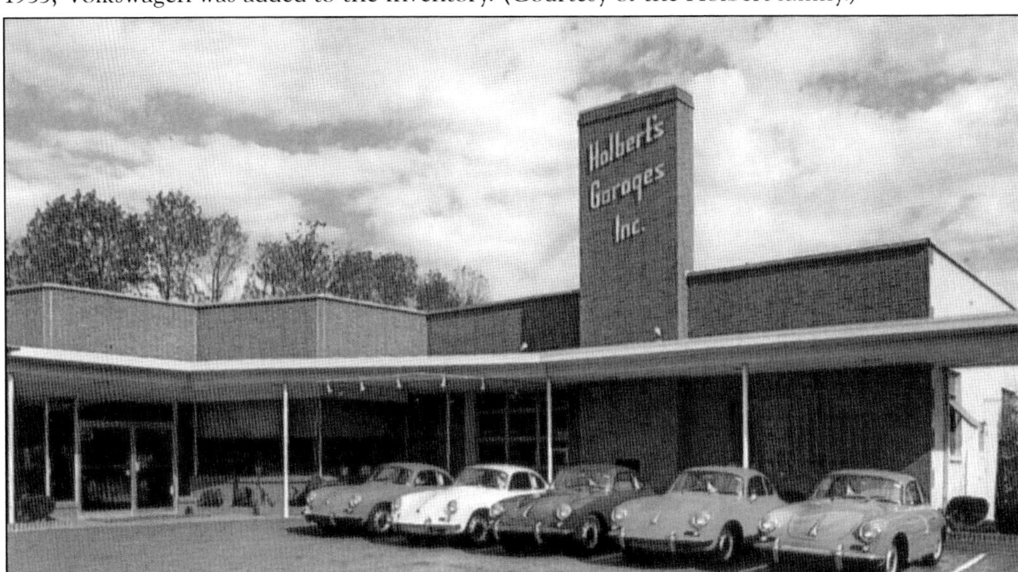

Bob Holbert built this structure, located behind the Hatboro Federal Savings at 1409 Easton Road, and used it from 1959 through 1969. The postcard pictured here shows the dealership with a row of classic 356B Porsches for sale. After 1969, the dealership relocated to larger accommodations next door and later expanded again a little farther down the road. The Thompson Organization purchased the dealership from the Holbert family in December 2010.

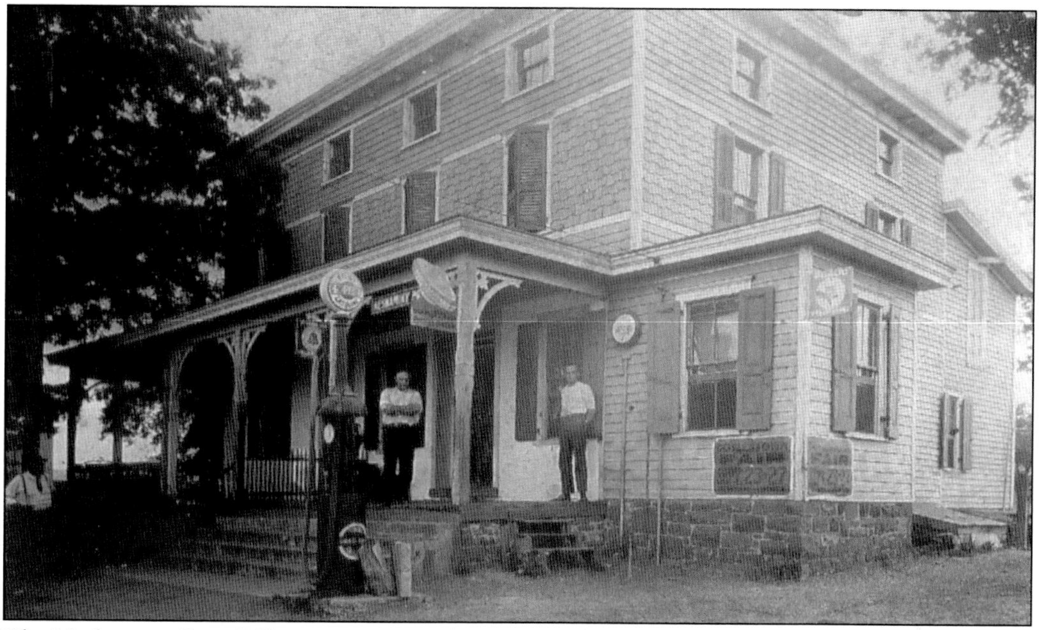

The Neshaminy Post Office was organized in 1865 with Daniel S. DuBree as postmaster. On July 26, 1867, John H. Worthington was appointed postmaster at Neshaminy. The post office at this time was located in the Worthington General Store. Frank L. Worthington ran the business from 1869 until 1883, when Walter S. Worthington took over. (Courtesy of David Paterson.)

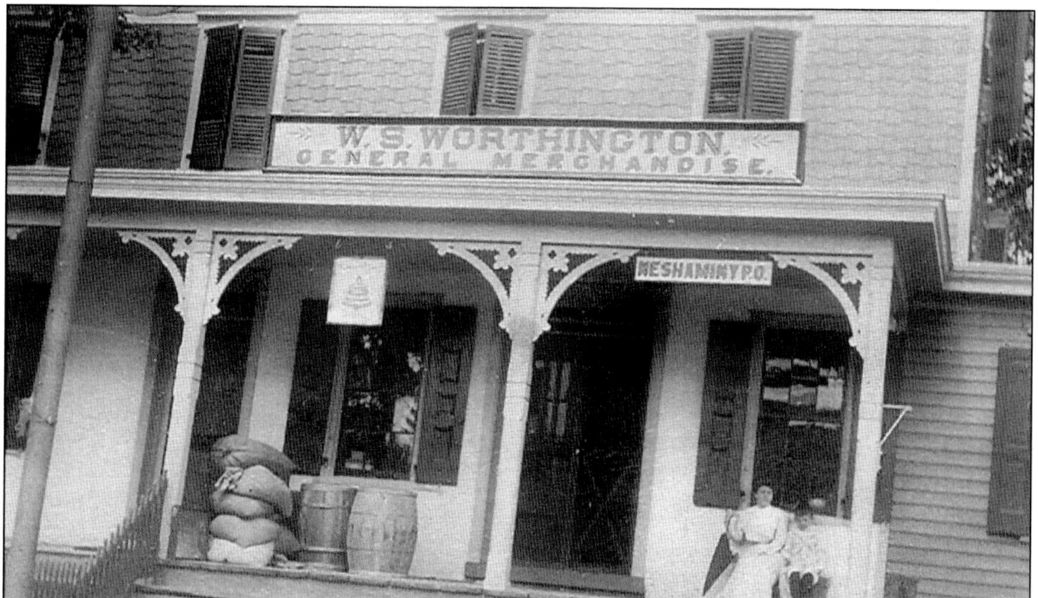

This view of the entrance of Worthington's General Store was taken in the 1920s. After Walter's death, sons David and Ralph owned and managed the store. The first unofficial firehouse was located in a garage behind the store, and at the top of the garage sat a bell to summon the firefighters in the event of a fire. The store was razed in 1960 when Easton Road was widened.

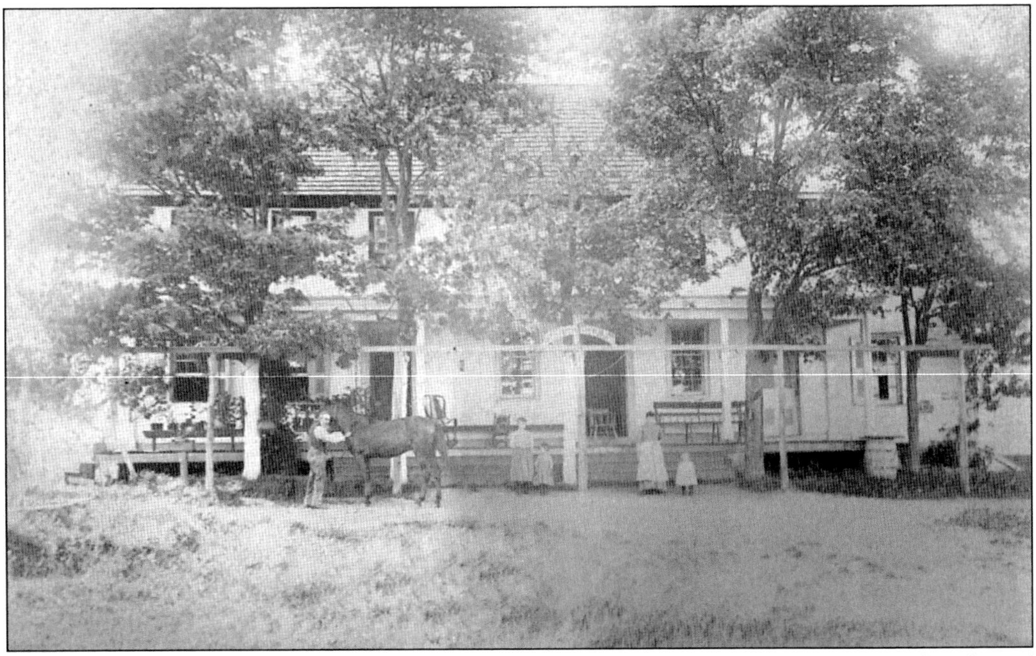

The Green Tree Inn (also known as Eells Foot) was constructed around 1834 on a wedge-shaped property between County Line Road and Limekiln Pike. When built, it was part of an 18-acre parcel. The property was divided into small fields, an orchard, and a wooded area. (Courtesy of Sandra (Hacking) Eckert for the Holt family.)

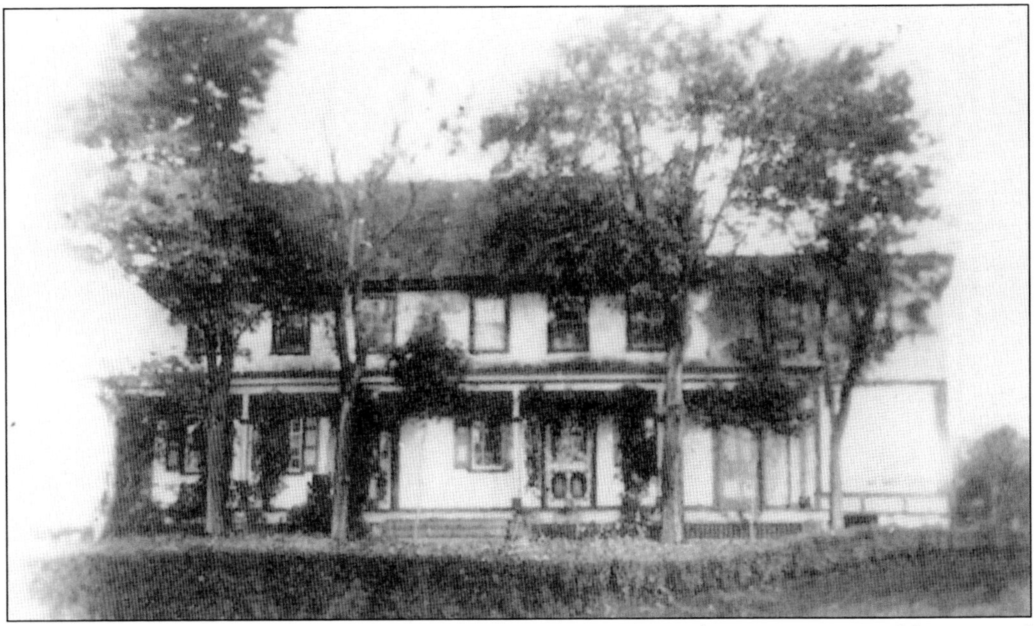

The tavern was a large structure originally built of stone and stucco. Many additions and modifications were made to the building over the years. Records indicate that Jacob Kephart was owner of the property in the 1830s, when he purchased it for $3,750. The property was later sold to William Snare. Rowland Dannehower eventually came to own the inn, only to sell it to John Kenderdine in 1867.

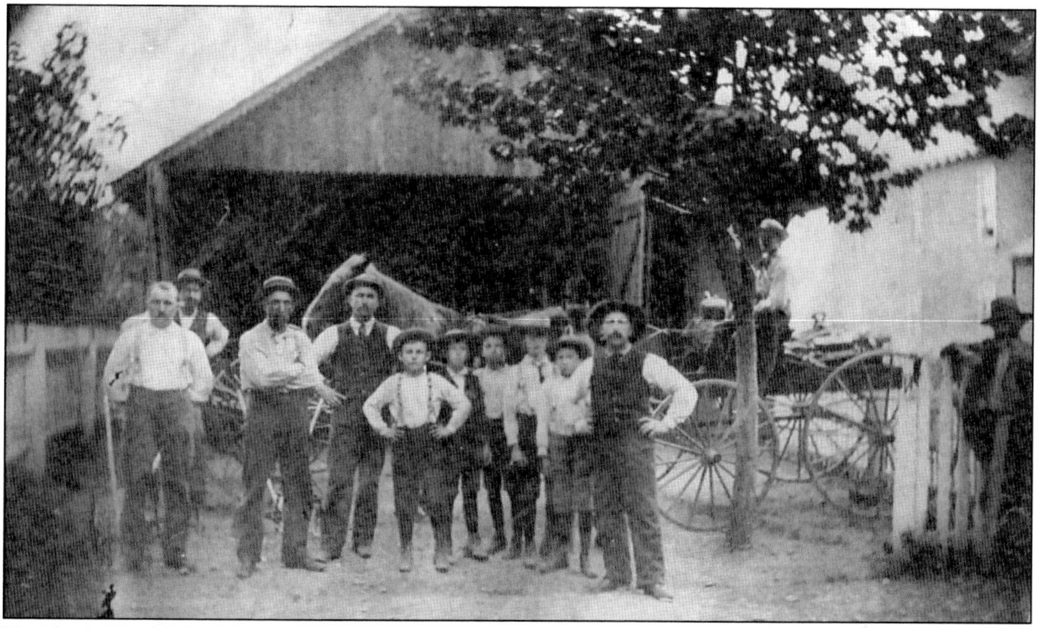

Kenderdine sold the inn to Elwood Holt for $4,300 in 1875. Pictured here during Holt's ownership is a group of farmers. Holt sold the inn to Harry Baker for $5,000 in 1891. Later, the Nash family would buy the property to use as a home. (Courtesy of Sandra (Hacking) Eckert for the Holt family.)

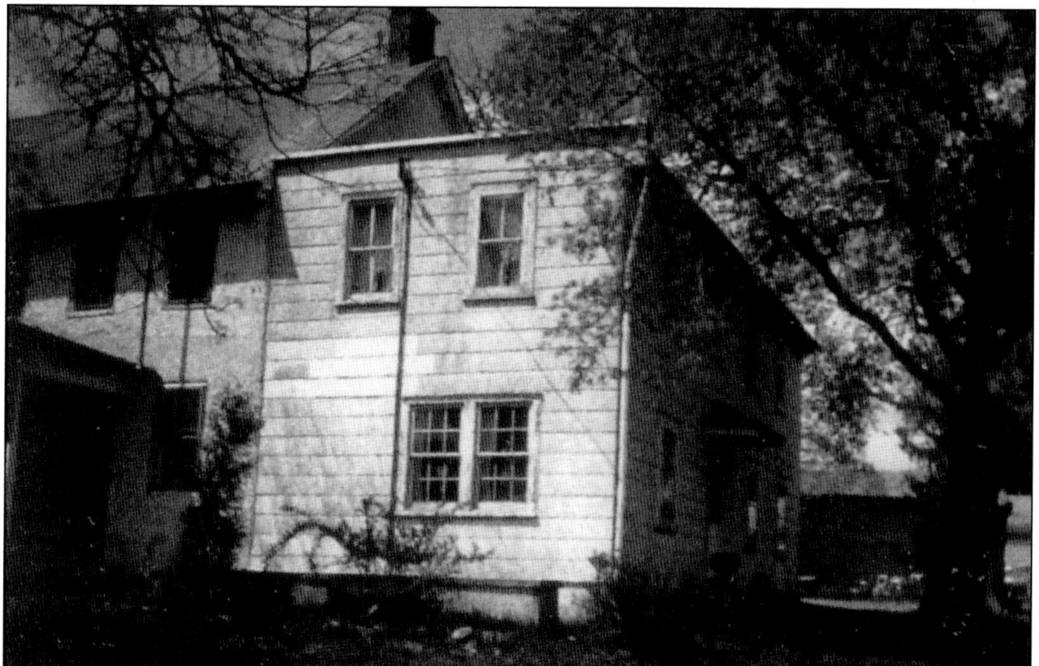

In 1933, Abram Nash submitted plans to build houses on part of the former tavern property. The Woodlawn Homes development on Woodlawn Avenue was originally built for the descendants of the Nash family. The inn was torn down in 1984 to make way for a landscaping business, which in turn was torn down in 2007 to make way for the Warrington Square Shopping Center. (Courtesy of Barbara Case.)

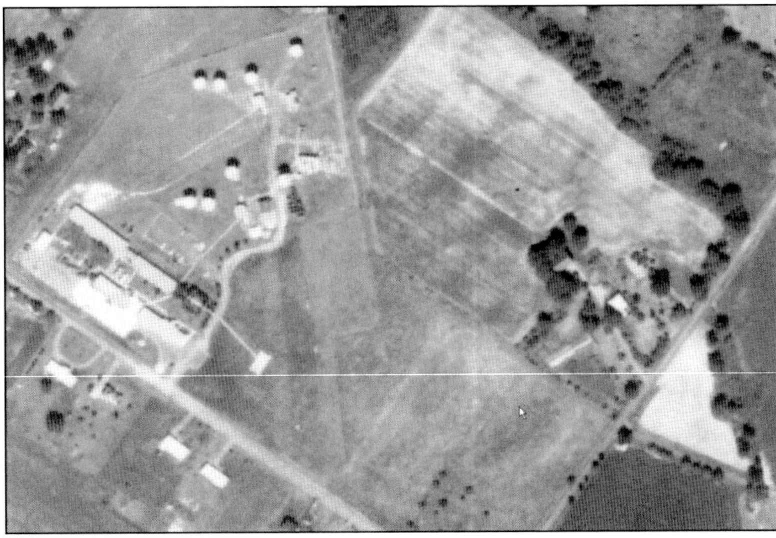

In 1954, two properties in the western part of the township, off Folly Road near County Line Road, were conveyed to the federal government. They were a 27.5-acre parcel located at Folly and Bradley Roads and a 23.7-acre parcel located south of Folly Road. Shown here is a 1965 aerial view of the fire-control area.

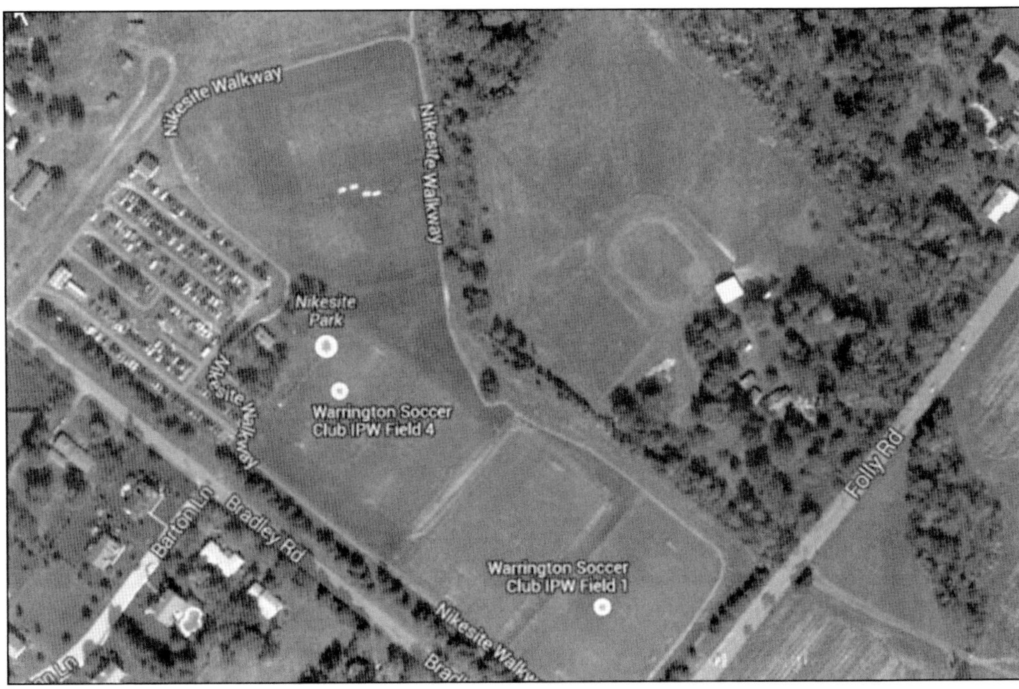

In the mid-1950s, the Philadelphia District of the Corps of Engineers supervised the construction of a circle of 12 Nike Ajax missile sites, averaging 25 miles from the city center. They were constructed to protect Philadelphia in the event of a Russian missile attack. Each Nike site had two sections, an integrated fire-control area and a launcher area. The fire-control area at the Eureka/Warrington site, now known as Igoe-Porter-Wellings Memorial Park (Upper Nike), included radar detection devices (which would warn of potential targets), barracks, a mess hall, two headquarters buildings, and fire-control facilities. This Google aerial view from 2010 shows where the fire-control area was located. (Imagery (c) 2014 DiditalGlobe, US Geological Survey, USDA Farm Services Agency, map data (c) 2014 Google.)

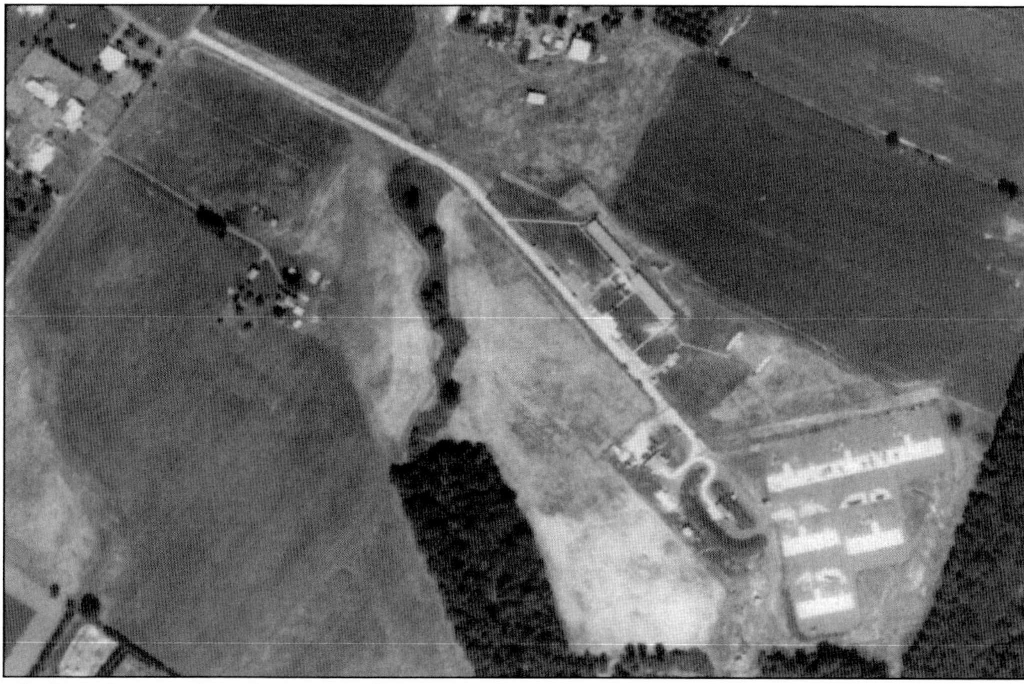

The launcher area (now known as John Paul Park at Lower Nike) was the location of the underground magazines that housed the launchers and missiles. In addition, a missile-assembly and -testing building, a missile-fueling building, and a structure that housed a generator were located on this parcel. Shown here is a 1965 aerial view of the launcher area.

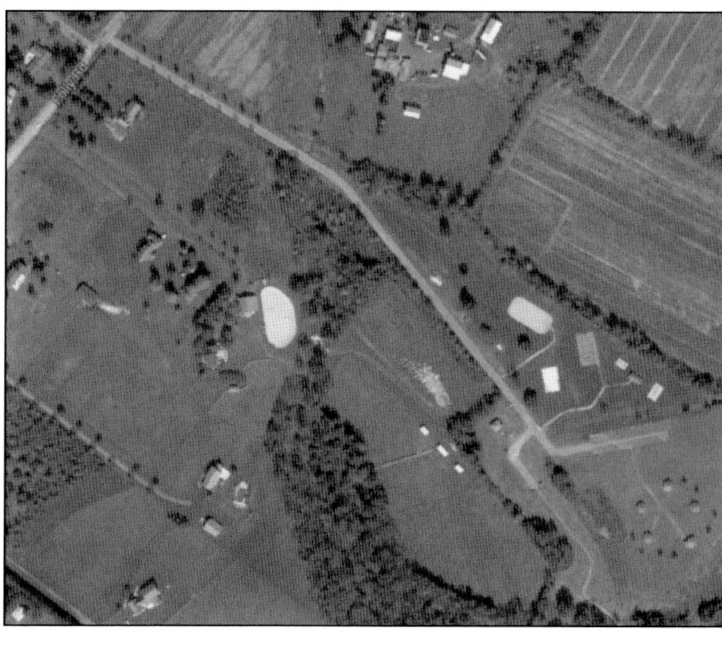

After 1969, all sites were declared surplus property by the US government. On Memorial Day 2000, the people of Warrington dedicated a bronze and stone marker to serve as a permanent reminder of those who came from all parts of the nation to defend the Philadelphia area. Shown here is a Google aerial view from 2010 of where the launcher area was located. (Imagery (c) 2014 DiditalGlobe, US Geological Survey, USDA Farm Services Agency, map data (c) 2014 Google.)

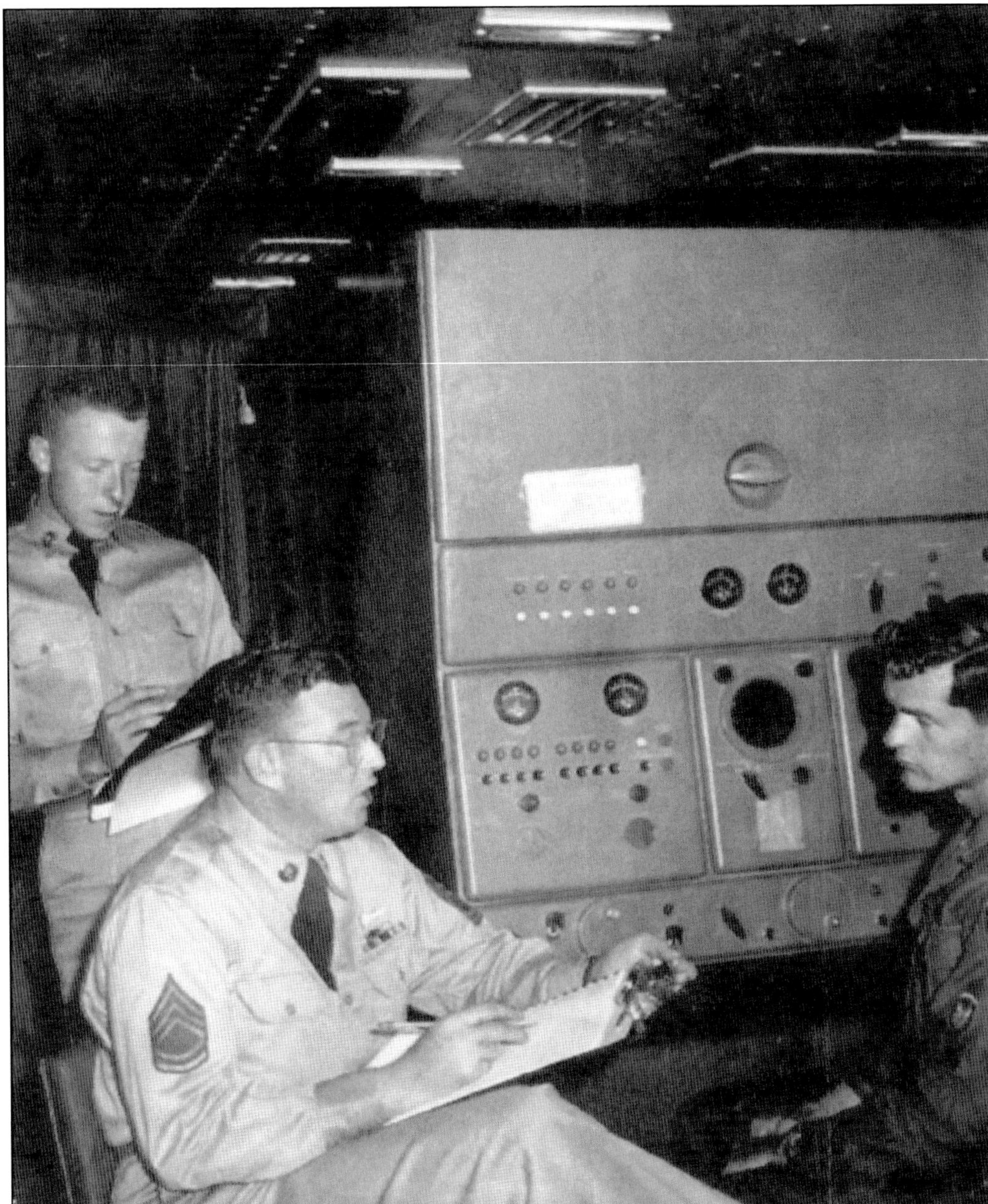

Some 200 officers and men were stationed at Site 99 at any given point in time. No missiles were ever fired from the Nike base in Warrington, or at any other such unit in the United States, because the nation never came under attack from the Soviet Union. In 1969, all Nike sites in the continental United States were declared obsolete with the development of nuclear intercontinental missiles. Pictured here around 1956 is an enlisted soldier being tested on radar-operator protocol procedures at the Warrington site integrated fire-control area. (Courtesy of Joe Desiderio.)

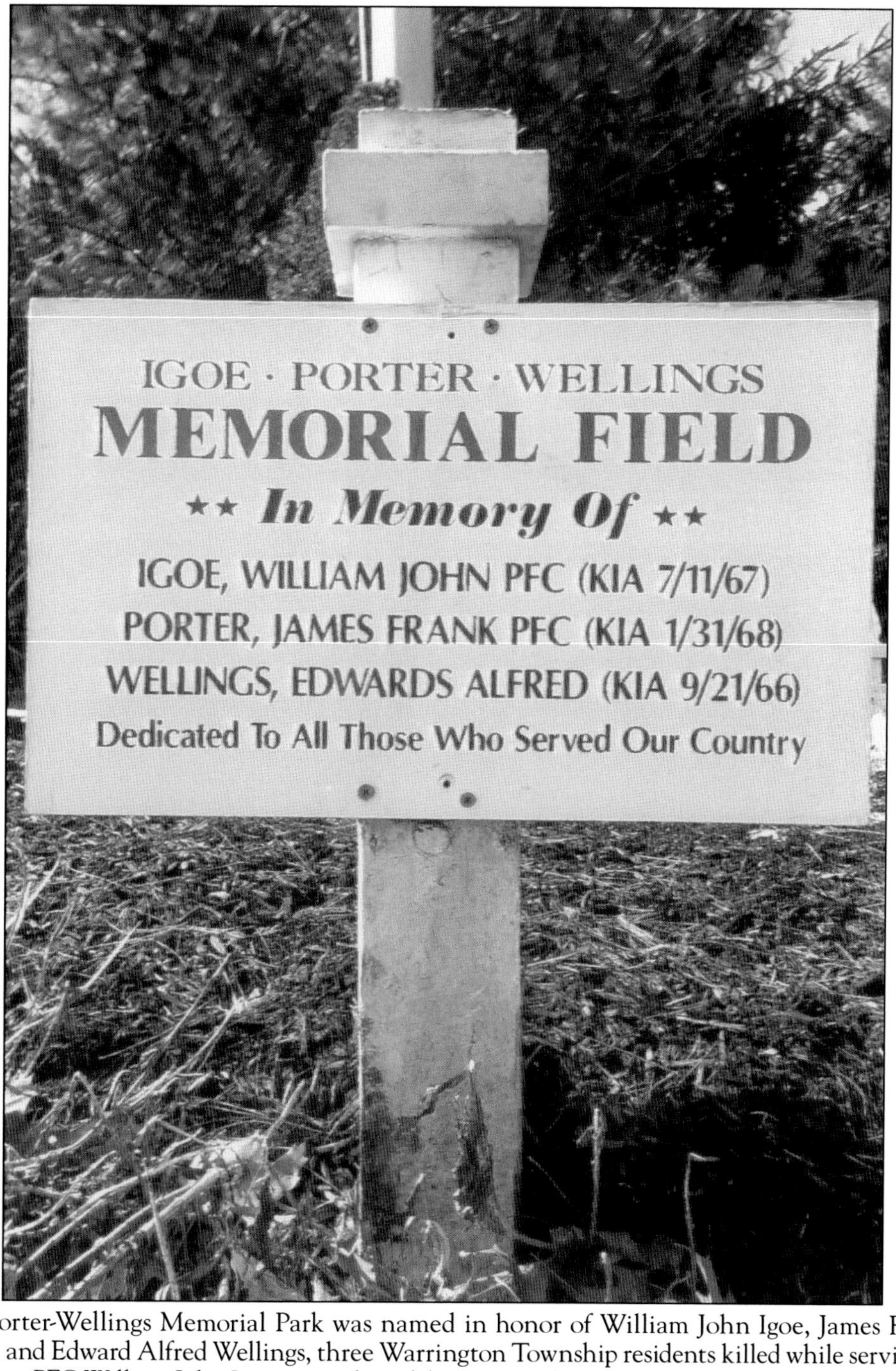

Igoe-Porter-Wellings Memorial Park was named in honor of William John Igoe, James Frank Porter, and Edward Alfred Wellings, three Warrington Township residents killed while serving in Vietnam. PFC William John Igoe, a member of the Army Selective Service-Armor Reconnaissance Specialist, 1st Infantry Division, served the country until July 11, 1967, in South Vietnam. PFC James Frank Porter, a member of the Army Medical Corps, Company D, 4th Medical Battalion, served until January 31, 1968, in Quang, South Vietnam. PFC Edward Alfred Wellings, a member of the Marine Corps-Rifleman USMC, 3rd Marine Division, served until September 21, 1966, in Quang Tri, South Vietnam.

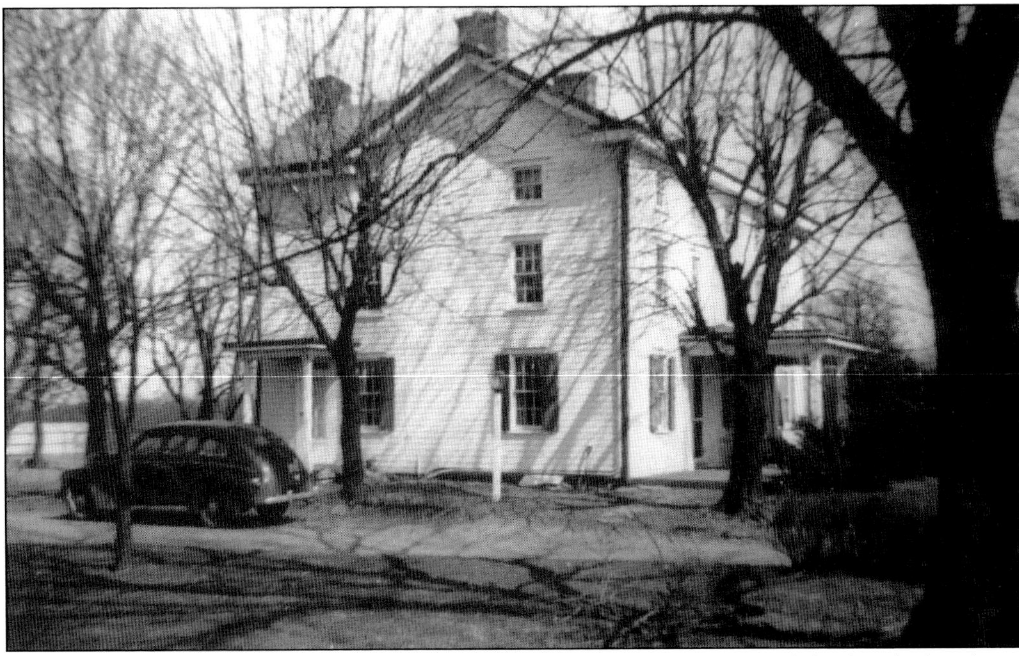

Washington Cadwallader assisted in the cultivation and improvement of the family farmhouse built in 1805. Located on Bristol Road, the farm was situated within a mile of the Warrington Post Office. This commodious two-story structure stands on an elevation and still commands a splendid view of the surrounding country. (Courtesy of Alby Cornell.)

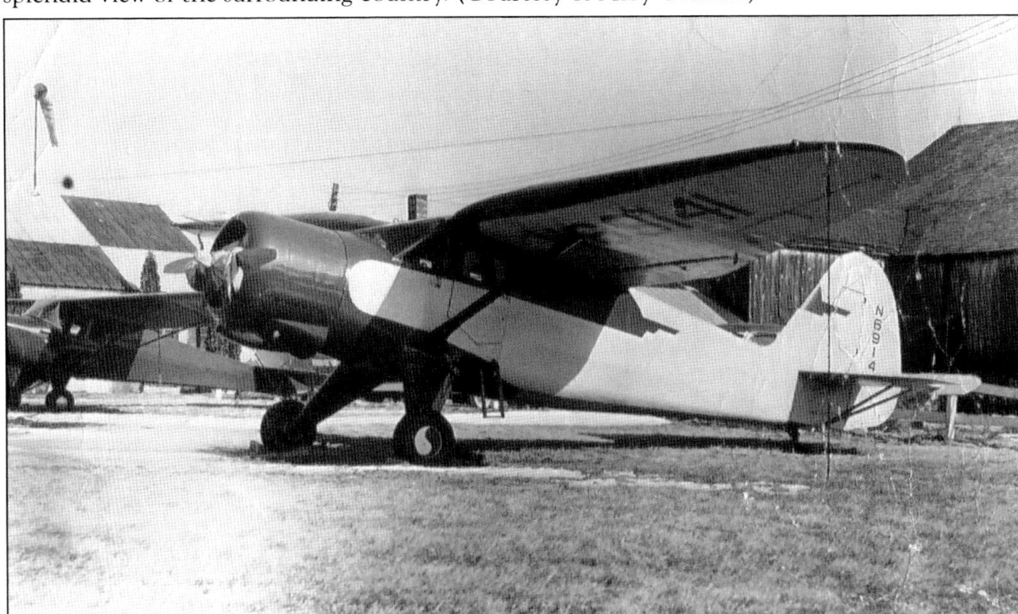

The Cornell family bought the Cadwallader property and built the Warrington Airfield shortly after World War II, when Norman Cornell gave part of his property to his son Ernest. Services at the airfield included flight lessons, transportation, and plane storage. This photograph, taken around 1960, is of a Stinson V-77 with a Taylorcraft parked behind it at the Warrington Airfield. (Courtesy of Alby Cornell.)

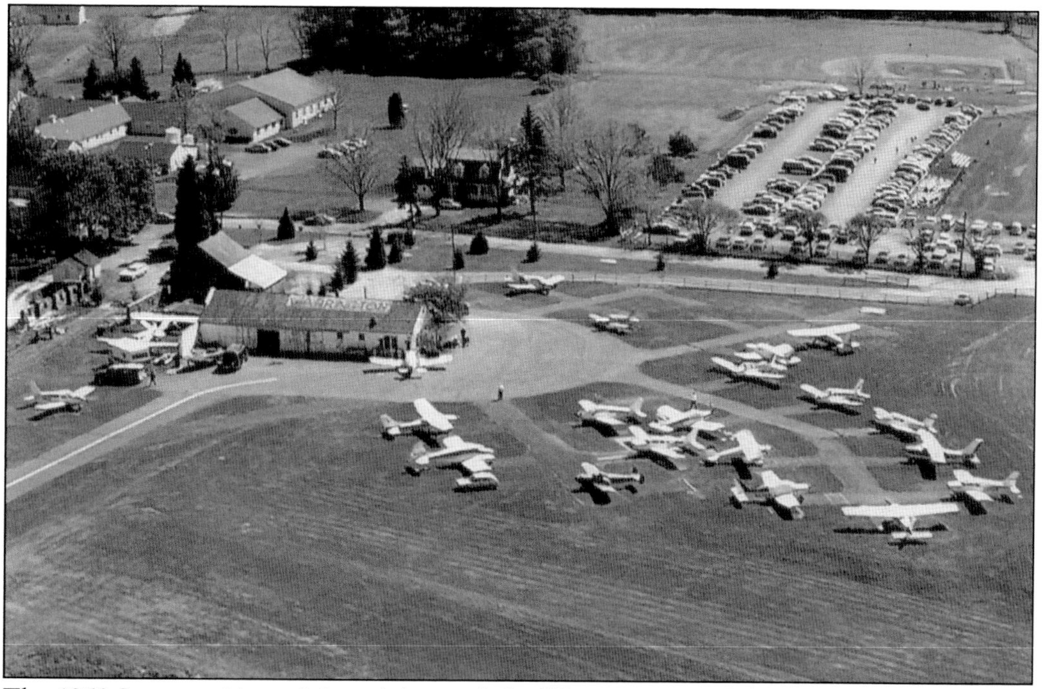

The 1960 *Jeppesen Airway Manual* depicted the Warrington Airfield as having two unpaved runways (2,800-foot runway 6/24 and 1,500-foot runway 16/34), along with two buildings at the south end of the field. The airfield was known for providing shuttle services to the Harrisburg and Philadelphia airports. This c. 1990 photograph shows the airport still in use. (Courtesy of Alby Cornell.)

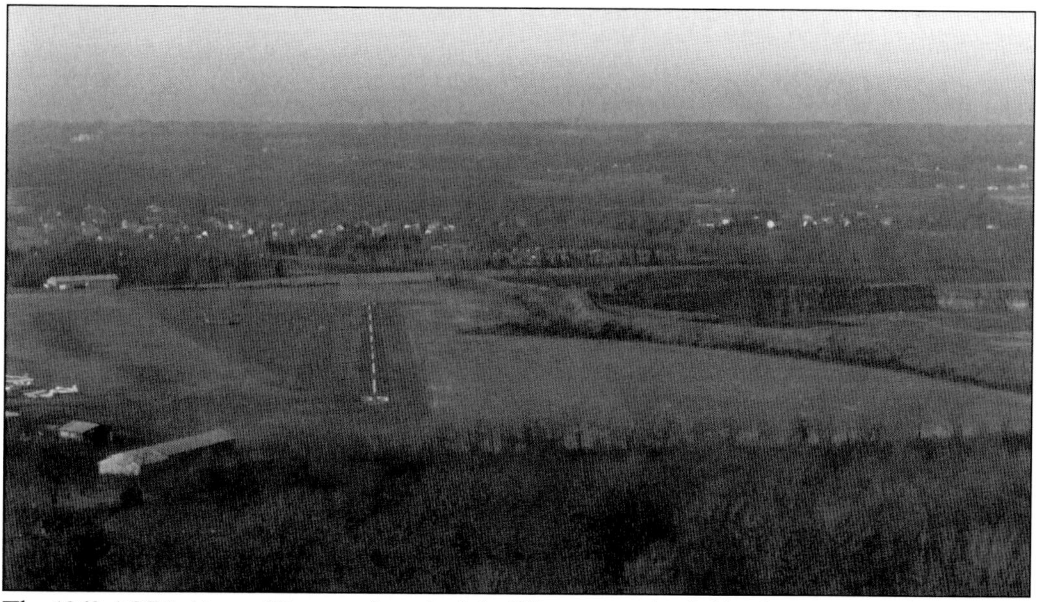

The 1962 AOPA *Airport Directory* described the Warrington Airfield as having two runways, with the longest being the 2,800-foot sod runway 6/24. In 1973, the longer runway was paved. Pictured here is a view from a final approach on runway 35 from the late 1980s. The Warrington Airfield closed on January 1, 1991. (Courtesy of Alby Cornell.)

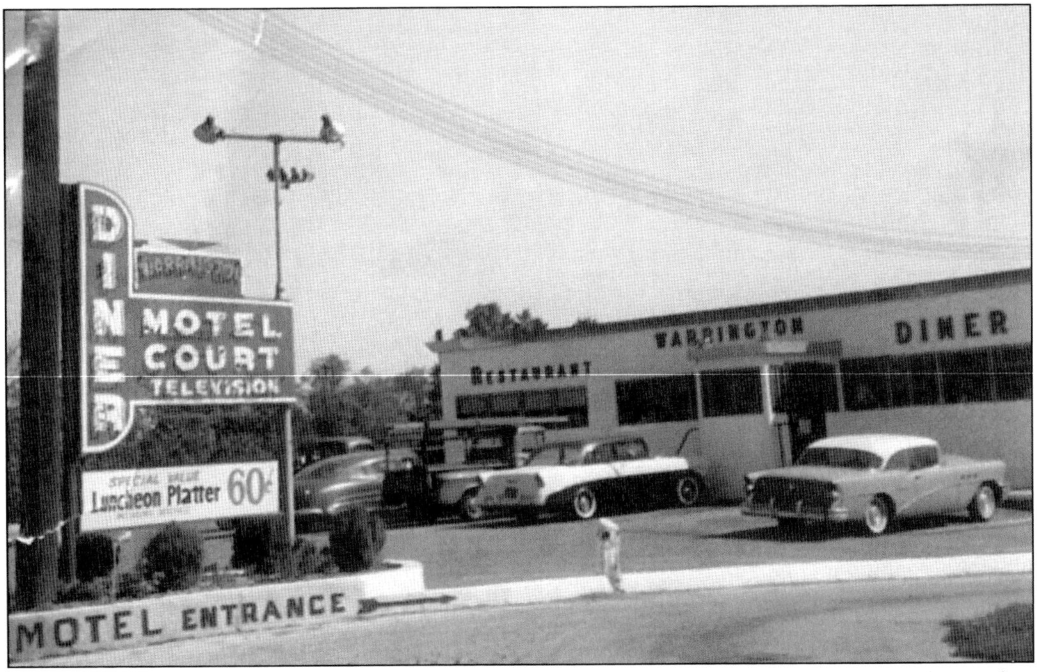

The Warrington Motor Lodge and the Generations at Warrington restaurant were located at 701 Easton Road (near the corner of Easton and Street Roads). In the early 1950s, Joe Elnitski, a police officer from Philadelphia, started the business as a diner and a few motel cabins. Some of these cabins started their lives as chicken coops. (Courtesy of the Leventhal family.)

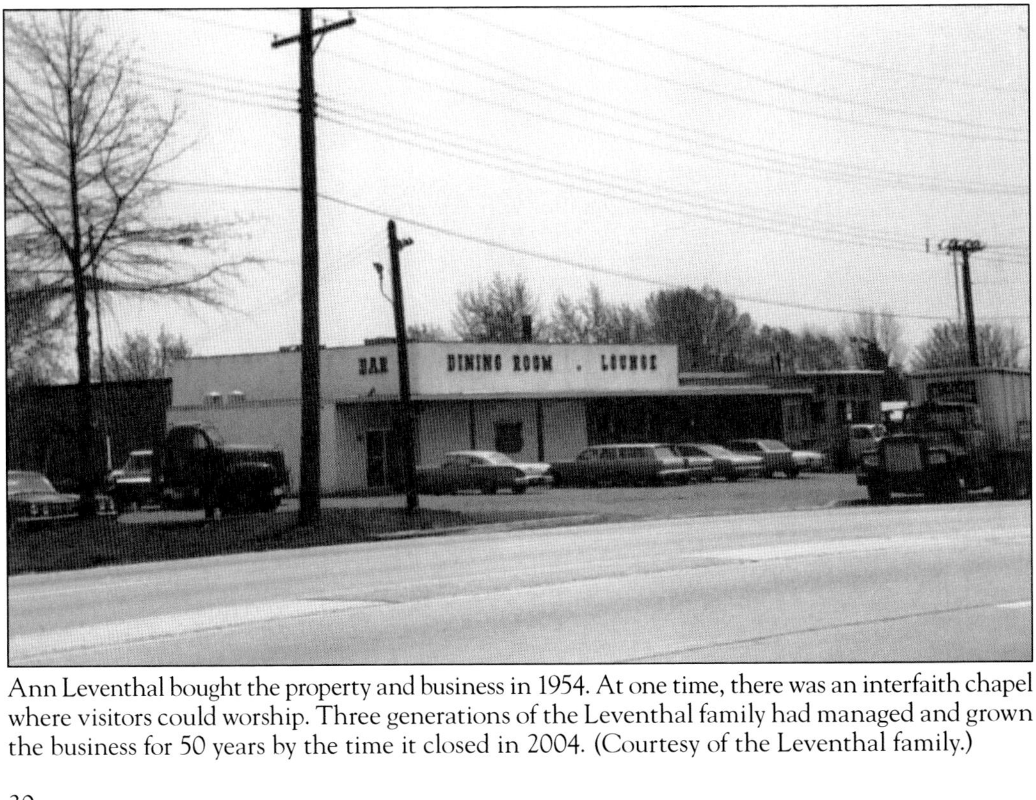

Ann Leventhal bought the property and business in 1954. At one time, there was an interfaith chapel where visitors could worship. Three generations of the Leventhal family had managed and grown the business for 50 years by the time it closed in 2004. (Courtesy of the Leventhal family.)

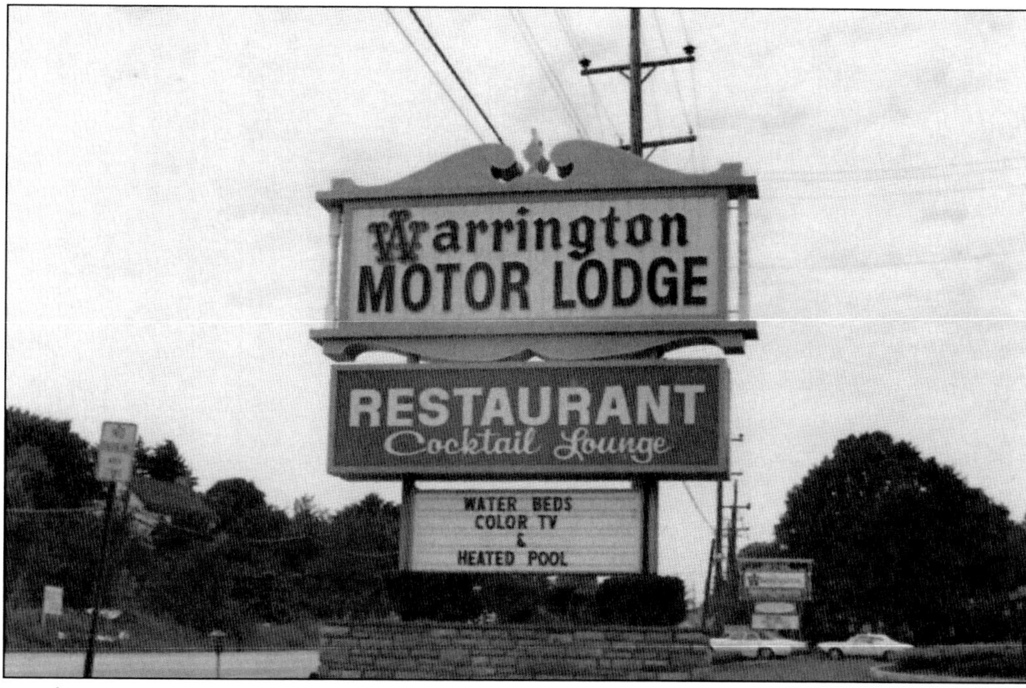

In advertising, rooms at the motel were described as "Guest room with 1 double bed and sofa sleeper or 2 double beds spacious designed to make you feel at home. Of course there are televisions and direct-dial telephones in every room." (Courtesy of the Leventhal family.)

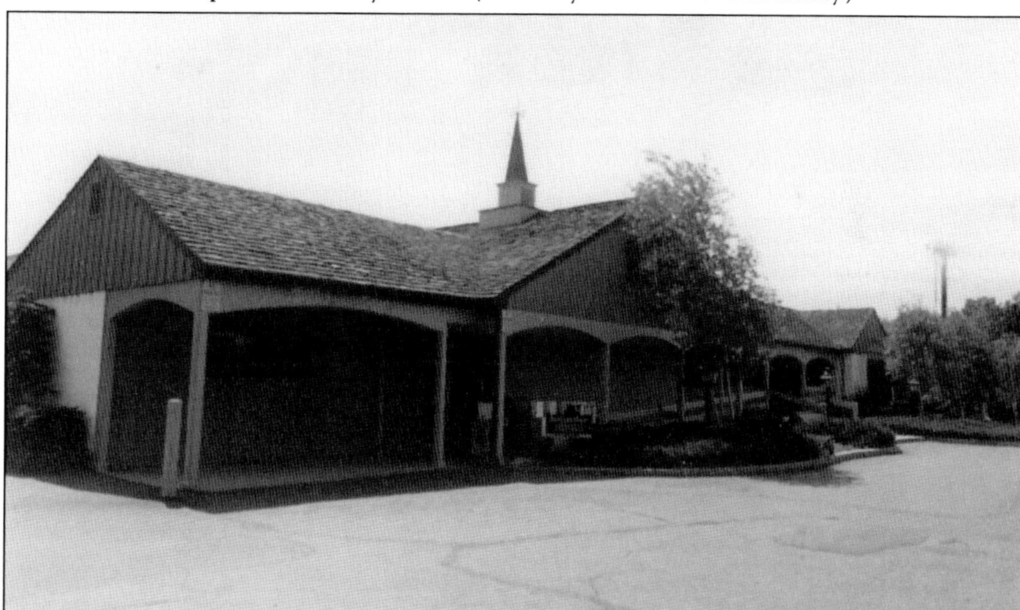
At the time of closing, the property included a large restaurant, a banquet facility that could accommodate up to 750 people, 66 motel rooms, and 10 apartments. All the rooms were on the ground level and were spread out on 12 wooded acres. The rooms, restaurant, and banquet facilities were taken down to make way for the Valley Square Shopping Center. (Courtesy of the Leventhal family.)

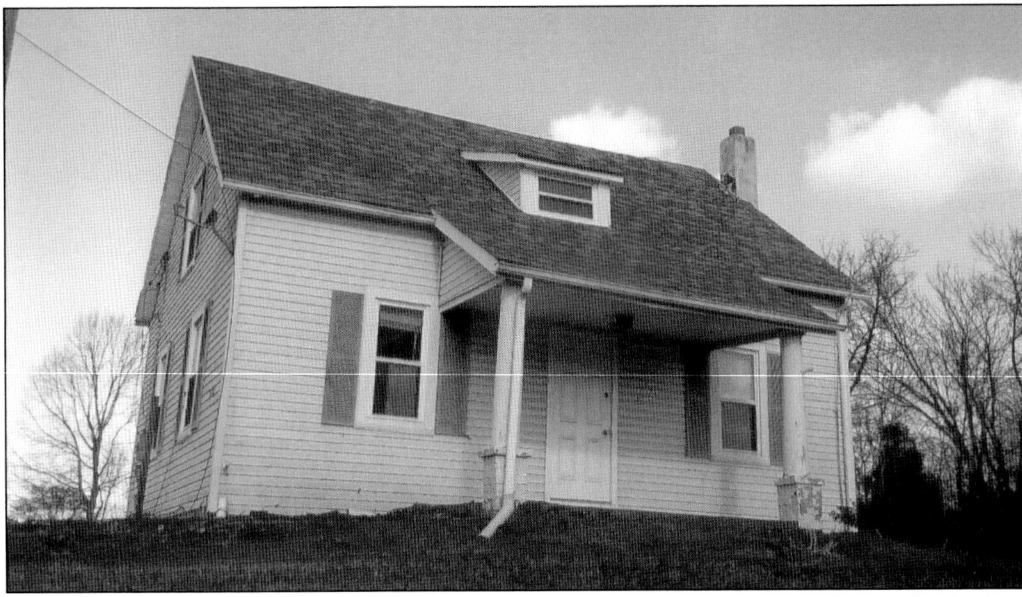

Demolished in 2011 due to the construction of the 202 Parkway, the Phelps house (built about 1875) was located on the corner of County Line Road and Stump Road. The house had four rooms on the main floor and two bedrooms on the second. The foundation was constructed of stone and mud mortar; floor jousts were hewed trees placed about two feet apart.

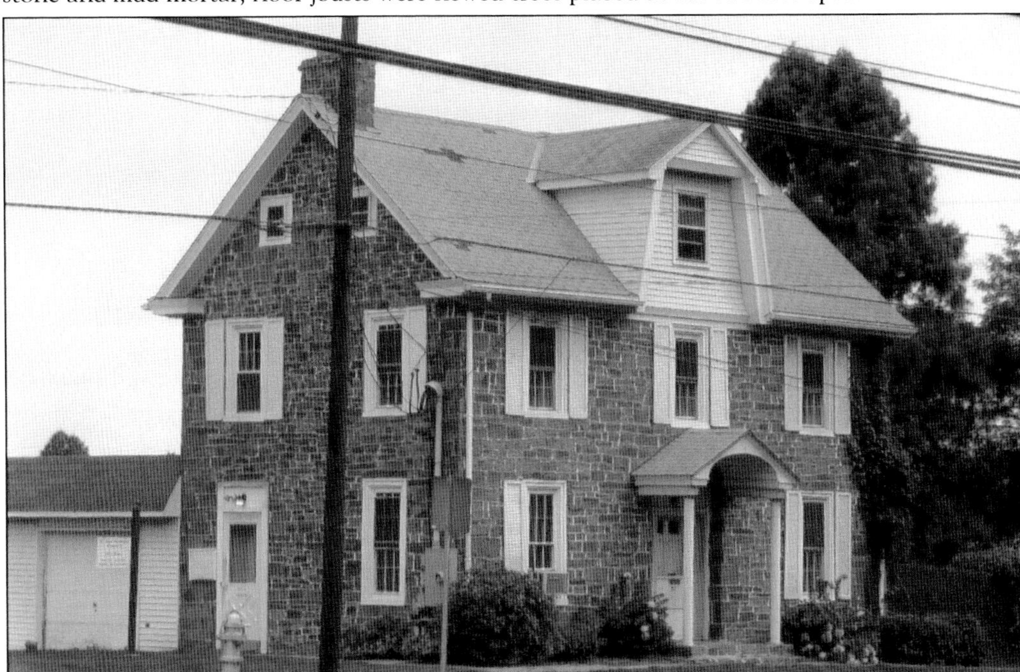

Located on the corner of County Line Road and Upper State Road, this stone house was built around 1840 by John Harp and was part of the hamlet called Harp's Corner. John Harp is buried in Pleasantville United Church of Christ Cemetery. This house later became the office for St. John Neumann Cemetery when it opened in 1982. It too was demolished for construction of the 202 Parkway.

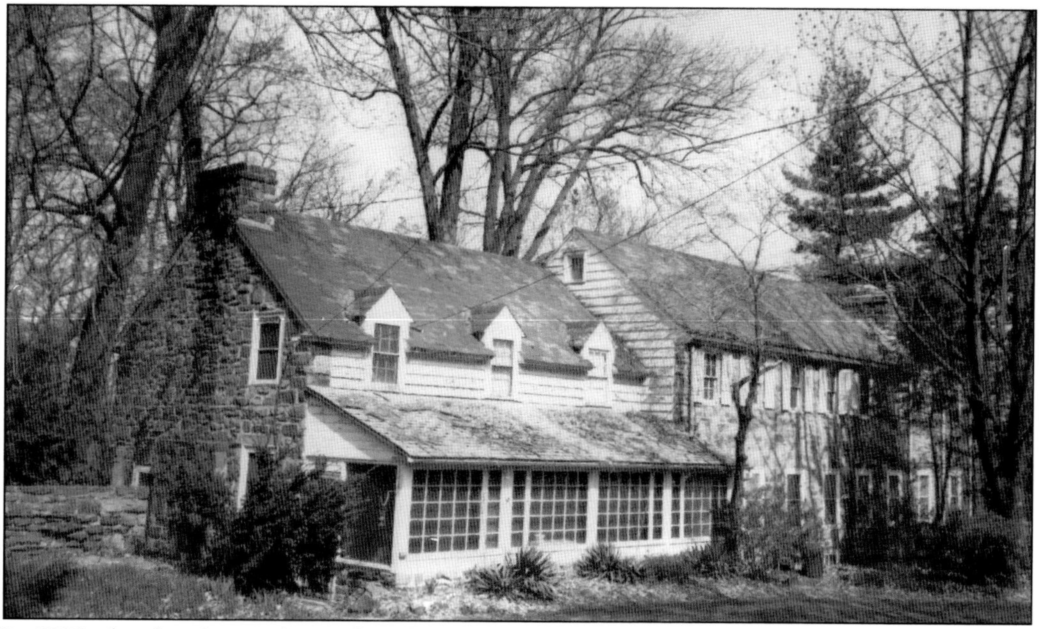

In 1983, this farmhouse, located on Easton Road in front of the entrance to the Warrington Quarry, was being considered for use as a new location for the township's municipal offices. This house, built around 1840, was constructed of stone. Township offices never moved to this location, and the home was razed in the early 1990s.

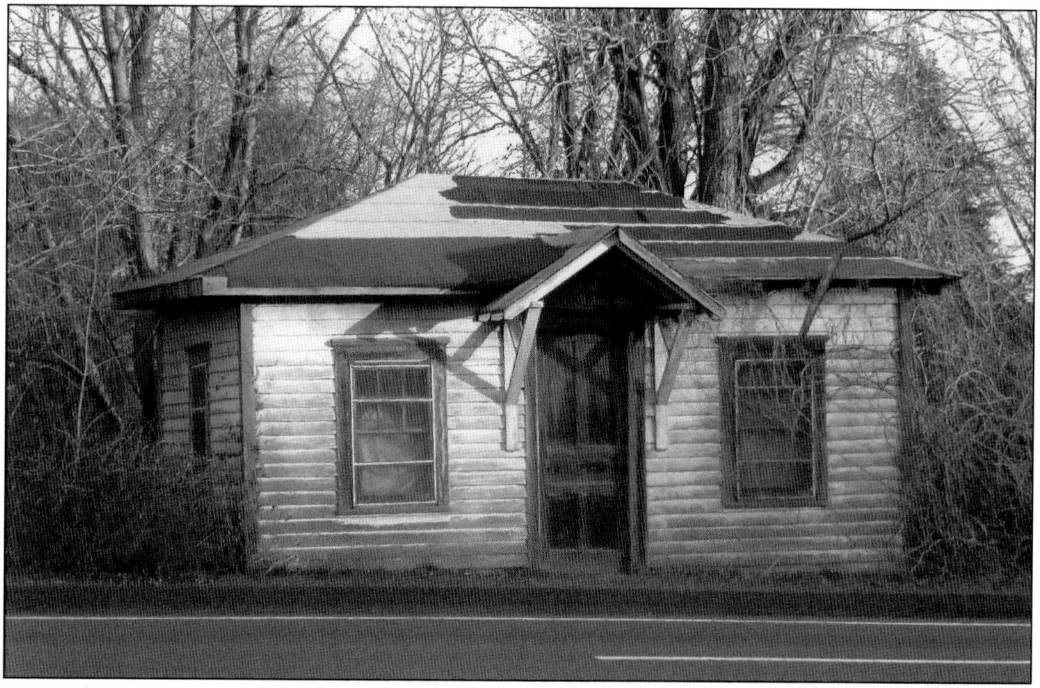

Located at the corner of Easton Road and Georges Lane was this small wood-frame shack. Built in the early 1920s, it was used as the sales office for the Crestwald housing development. The Great Depression ceased the construction of the planned houses, and the structure, vacant for many years, was razed in 2013.

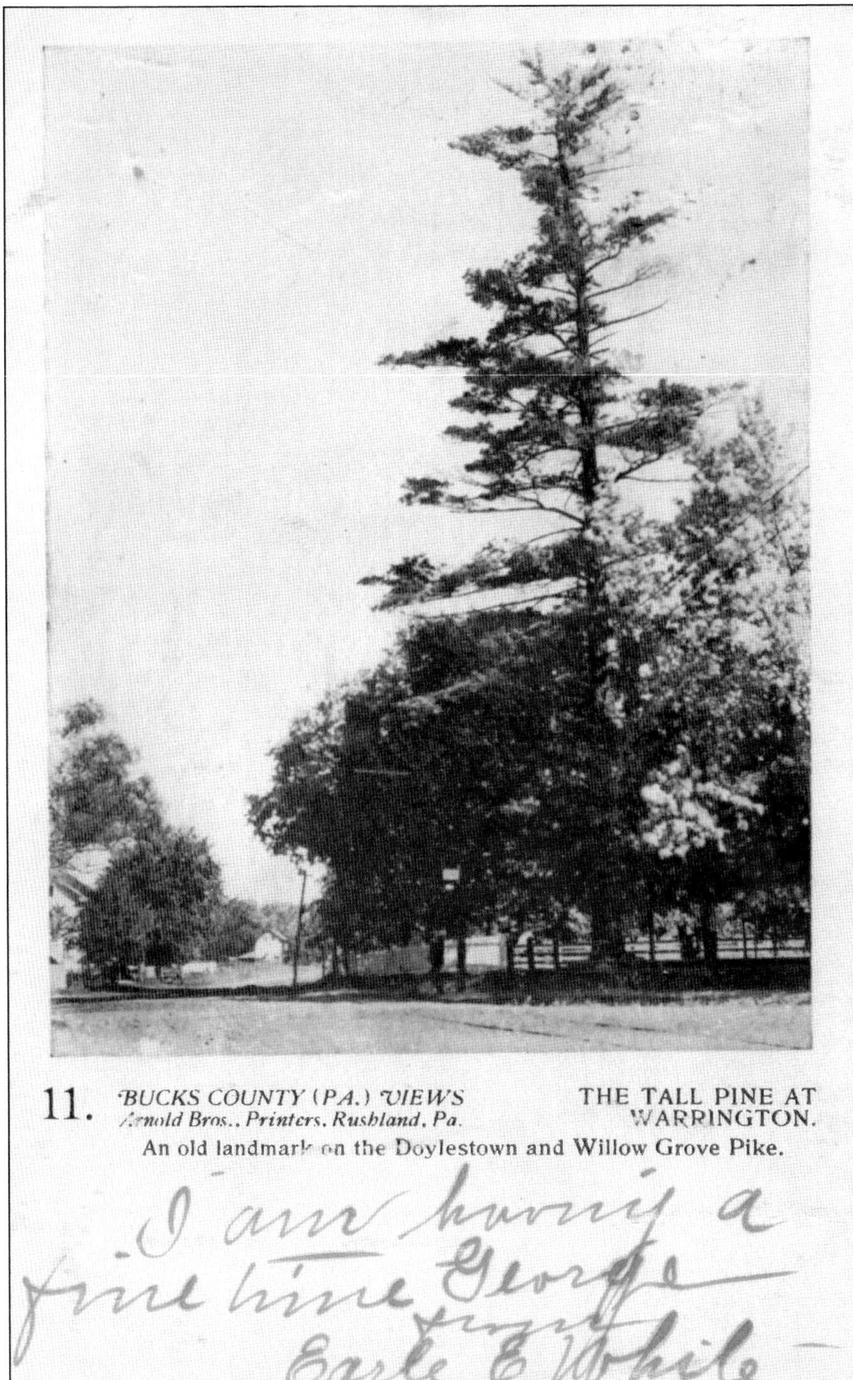

As described by Phebe Westcott Humphreys in 1905, "At Warrington is a tall pine tree, claimed to be not only the tallest, but the oldest of any tree in the vicinity. It is a noble monarch of the original forest, and can be seen ten or twelve miles away, as it stands on the highest point of land in Bucks County." The tree was damaged by lighting in 1910 and was taken down five years later. (Postcard published by Arnold Brothers.)

Two

Prominently Important Structures

The Warrington Historic Commission and the Warrington Historical Society reviewed all known eligible Warrington Township historic properties in 2013. The 24 structures mentioned in this chapter received the highest ratings based on the follow criteria:

Event—The property makes a contribution to the major pattern of American history.
Person—The structure has an association with significant people of America's past.
Design/Construction—The distinctive characteristics of the buildings architecture and construction meet a certain standard, including having great artistic value or being the work of a master.
Information Potential—The property has yielded or is be likely to yield information important to history.
Future Security—The structure's integrity or existence is jeopardized by future development.

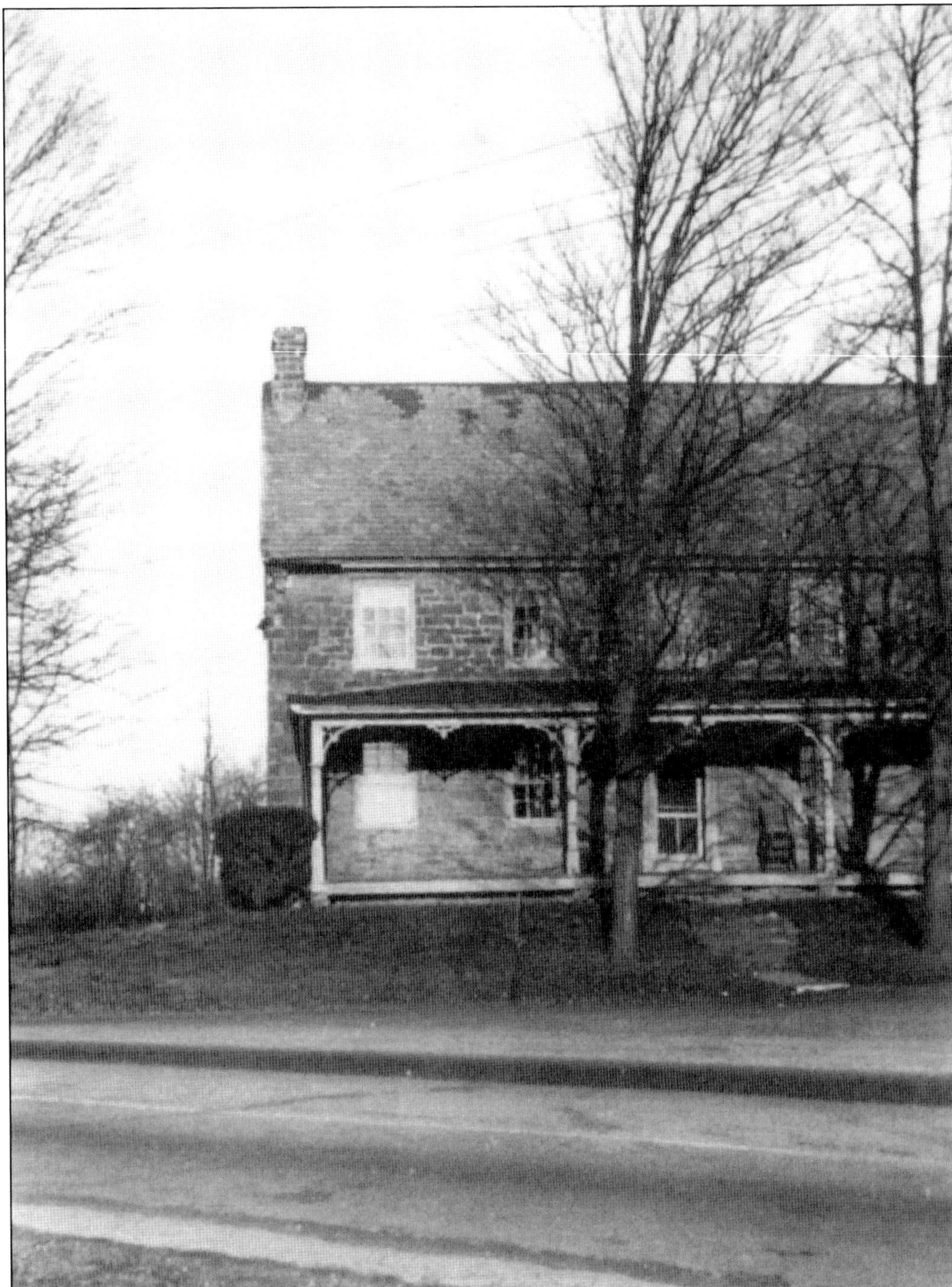

In 1790, John Barclay purchased the property located at the corner of Easton and Bristol Roads, where he would later begin construction of this Colonial stone mansion in 1799. In 1803, shortly after the construction was completed, Barclay's wife, Jane, passed away. Deciding to move back to Philadelphia, John Barclay conveyed the mansion to his son James for the price of "one silver dollar." (Courtesy of the Barness family.)

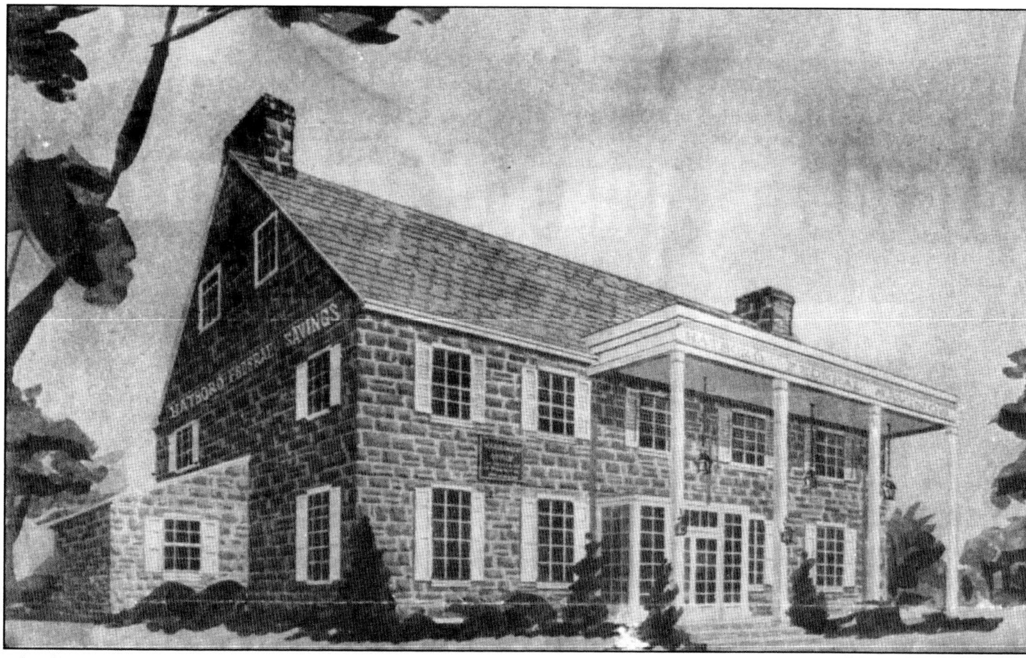

The house was purchased by Benjamin Hough in 1833. During Hough's ownership, it is documented that the future Civil War commander and US president Ulysses S. Grant visited the homestead in 1843 and 1853. In 1856, the property was bought by Robert Radcliff and then conveyed by him to his son Elias H. Radcliff in 1864.

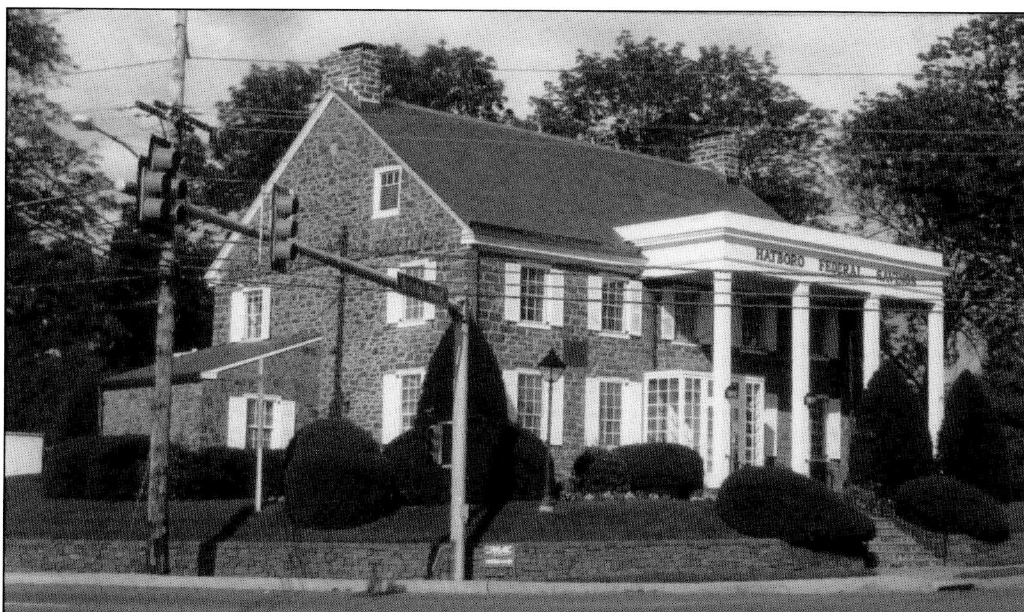

In 1963, the building was purchased by Hatboro Federal Savings from the Radcliff family. After restoration and modifications were made to the structure, a three-day grand-opening celebration took place at the new Warrington branch location on April 9, 1964. During each day of the grand opening, an 11-inch, portable, black-and-white General Electric television was given away as a prize.

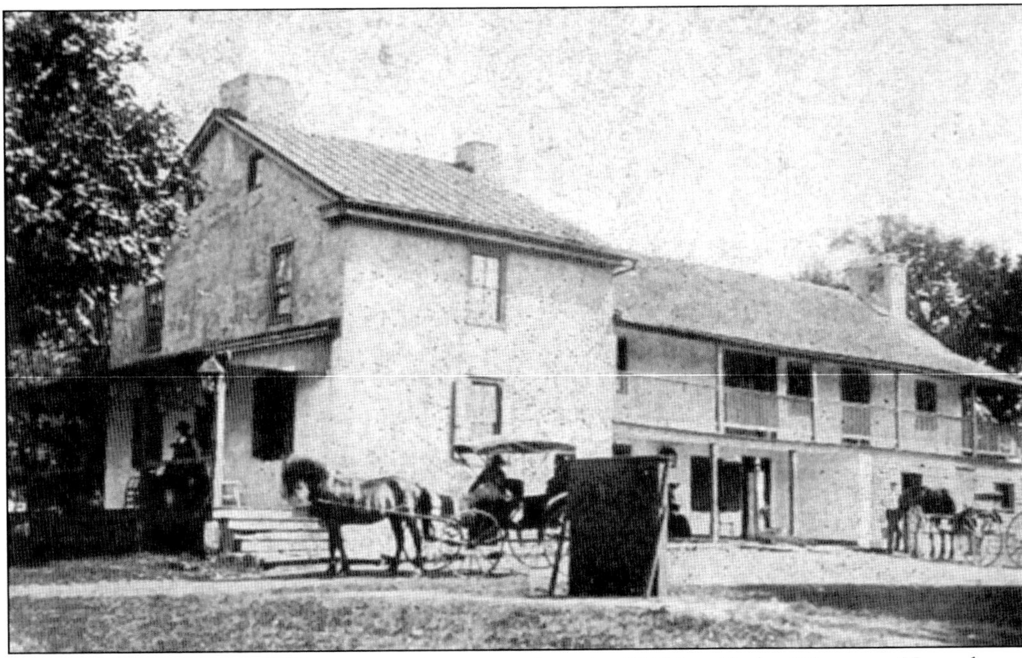

This photograph of the Warrington Inn was taken in 1905 by Phebe Westcott Humphreys, the author of *The Automobile Tourist; Motor Car Journeys from Philadelphia, with Historical and Descriptive Notes*. She mentions the tall pine tree and the "Warrington Hotel" upon making a return trip to Philadelphia from Wrightstown via the Bristol Pike.

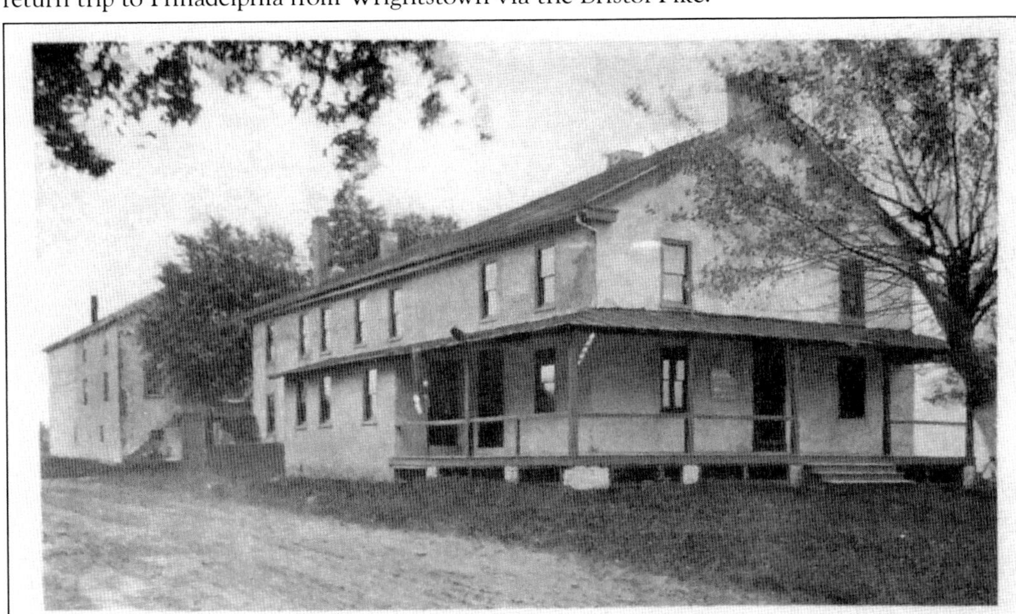

Craig's Tavern was the first tavern to be opened in the township. It was located at the corner of Easton Road and Bristol Road. John Craig received his first tavern license for this site in 1757. Today, located at 1373 Easton Road, it is the township's last old-time tavern. (Postcard published by Arnold Brothers; courtesy of Hatboro Federal Savings.)

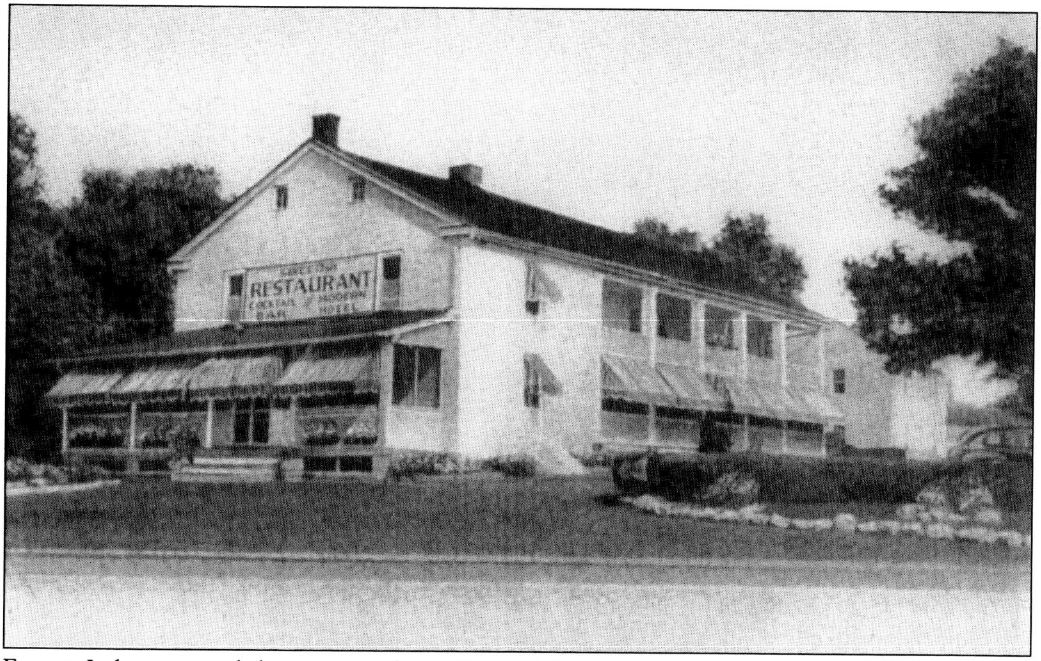

Francis Lukens owned the property from 1814 to 1824 and again from 1831 to his death in 1842. In 1860, while being sold at a sheriff's sale, the inn was described as "a substantial convenient two-story stone Hotel, with kitchen attached, with 15 rooms, and double piazza on each front, a good stone barn, sheds; carriage, ice, wood and hog houses; almost all kinds of out buildings."

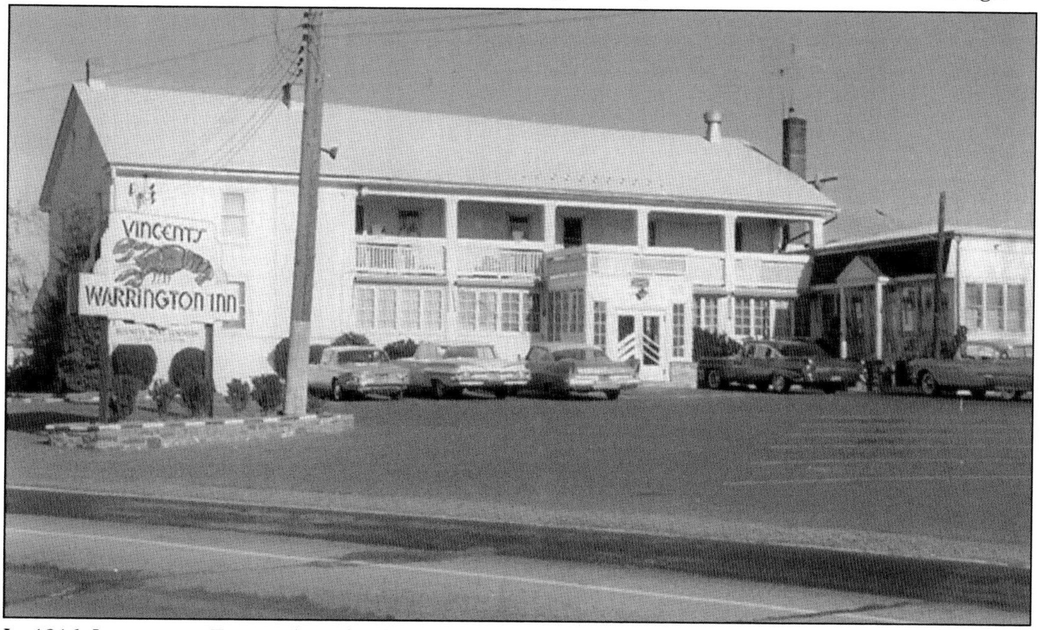

In 1916, Innocenzo Fererro bought the inn and named it the Warrington Inn. Frank Conti leased it from 1932 until he bought the Cross Keys Inn in Doylestown. In 1941, Fererro's nephew Vincent Coggiola purchased the inn and added "Vincent's" to its name. It was expanded and remodeled several times. Coggiola's sons took over until the property was sold in 1996. Today, the location is known as Villa Barolo.

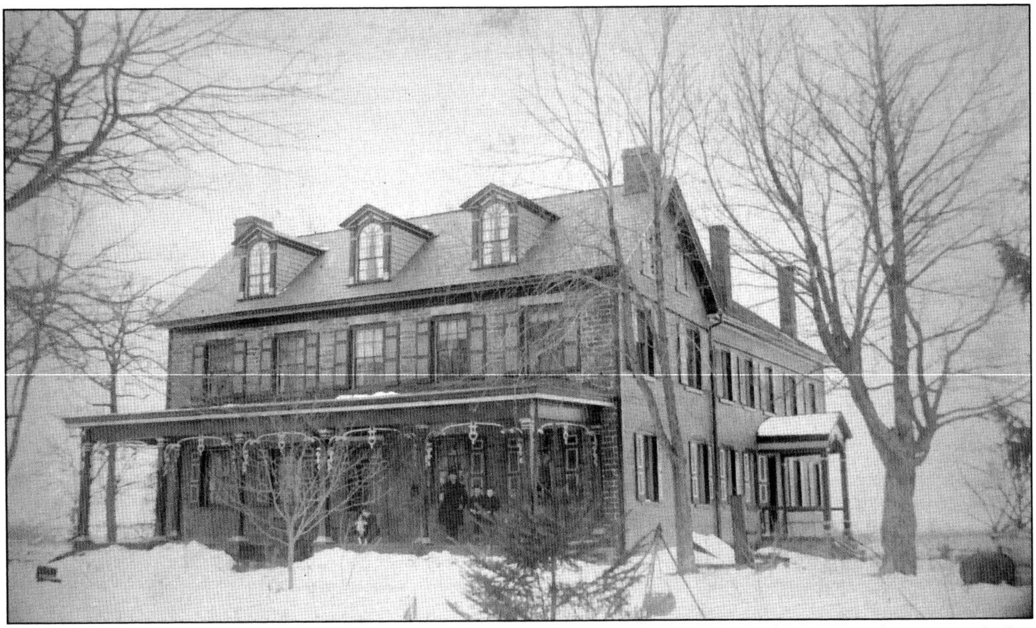

The "mansion-house" at 850 Easton Road was built by Rev. Nathaniel Irwin, who owned the property from 1785 to 1812. Irwin, a well-known minister at the Neshaminy Presbyterian Church in Warwick, demolished a house that was originally built on the property in 1734 and constructed a new one in 1809. At the time of this c. 1890 image, the home was owned by the Dobbins family. (Courtesy of Alberta Titus Mininger and Charles Titus.)

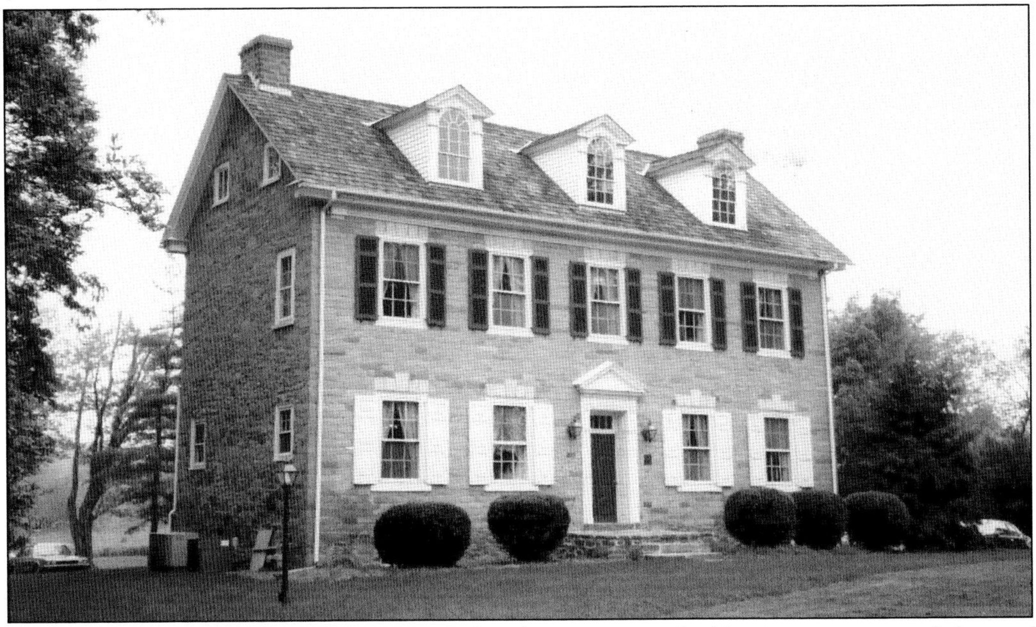

The front of the Irwin home facing Easton Road is constructed of finely cut stone, and the roof is topped with cedar and three ornate dormers. In 1858, Perry McNeille bought the property and enlarged the home with a long ell at the rear. The Dobbins family purchased the property in 1878. This home received a certificate and plaque from the Bucks County Heritage Conservancy in 1981.

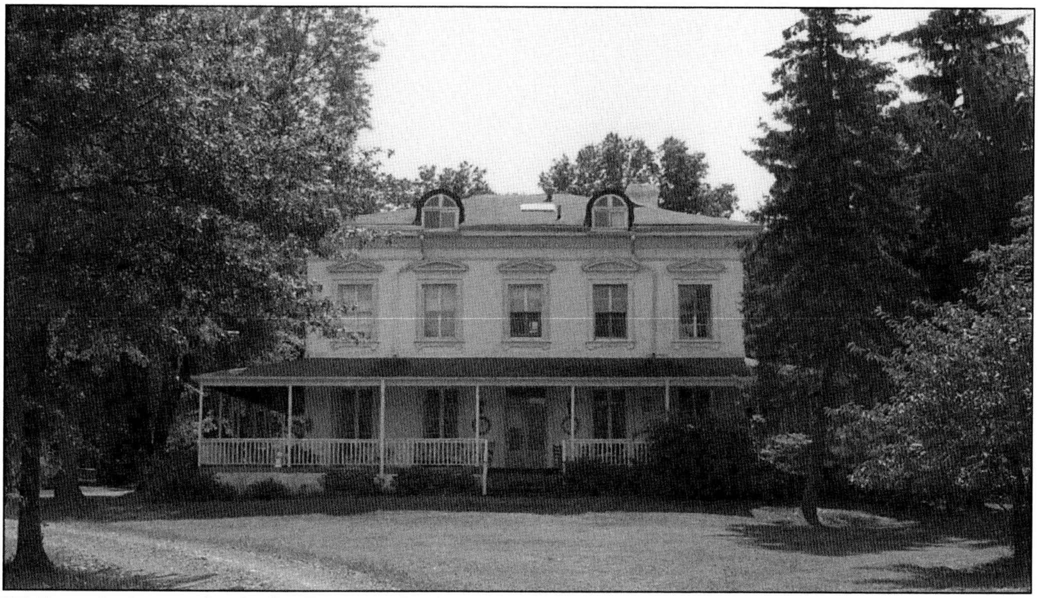

William R. Brown built this home, which was once known as "Brown's Folly" and the "Deserted Mansion." According to the *Bucks County Intelligencer* in 1874, "By the original specified plan the building was to have cost $10,000; but by alterations of the plan, as well as from other causes, $28,000 was expended before the building was completed. Together with other pecuniary losses, caused his failure, and the house was sold at sheriff's sale."

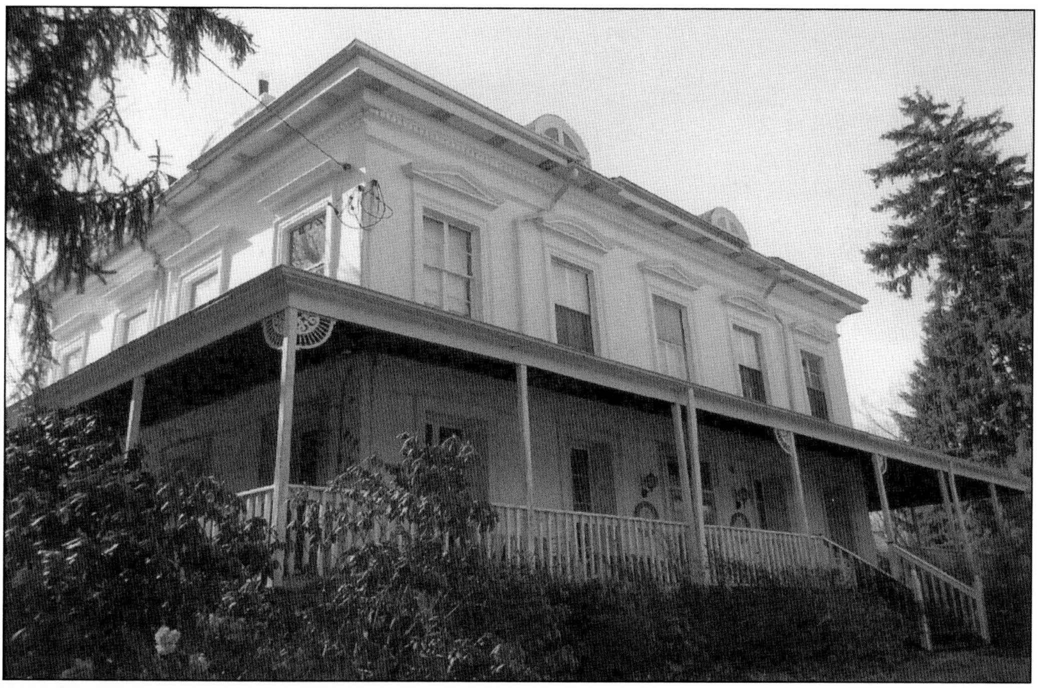

Another story states that when the house was nearly done, Brown rode out one day to examine the work. A messenger, who had followed him from town, gave him a letter telling him that his bride-to-be had eloped with a mutual friend. Without hesitation, he simply turned, closed the door without locking it, mounted his horse, and was no longer heard from.

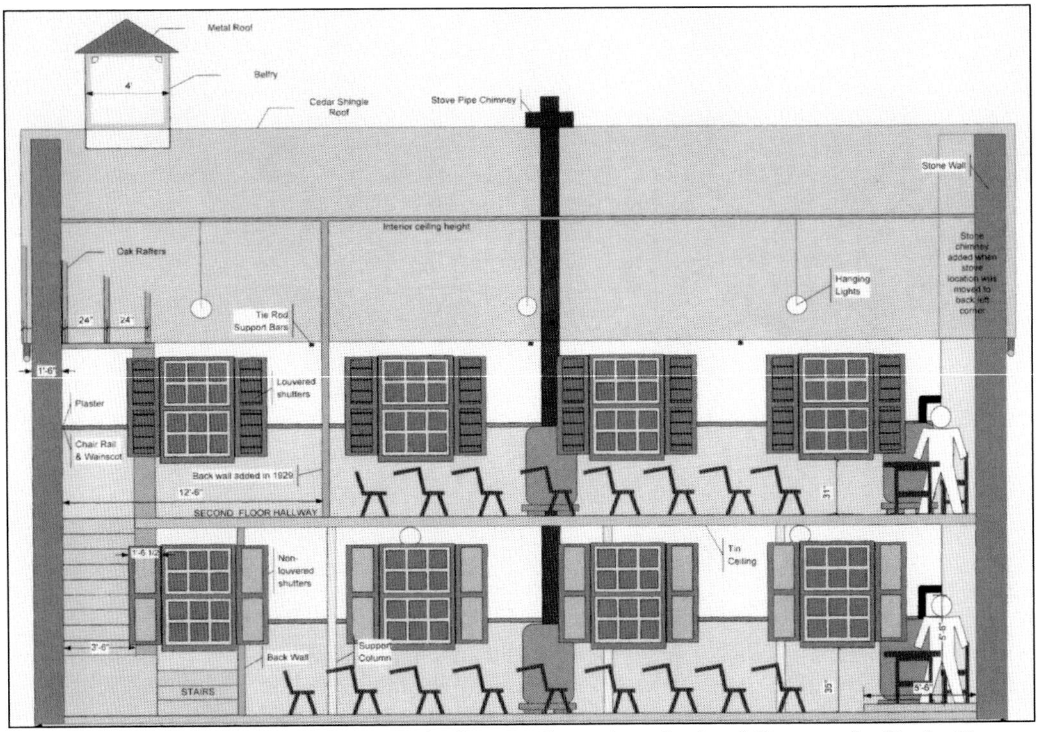

In 1808, the Warrington School House built in 1765 was described as follows in the Bucks County Deed (book No. 38, page 438): "A school house has been erected and used for many years and whereas the said school house is in a state of array and the erection of a new one contemplated and the function of the existing school house being such as to render it inconvenient."

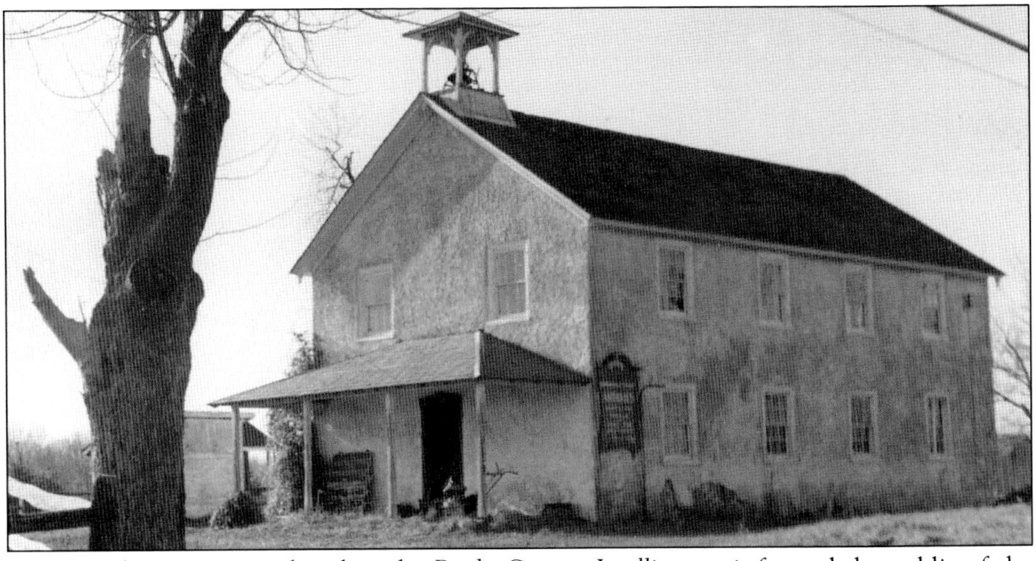

In 1851, advertisements placed in the *Bucks County Intelligencer* informed the public of the bidding process: "To Carpenters and Masons. The Board of School Directors of Warrington will meet at the school house near Newville, on Thursday, the first day of May, to receive proposals for building a school house; where the plan and specifications can be seen." The structure built is today located at 2524 Bristol Road.

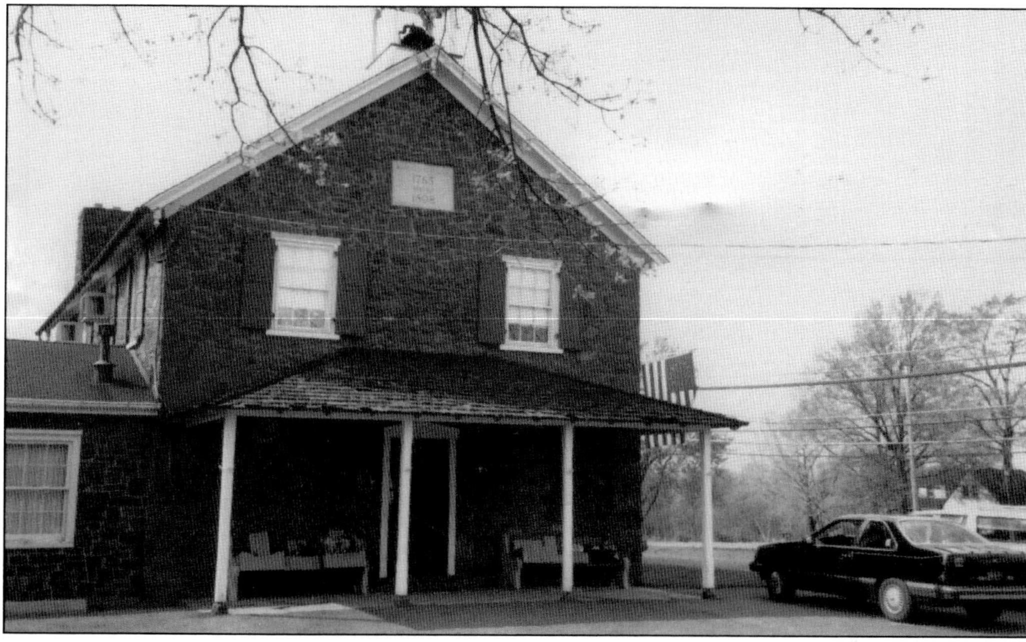

In 1909, the *Daily Intelligencer* reported that "entertainment was given by the pupils of the Warrington School. The net proceeds were $19 that will be used to purchase a bell. A large copula containing a bell has been erected on the Warringtonville schoolhouse during the past week. It greatly improves the looks of the building, and the sound of the bell can be heard all over the school district."

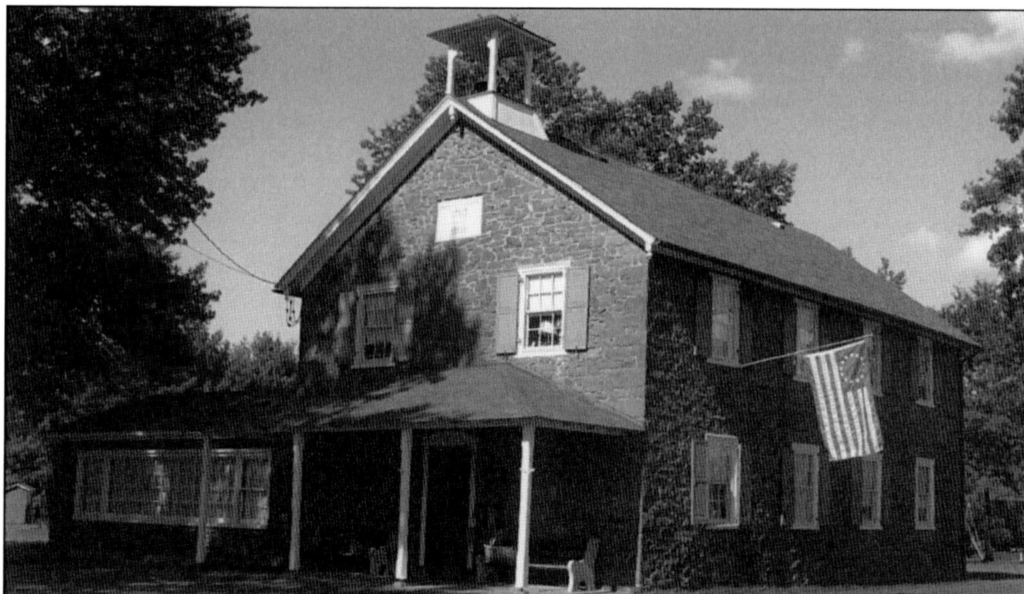

The Warrington School House was the first township school to have electricity. As documented in the November 19, 1939, Warrington Township School Board meeting minutes, "It was decided from a reliable electrician an estimate of the cost of wiring the Warrington School House for the installation of electrical lights. Complaints have been made by the patrons due to on dull or cloudy days pupils could not study for the lack of sufficient light."

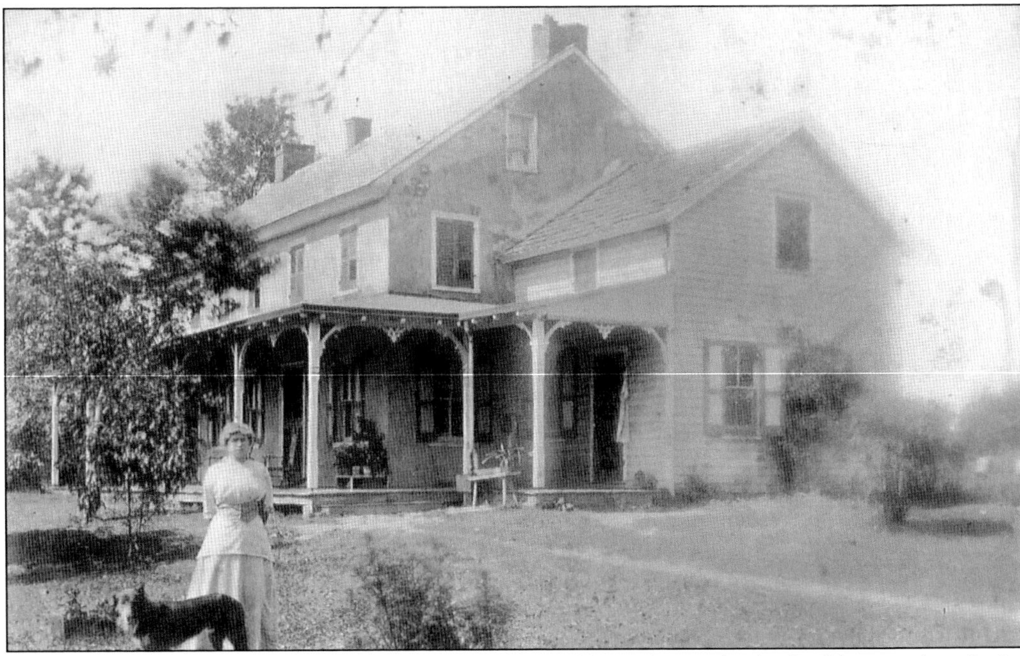

John George Weisel lived in this house located on Mill Creek Road. The building is classified as new on the 1798 federal direct tax assessment, with Michael Moyers documented as owner of the farm. The property, while owned by the Weisel family, consisted of 86 acres and included a sawmill and a chopping mill that drew power from the Mill Creek, which ran through the property.

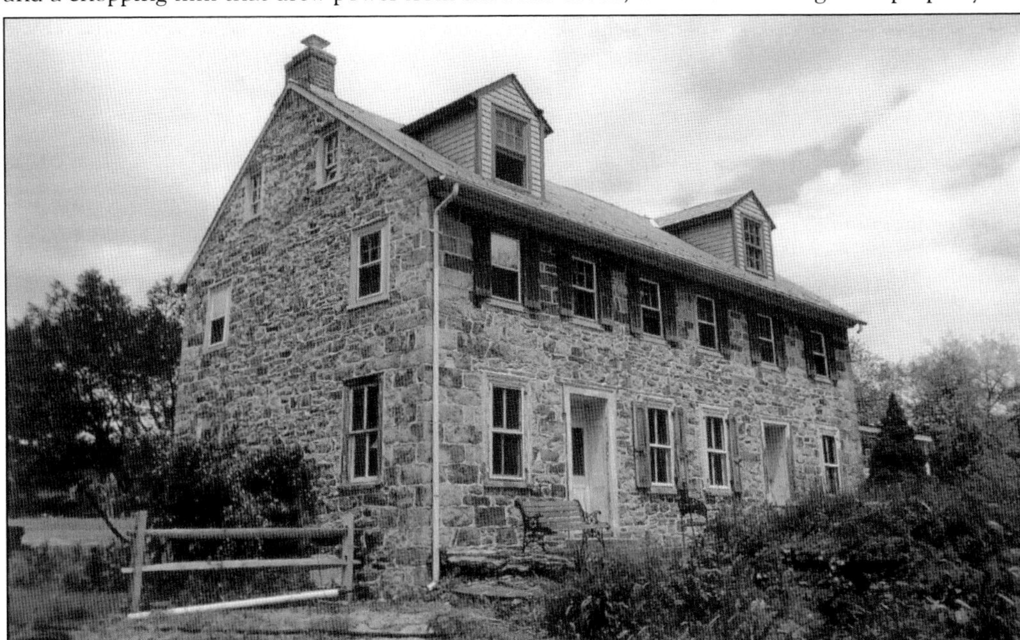

In the mid- to late 1800s, the three sons of John George Weisel (Henry, Samuel, and Aaron) lived on adjoining farms between Mill Creek, Stump, and Pickertown Roads. Upon Samuel's marriage to Catherine Kober in 1851, he took possession of the farm and the mills from his father. The mills on the property were torn down by 1906.

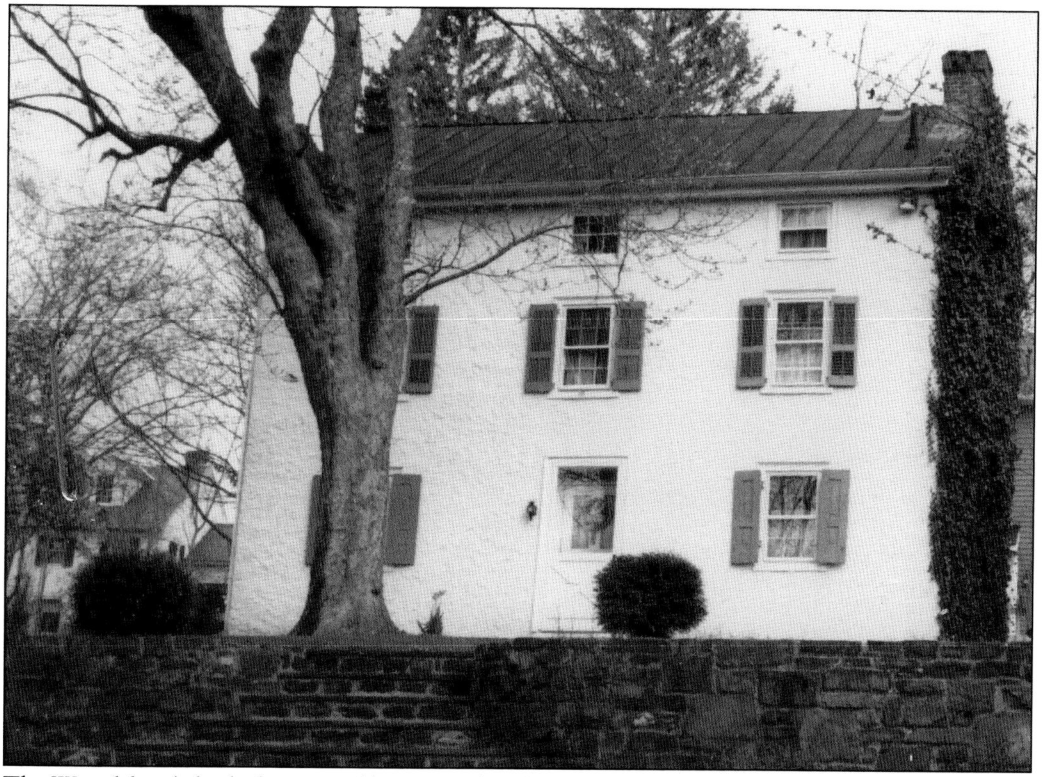

The Weisel family built this second house on their land. John George Weisel and his wife, Catherine Scheib, moved there after their son Samuel took possession of the farm. Built about 1850, it is situated closer to the property's lane and Mill Creek than the older house on the property.

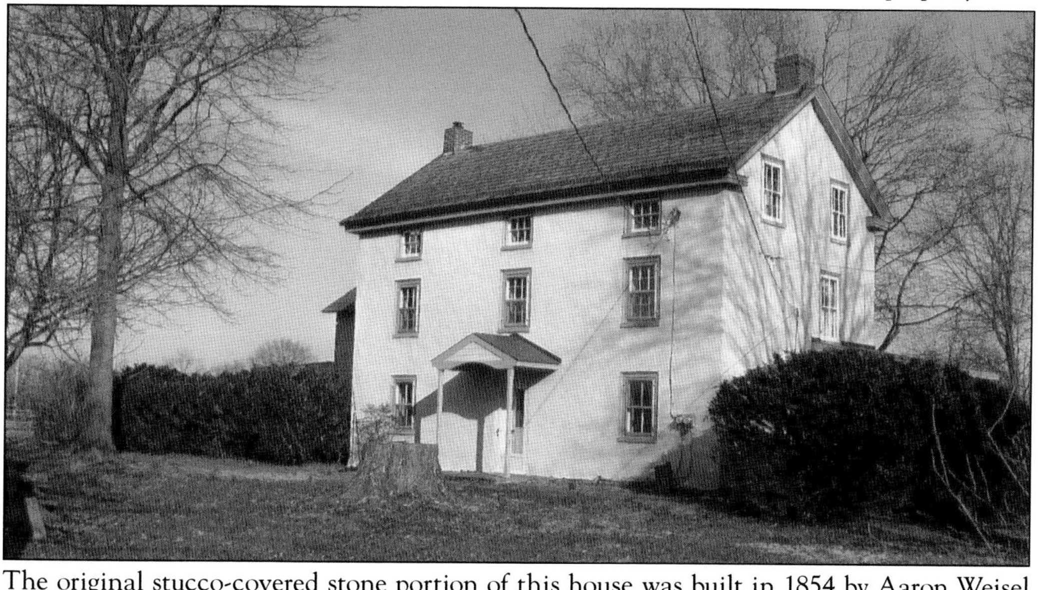

The original stucco-covered stone portion of this house was built in 1854 by Aaron Weisel (February 25, 1831–September 20, 1916). Aaron married Maria Kober and had six children. This farm, in the 1850s, was comprised of 55 acres. Today, the house and barn still stand and are part of a 10-acre parcel.

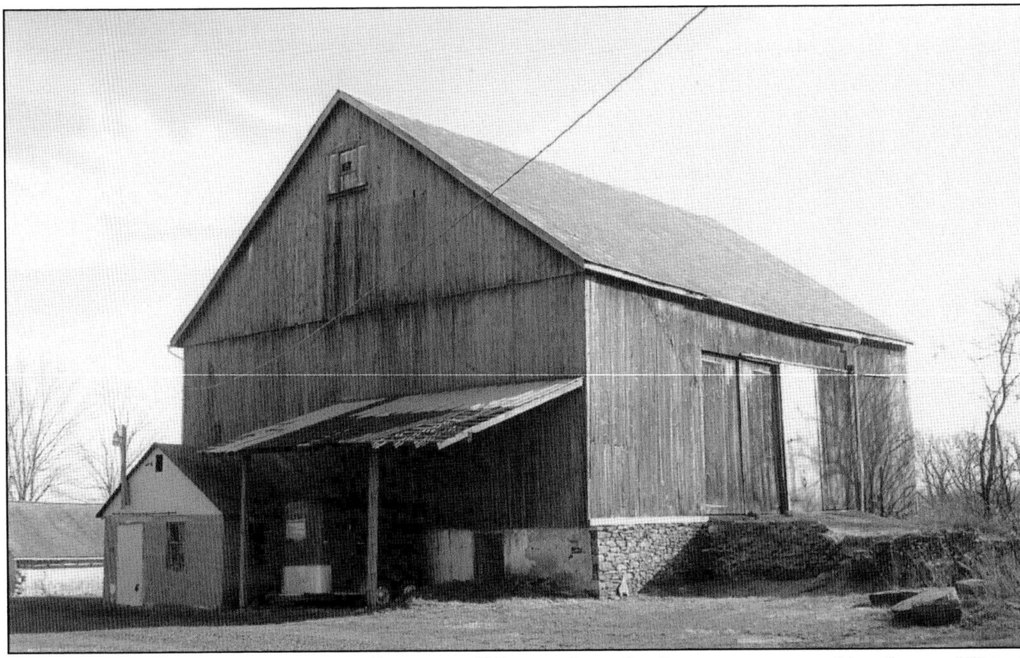

The Pennsylvania bank barn seen here is still located on the farm once owned by Aaron Weisel. The barn was built in the mid-1800s to be used for animal shelter, hay threshing, and storage for grain and hay. This large barn is 104 feet long by 55 feet wide and has a height of 50 feet. Until recently, the barn had in place its original slate roof.

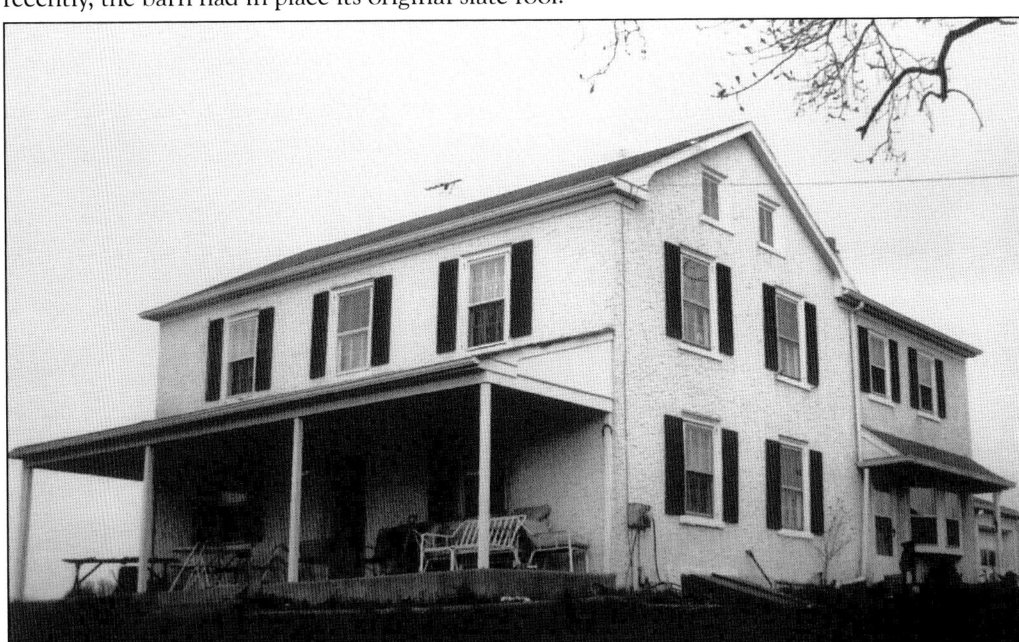

Henry Weisel built a house on the 69 acres of land he owned along Pickertown and Mill Creek Roads. The farm and home of Weisel were well known in the area, being prominently displayed in J.D. Scot's 1876 atlas of Bucks County. The house and farm buildings were razed in 2000. (Courtesy of the Weisel family.)

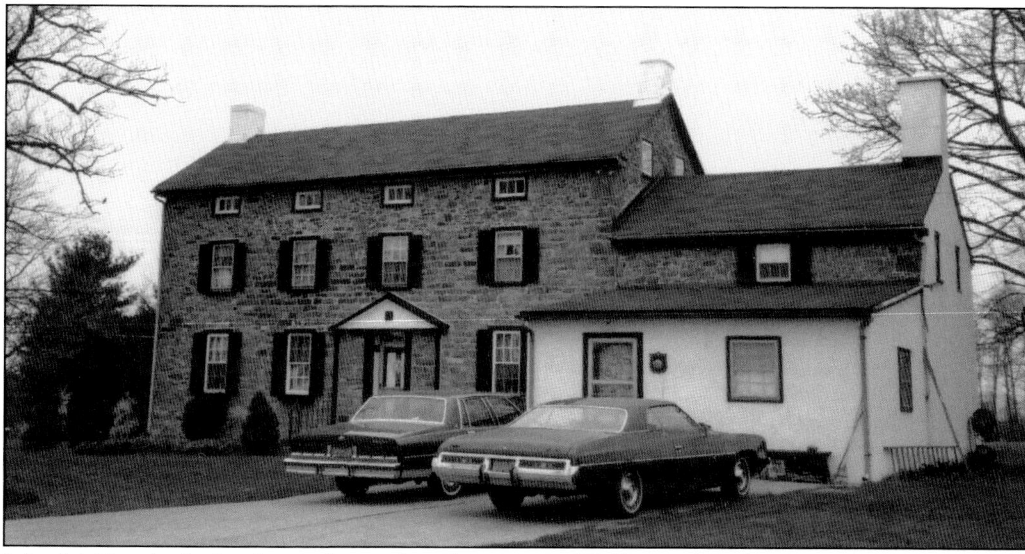

John McNair built this home, located at the corner of Folly Road and Street Road, around 1845. William and Dorothy McNaney bought the home and 37 acres in 1965. In 2000, the McNaneys sold off 30 acres of the property for development, retaining the remaining 7 acres. This home received a certificate and plaque from the Bucks County Heritage Conservancy in 1981.

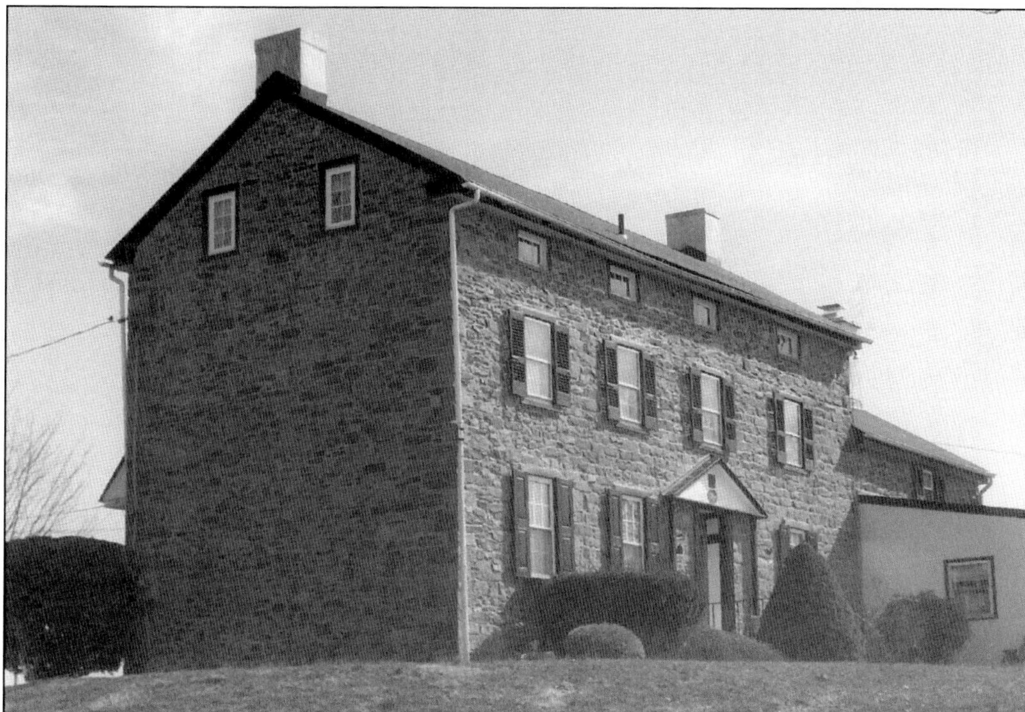

The south side of the house (facing Street Road) was constructed of nicely cut stone, while the remaining walls were constructed of random stone. Originally, the house was covered in stucco. Its removal revealed evidence that the 1845 section of the house had been enlarged at some point from two and a half stories to two and three quarters and that the width of the house had been expanded from three windows across to four.

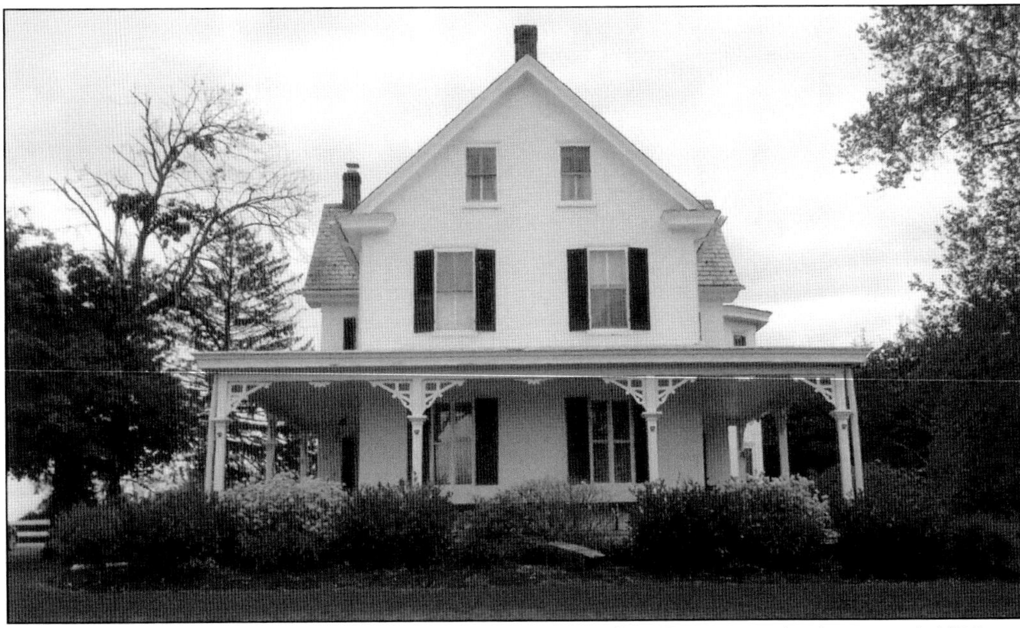

The center stone portion of this home, known as Yankee Farm, was built around 1825 and today sits across from the Central Bucks South High School on Folly Road. Built by Benjamin and Elizabeth Fulton in a design typical of the second quarter of the 19th century, the home commands a dramatic view. It is situated on a hill and employs a grand wraparound porch with elongated windows.

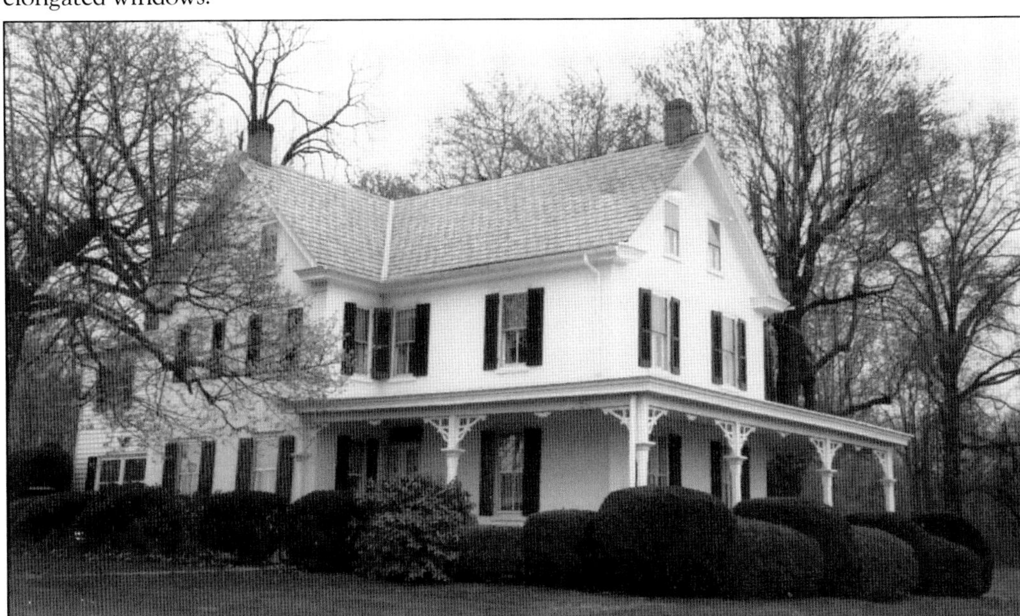

The Fultons made several improvements to the home during their 24 years of ownership. Around 1850, a two-story frame addition to the front (northwest) of the structure was built. This added a grander front entrance, a front foyer/staircase, and a wraparound porch to the home. In the 20th century, a kitchen wing was added to the back of the home. This wing was later rebuilt with a larger footprint.

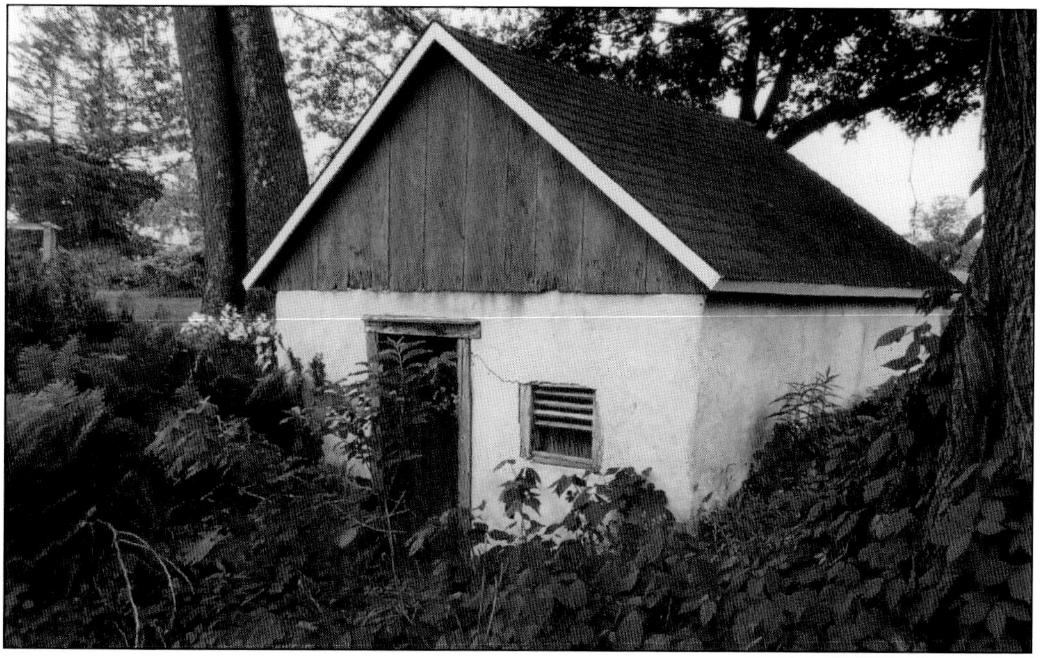

Several outbuildings are located on the property, including a small stone-and-stucco springhouse with a gable roof (pictured here), a machine shed, and a corncrib. A natural spring still provides ample water to the pond located in the front, near Folly Road. This pond at one time provided ice to area farms. (Courtesy of Frank and Connie Ace.)

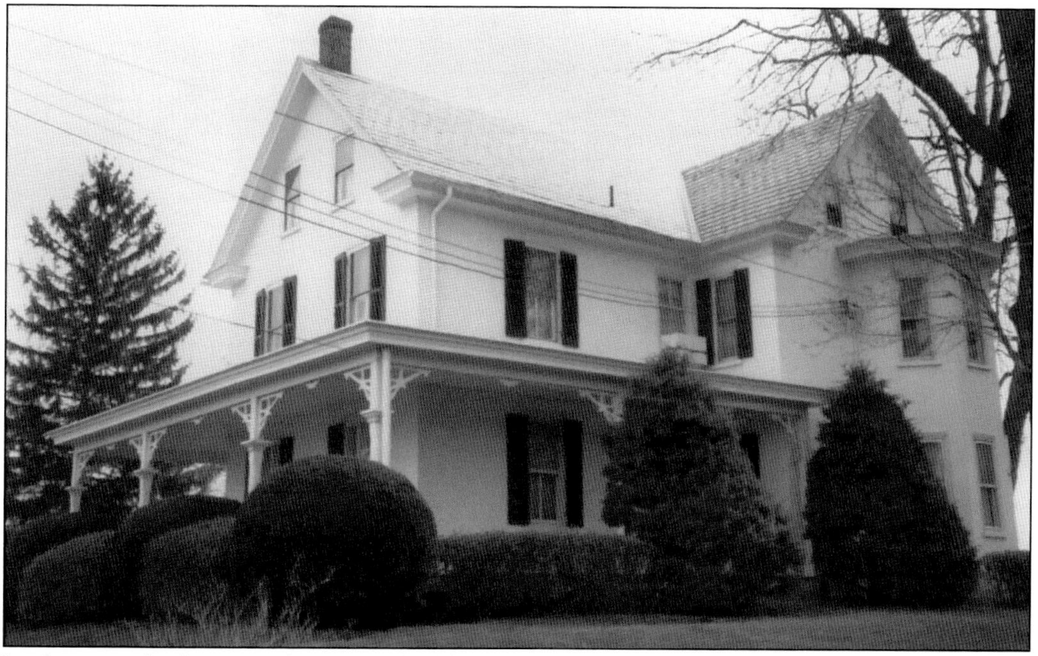

In the past, the house and property had been threatened by eminent domain so that the land could be used for the then to-be-built Central Bucks South High School athletic fields. This home, which has only been owned by two families in the past 100 years, received a certificate and plaque from the Bucks County Heritage Conservancy in 2000.

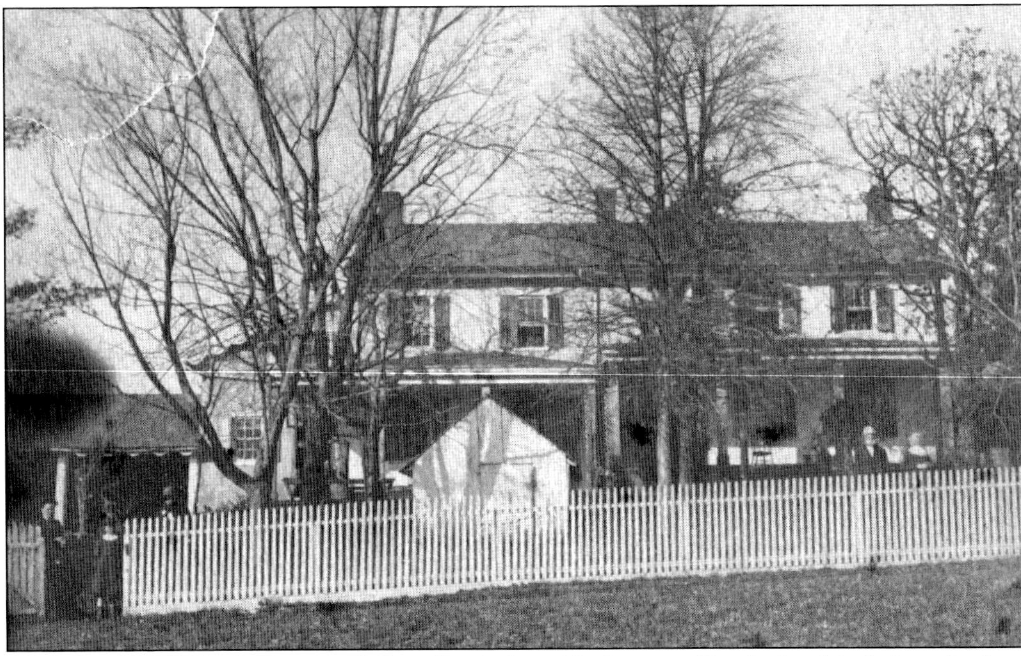

William and Elizabeth Long settled on land along Neshaminy Creek that his father, Andrew, purchased in 1735 for £256. William Long was taxed on 1 slave, 2 horses, 6 cattle, 20 sheep, 1 gristmill, 1 sawmill, and 240 acres of land in 1775. This picture of the Long house located off Bristol Road was taken around 1900. (Courtesy of the Harris family.)

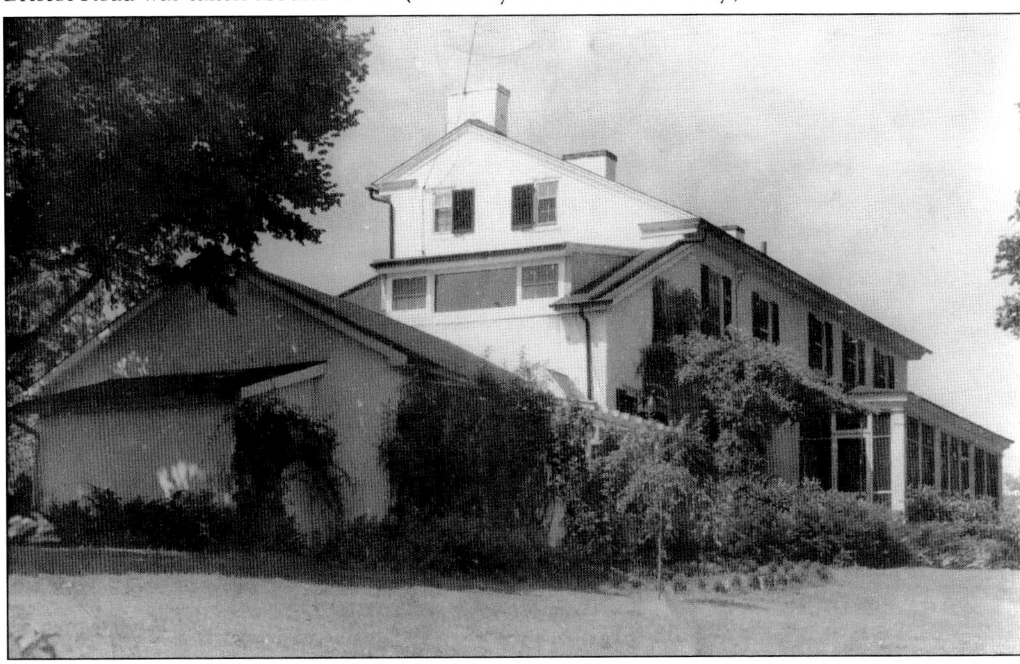

The Long house is pictured in 1953, when it was purchased by the Harris family. The northwest room of the homestead, built about 1760, was used as a hospital at one time during the American Revolution, probably while Washington's army lay encamped in Neshaminy's hills in 1777. (Courtesy of the Harris family.)

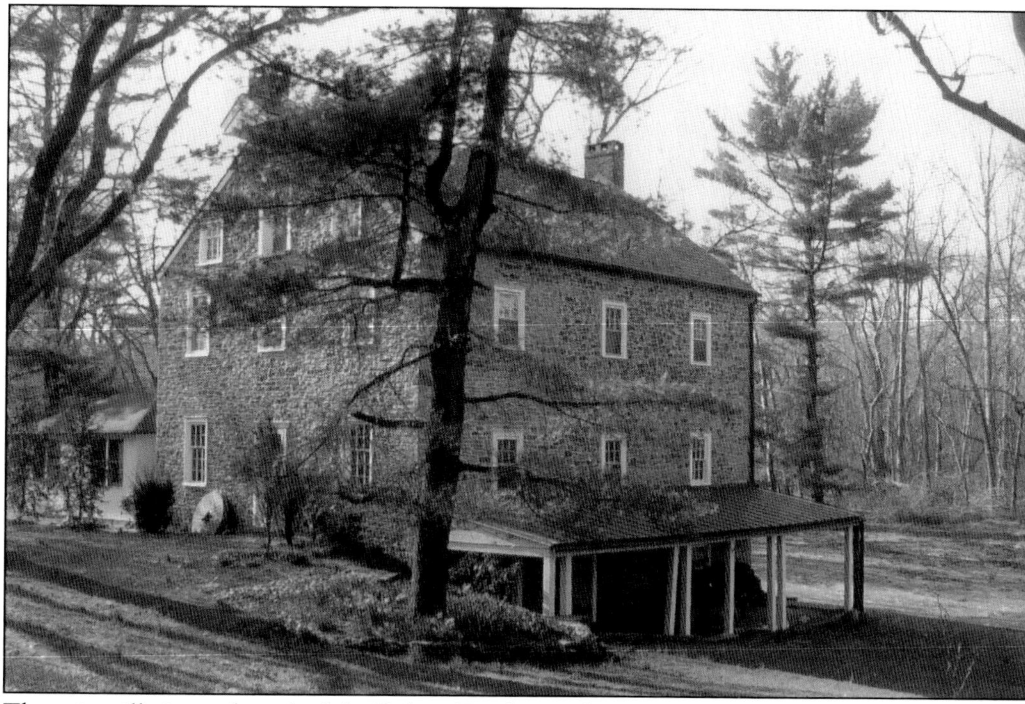

The gristmill pictured was built by Robert Tomkins, who owned the land from 1749 to 1759. The mill, located on Valley Road, operated under the name of Long Merchant Mill when the Longs owned the property. In 1936, Adeline McCord converted the mill into a residence with plans drawn by A. Oscar Martin.

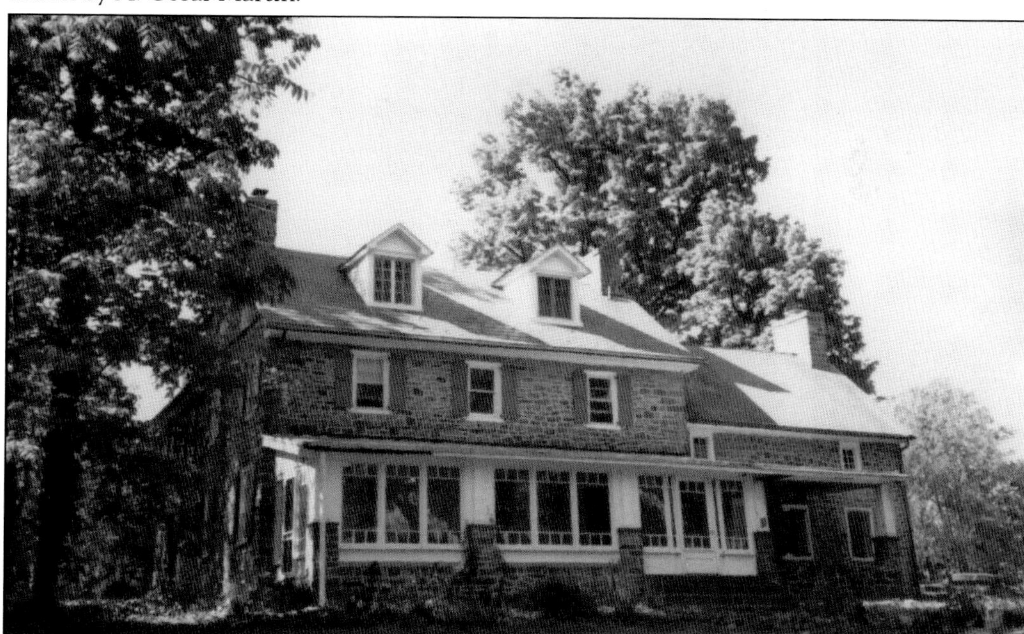

The rightmost portion of this home located off Valley Road is believed to be as old as the mill and is said to have been the miller's house. This photograph shows the large stone additions that were built onto house in the 1830s and the 1850s.

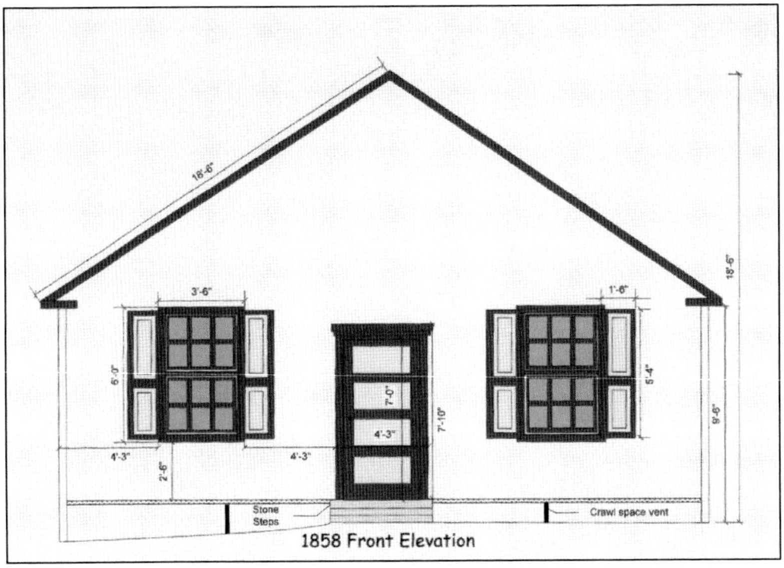

1858 Front Elevation

The prospect of a schoolhouse located at the corner of County Line Road and Folly Road, near the village of Pleasantville/ Eureka, Warrington Township, is mentioned as early as 1751, when Ephraim Leech created a will that conveyed one acre of land at the south corner of his property for the purpose.

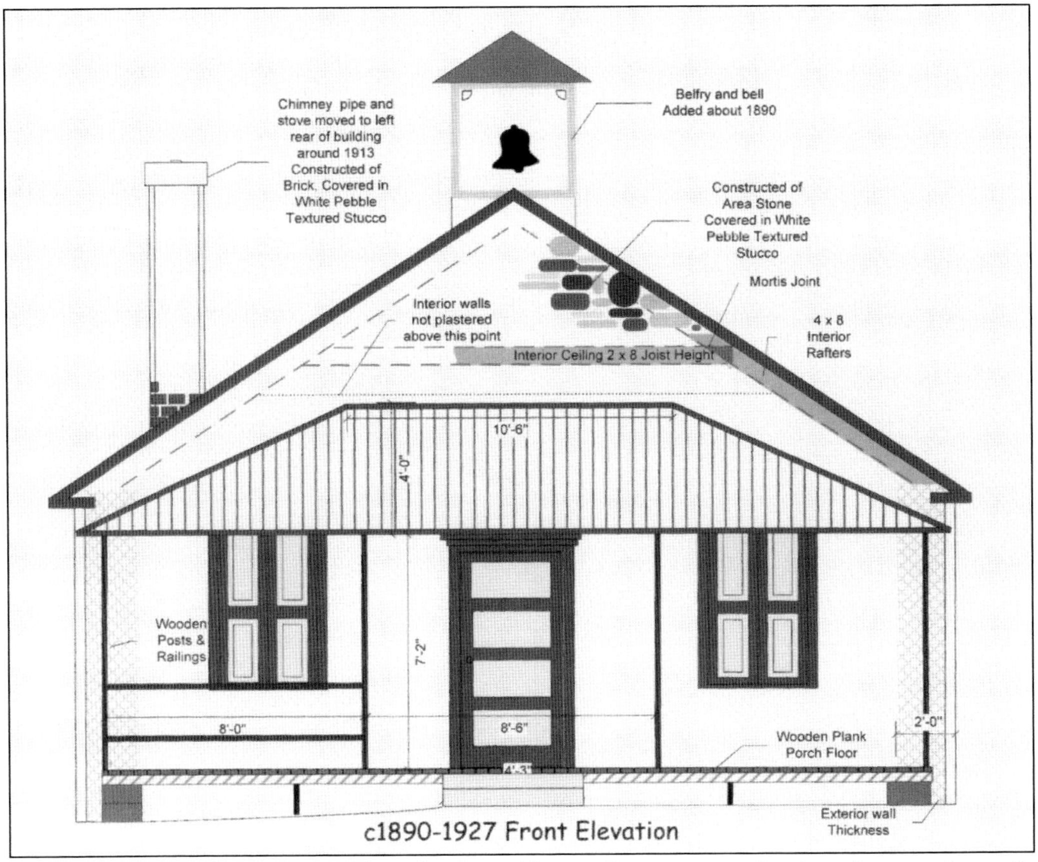

c1890-1927 Front Elevation

It was agreed that the patrons of the school would raise the necessary funds and put up the walls of a 28-by-35-foot house, which would be stone with a wall through it. The walls outside would be finished with a good common dash and the inside with three coats of plastering. The directors were to pay a reasonable price for putting the ceiling on.

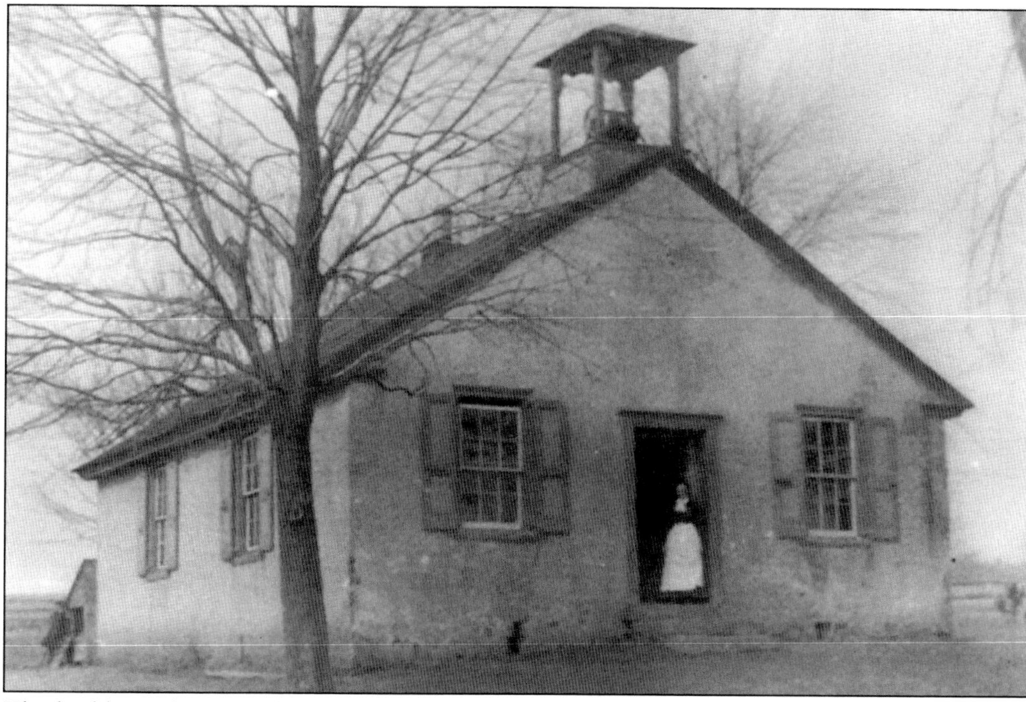

The building of a new schoolhouse on County Line Road is well documented in school board meeting minutes: "At a meeting of the board of school directors of Warrington district pursuant to adjournment at the County Line School room on June 11, 1857. Present: John L. Radcliff, Henry McKinstry, Abraham R. Kephart, Thomas S. Radcliff, and John Cozen. The meeting was for the purpose of making arrangements for building."

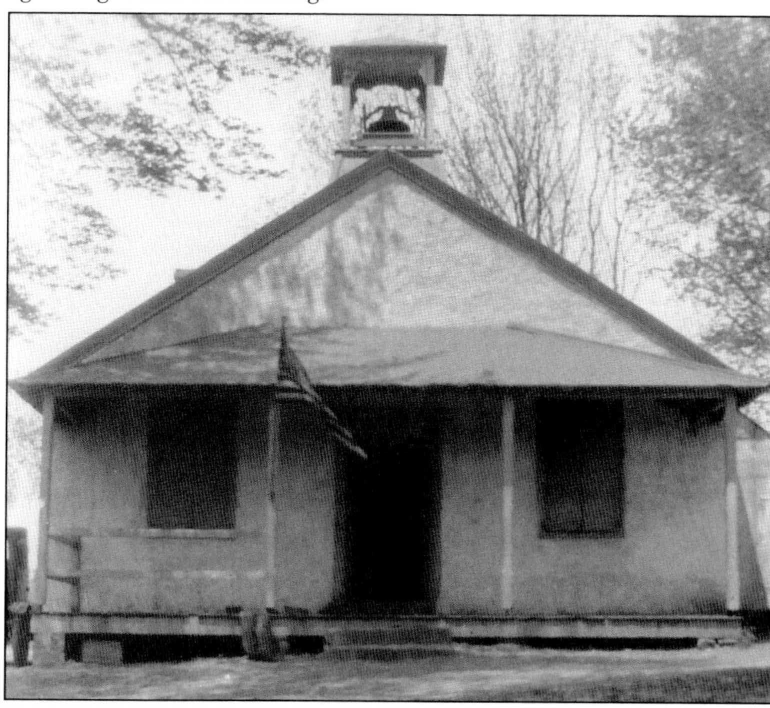

In April 1927, the need for a new, larger school was brought before the board. The existing school remained in operation until 1928, when the two-room Mill Creek School opened. Charles and Catherine Schlechter submitted a sealed bid for $2,000 to purchase the property and became the owners in August 1928. The Schlechter family first used it as a summer and holiday retreat.

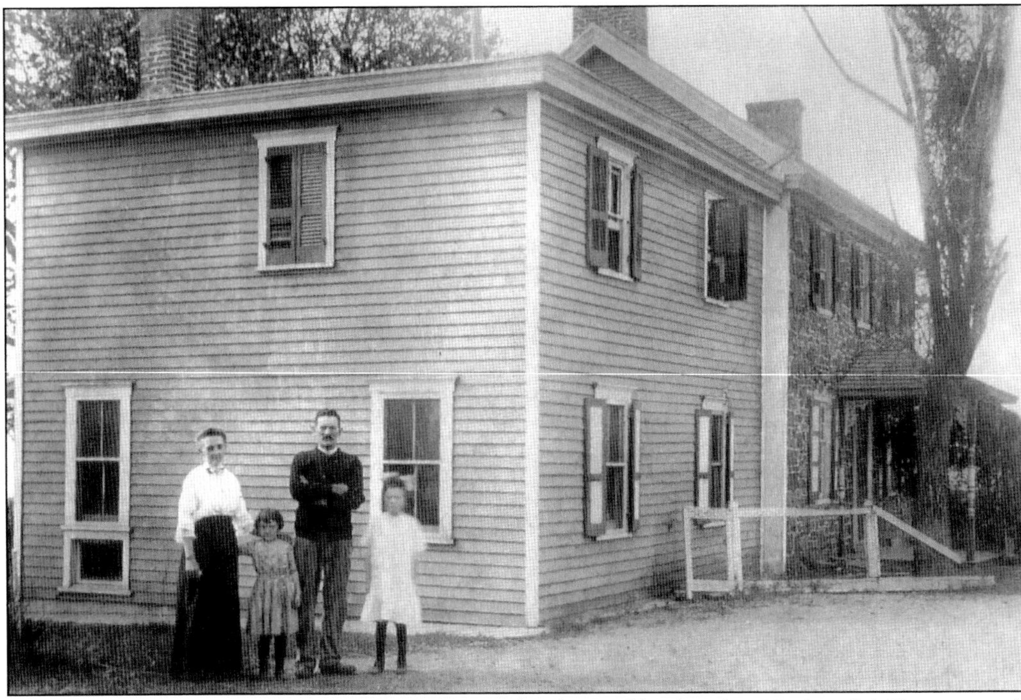

In 1823, John McKinstry purchased 27 acres so that he and his brother Nathan McKinstry could live in a log cabin while doing carpet weaving and farming. Around 1825, they constructed the original portion of the house with local red stone at 3263 County Line Road. There were a parlor and kitchen on the first floor and three bedrooms on the second floor. (Courtesy of Bob and Jane Henderson.)

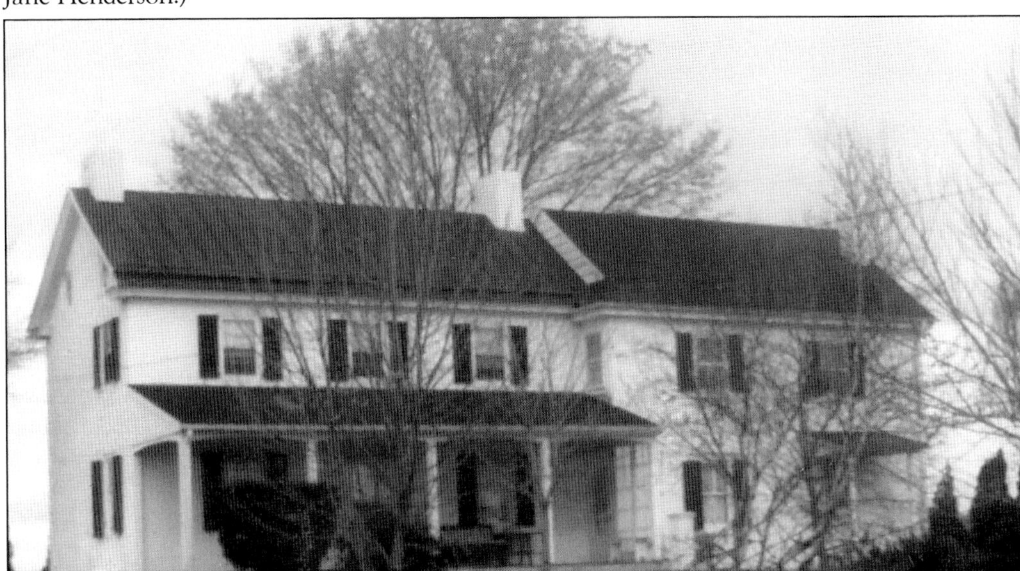

The need to build an addition on the home came in the early 1900s. The new frame addition included a bathroom, kitchen, and dining room on the first floor, plus a bathroom and two more bedrooms on the second floor. This house received a certificate and a plaque from the Bucks County Heritage Conservancy in 1982. (Courtesy of Bob and Jane Henderson.)

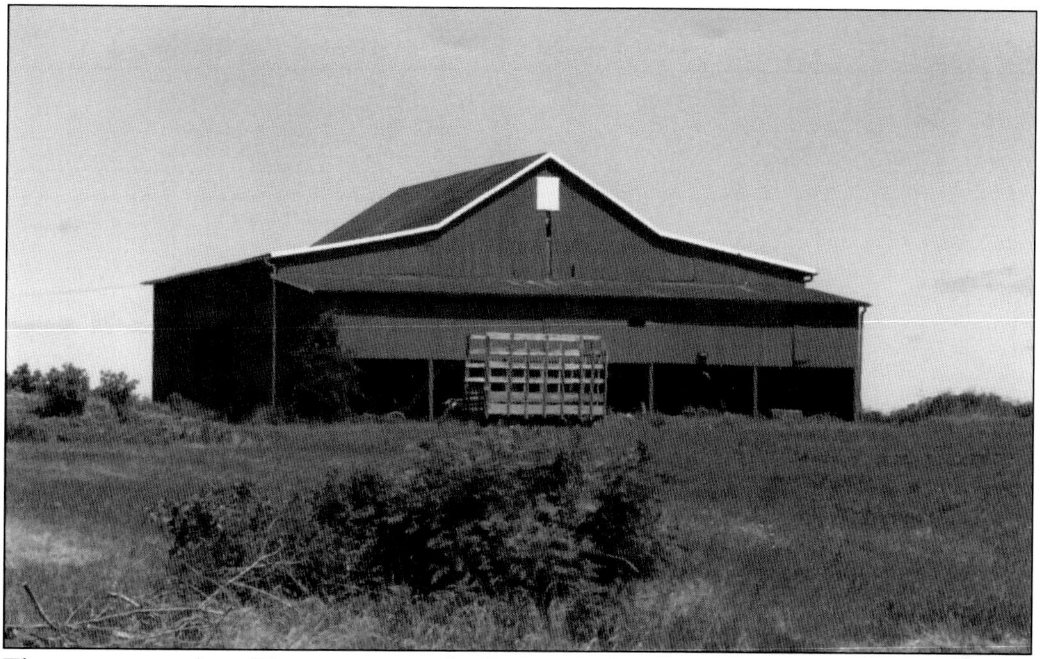

There were several small barns, a summer kitchen, an outhouse, two chicken houses, a woodshed, and a large hay barn on McKinstry's property. Pictured here is the large hay barn (built around World War I), which was dismantled in 2000 to make way for the housing development known as the Chase at Warrington Hunt. (Courtesy of Bob and Jane Henderson.)

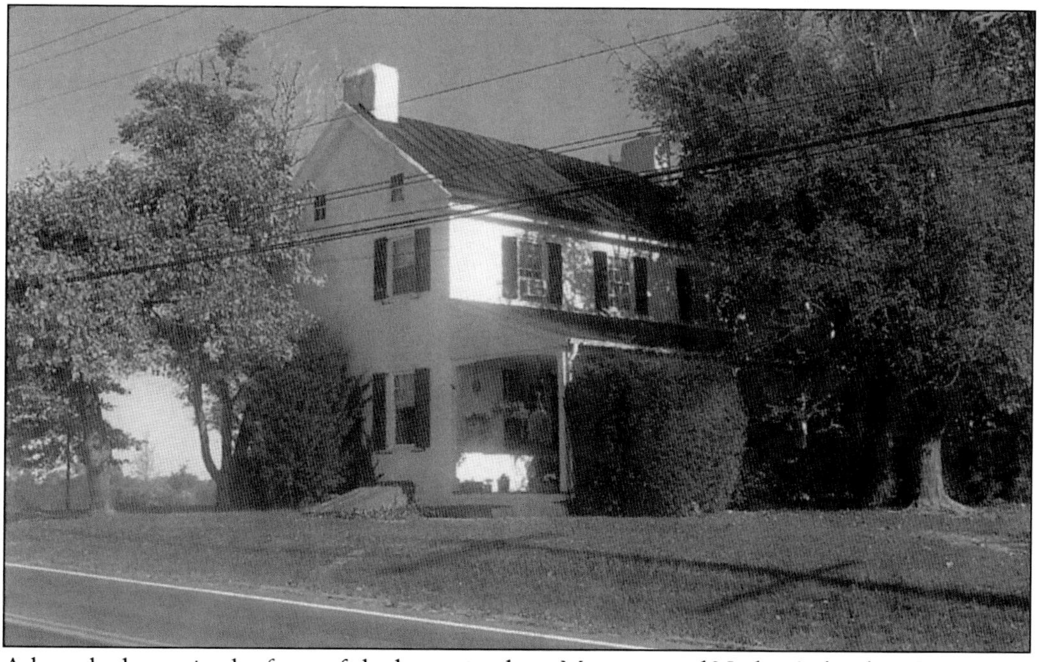

A large bedroom in the front of the house is where Margaret and Nathan's daughter Jennie was born in 1828. Later, Jennie's daughter Elizabeth Mae Kohler was born in the same room. The historical society is keeping a close eye on this property, as the Pennsylvania Department of Transportation has plans to widen County Line Road, which may affect its existence.

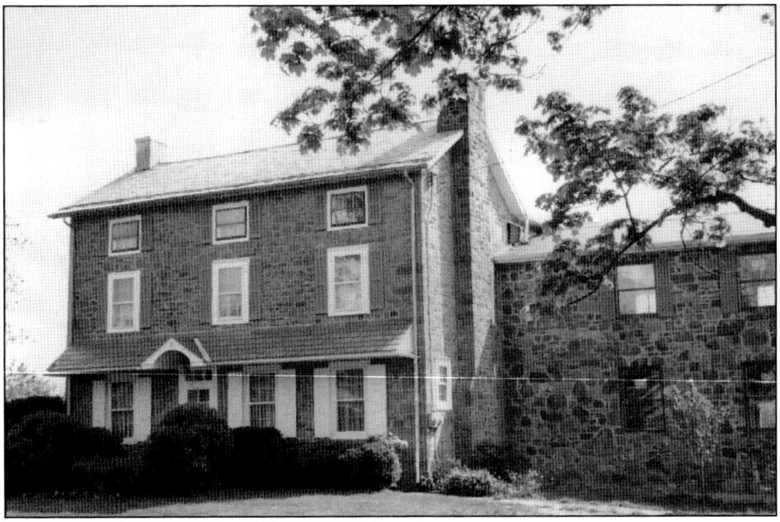

Located on Bristol Road, across from Kelly Drive, is the Bristol Springs Farm. The house pictured here has a date stone on it that states, "J and S Cozens 1856." James Cozens was known as a master mason and a longtime school board member. He built many of the schoolhouses and bridges in the area.

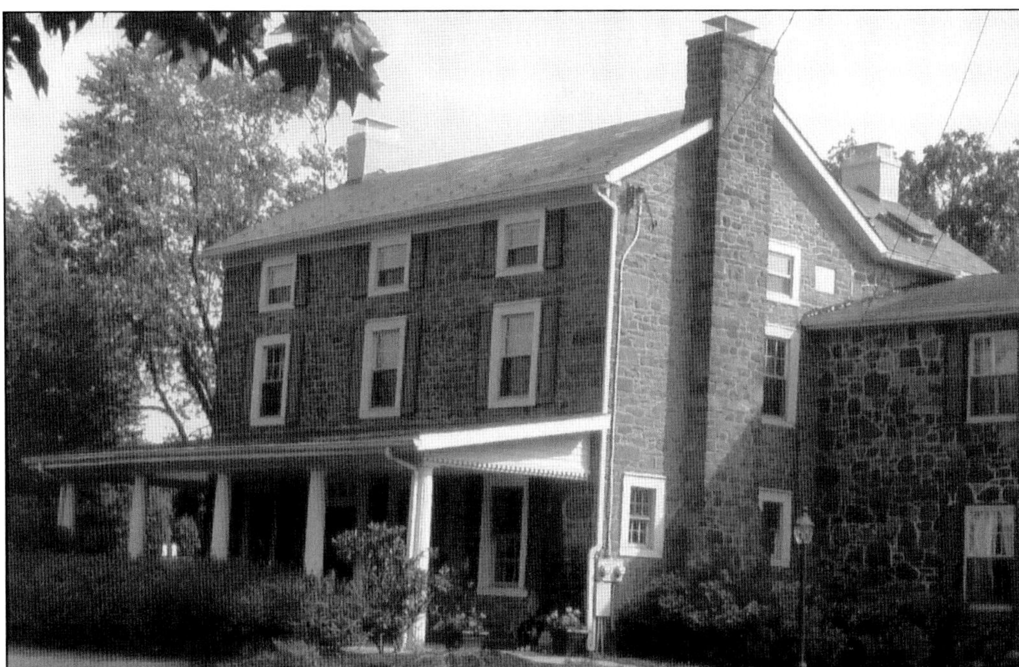

Charles Cadwallader was born September 14, 1917, at his grandparents' farmhouse. The farm consisted of 69 acres at that time. Charles remembers when the original red barn and silo burned down in 1925 or 1926, and neighbors pitched in and helped rebuild the barn. There were also a combination wagon house/woodshed and a thriving orchard. The pond that produced ice that was stored in the combined icehouse/springhouse is still there.

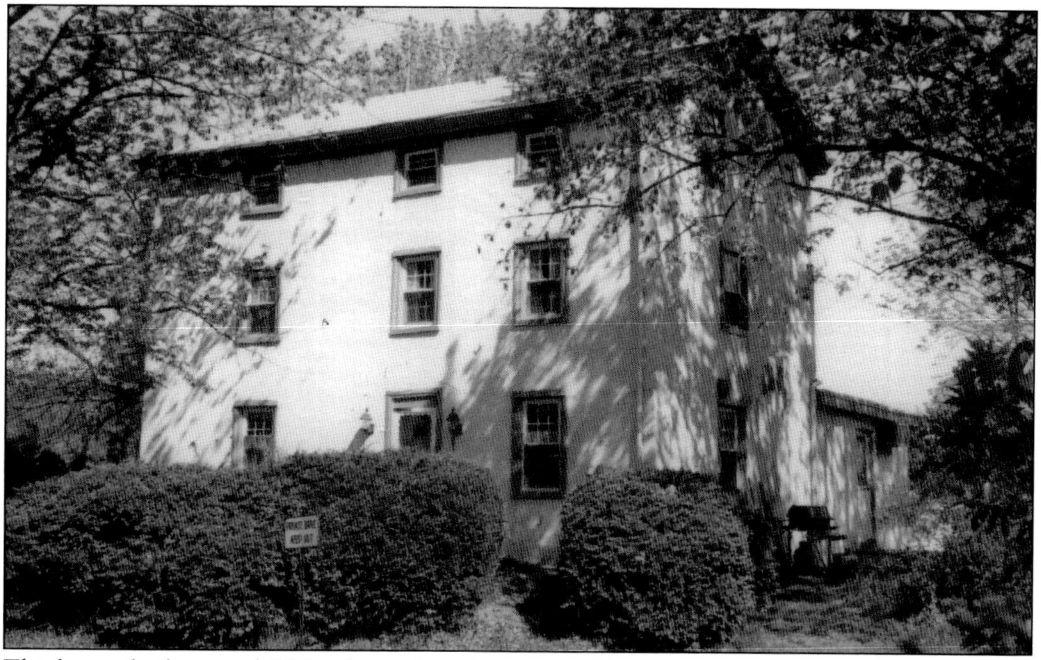

This house, built around 1750, is located on the corner of County Line Road and Bradford Avenue. It is one of the oldest known existing homesteads in the township. The stucco exterior shown in the photograph has since been removed to expose the stone exterior seen today. The 1850 map of Warrington Township produced by W.E. Morris lists the Rutheford family as owner.

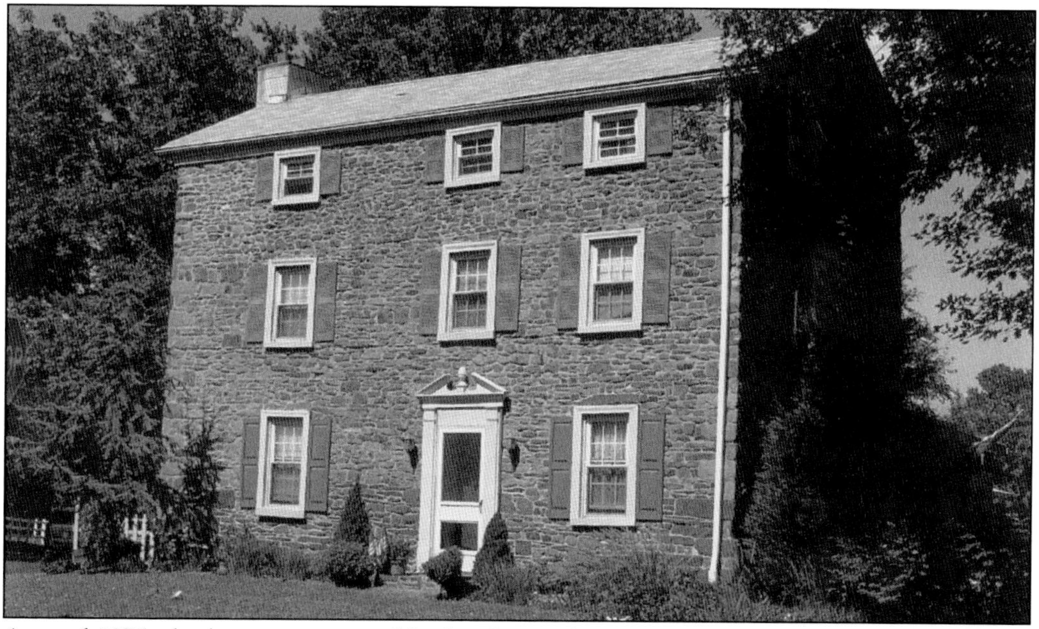

Around 1875, the house was owned by brother and sister Henry and Elizabeth Arnold, who were well-known local farmers, butchers, and merchants. Maps of the township from 1876 and 1891 document that the home was part of a 52-acre farm. Today, the historical society is closely monitoring this property, as the Pennsylvania Department of Transportation's plans to widen County Line Road may affect its existence.

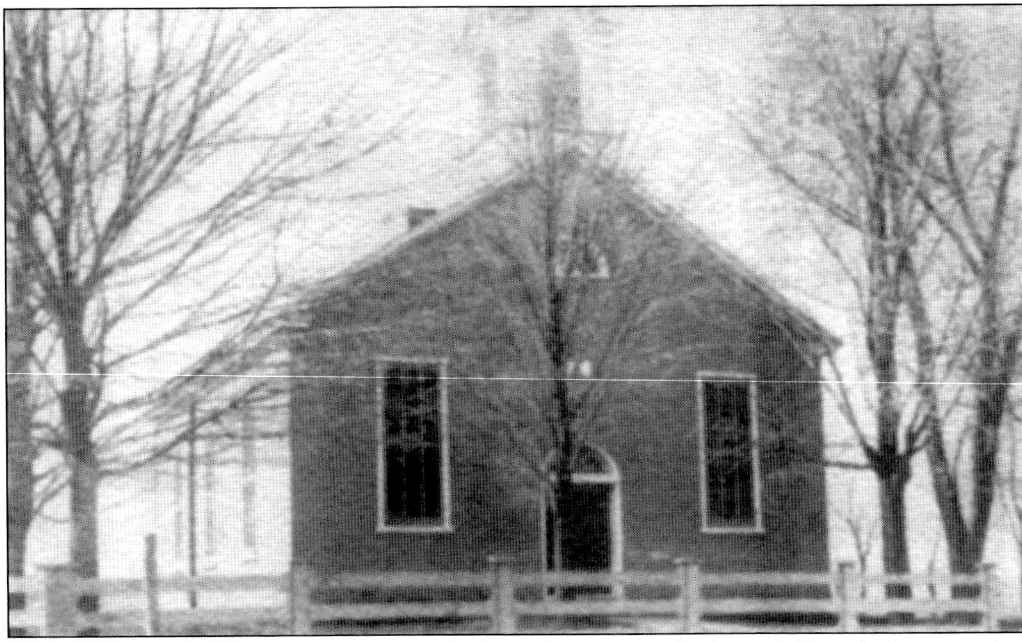

On October 19, 1840, a cornerstone was laid for the German Reformed Church. It was a plain brick structure, 60 by 51 feet. The building's dedication took place on May 19, 1841. After years of services, a farewell service was held on June 5, 1898. On the following day, workmen began to tear down the old building to construct a new one.

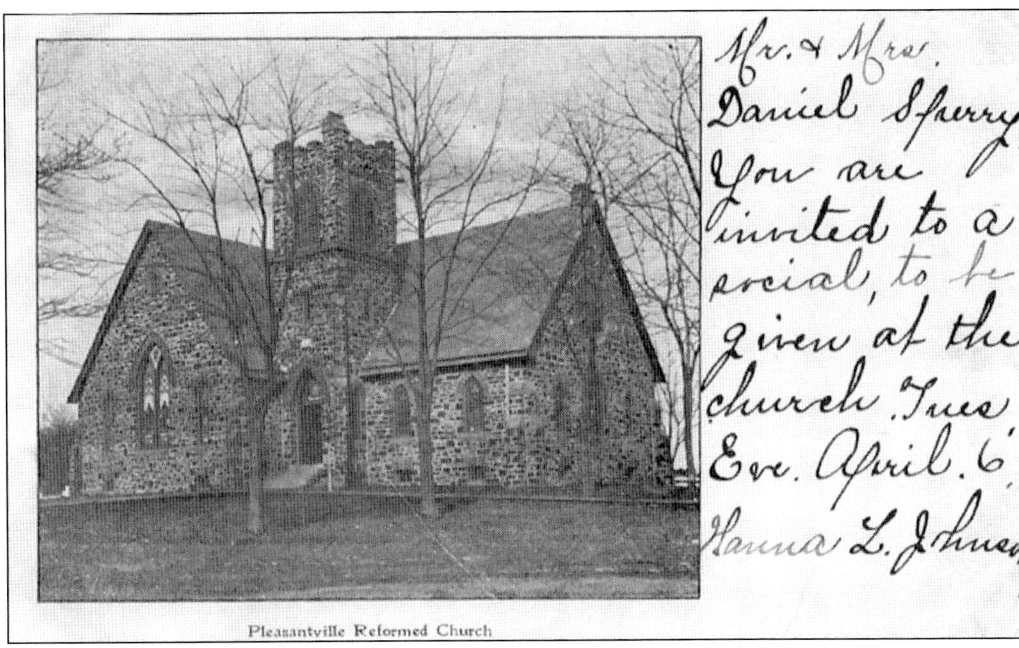

A vote was taken on March 20, 1898, in favor of a new church. Accordingly, a building committee was appointed, and architect A. Oscar Martin of Doylestown was employed to present plans for the new edifice, seen here around 1899 or 1900. The first service in the new church was held on Christmas Day 1898. The cost of the new building was $7,000. (Courtesy of Mark Hamilton.)

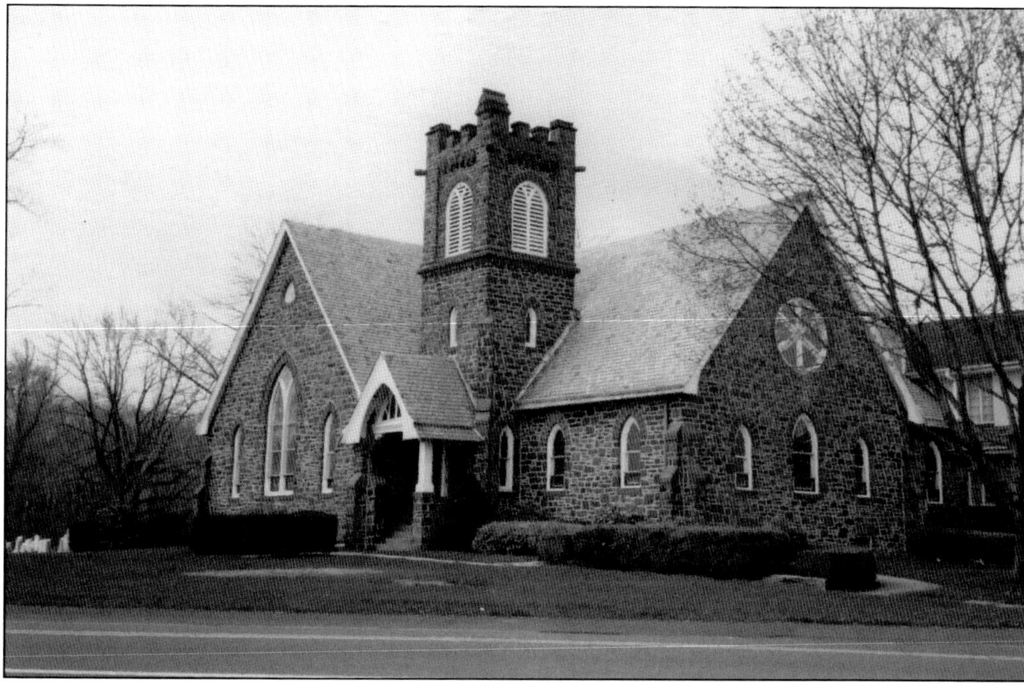

The bell in the belfry, dating to 1850, is from the original brick church. Around 1901, a portico was added to the front entrance, and a pipe organ was installed in the sanctuary in memory of Tilghman A. Hoover. In 1934, the church merged with the Pleasantville Evangelical and Reformed Church. In 1957, another merger took place, and the church became the Pleasantville United Church of Christ.

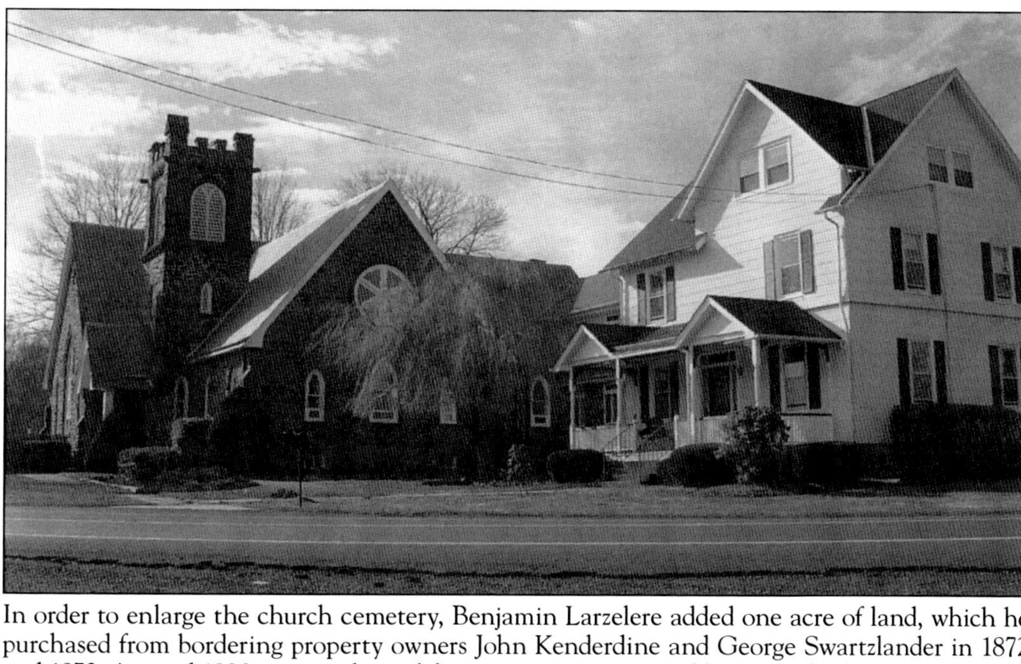

In order to enlarge the church cemetery, Benjamin Larzelere added one acre of land, which he purchased from bordering property owners John Kenderdine and George Swartzlander in 1872 and 1873. Around 1890, a second wood-frame structure, pictured here, was built on the property to be used a pastorate.

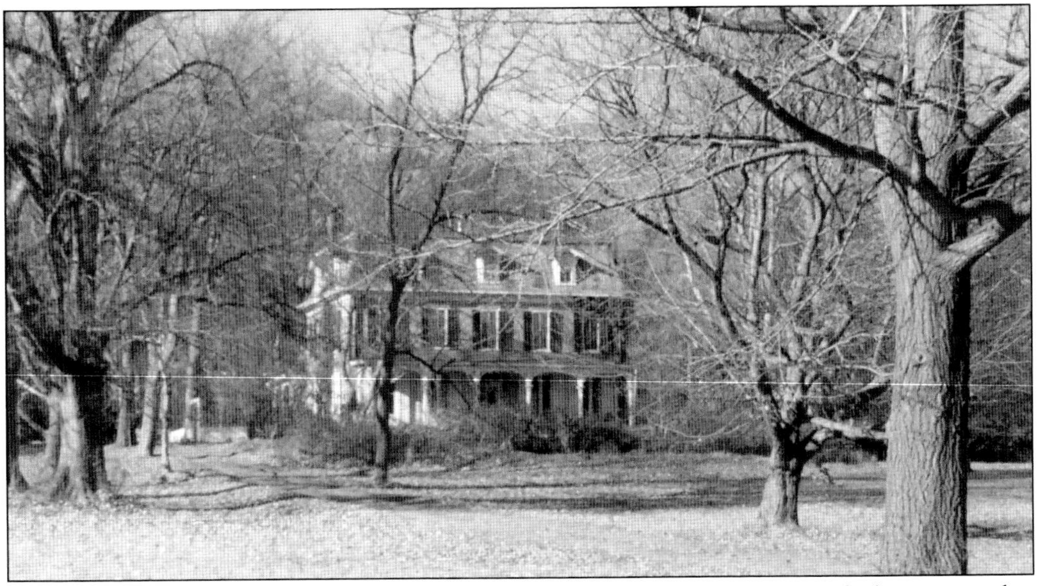

Broadlawns, once located at 1574 Easton Road, was built in 1872 by James Grier for his two maiden sisters (Mary and Elizabeth). The home is a Victorian mansion designed with French Colonial architecture and a mansard roof. The nine-bedroom house and large barn were constructed of sandstone quarried on the property. There were three covered porches that overlooked the grounds. (Courtesy of Scott Yates.)

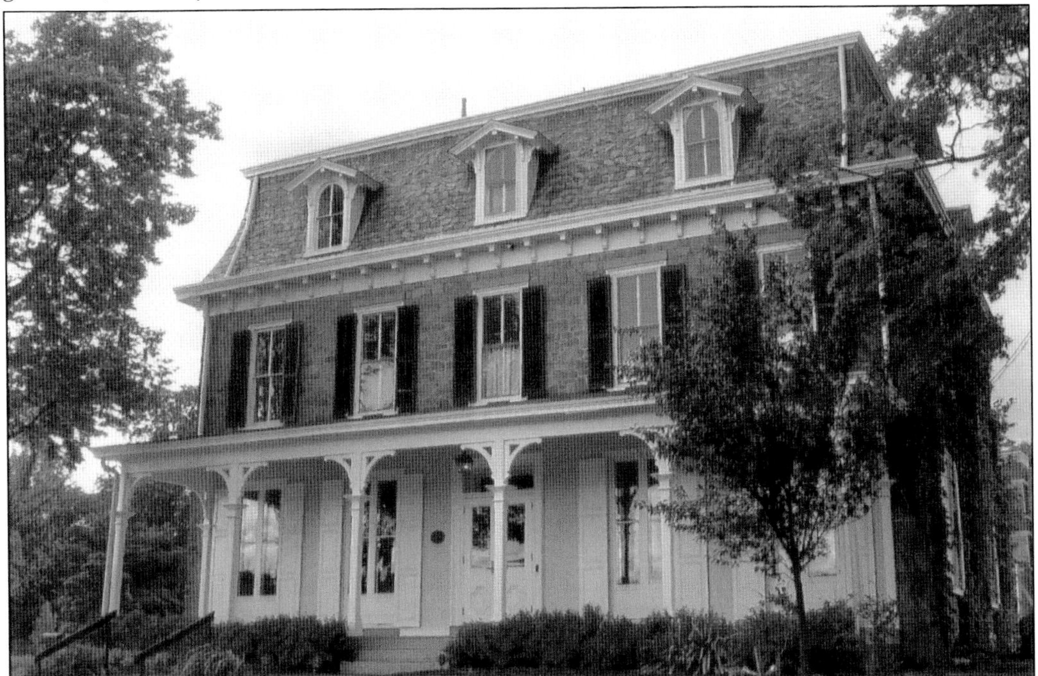

This house features a staircase that sweeps from the center entrance hall to the third floor. The large, stately drawing room is lined with tall windows. The library has a carved marble fireplace and ceiling-height bookcases. The dining room showcases a crystal chandelier, and the kitchen has a stately fireplace.

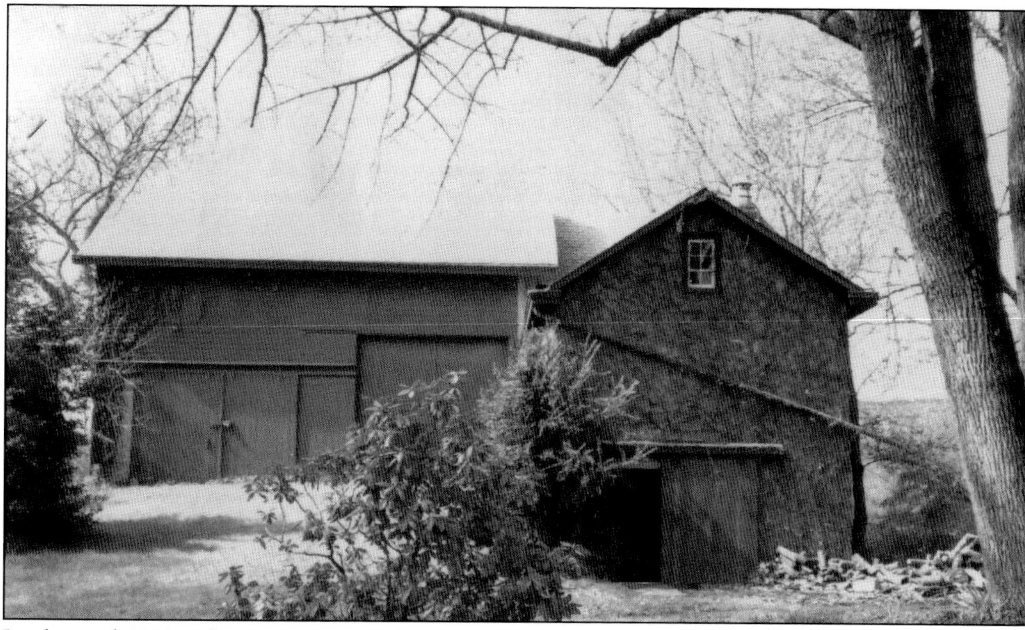

In the mid-1900s, the property was described as a Victorian home with several outbuildings set amid open lawns and towering oaks on 31 acres in Warrington. The Broadlawns and 31 acres were purchased in 1945 by Dr. John S. Prickett (chief radiologist of Doylestown Hospital from 1939 until his retirement in 1970) and his wife, Elsie. The couple hired Ralph Land to renovate and preserve the Victorian mansion.

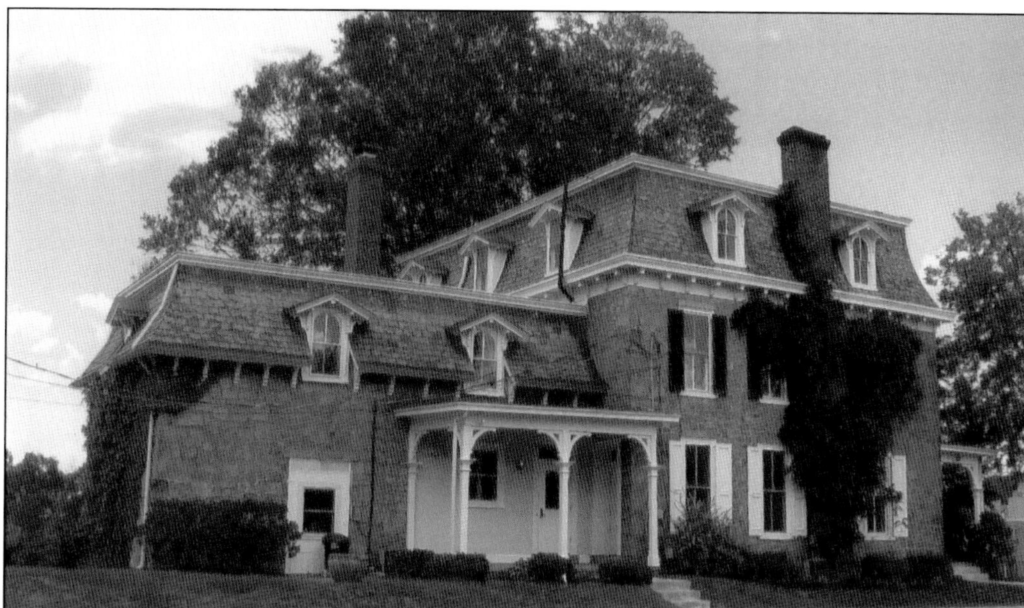

In 1994, the home and property were showcased as the Bucks County Designer House, which benefited Doylestown Hospital. The house was sold by the Prickett family in 2002. During the development of the property, all the farm buildings were removed. The house is now located at the center of the Stone Manor Corporate Center and is currently in danger of having its zoning changed from commercial (offices) to residential (apartments).

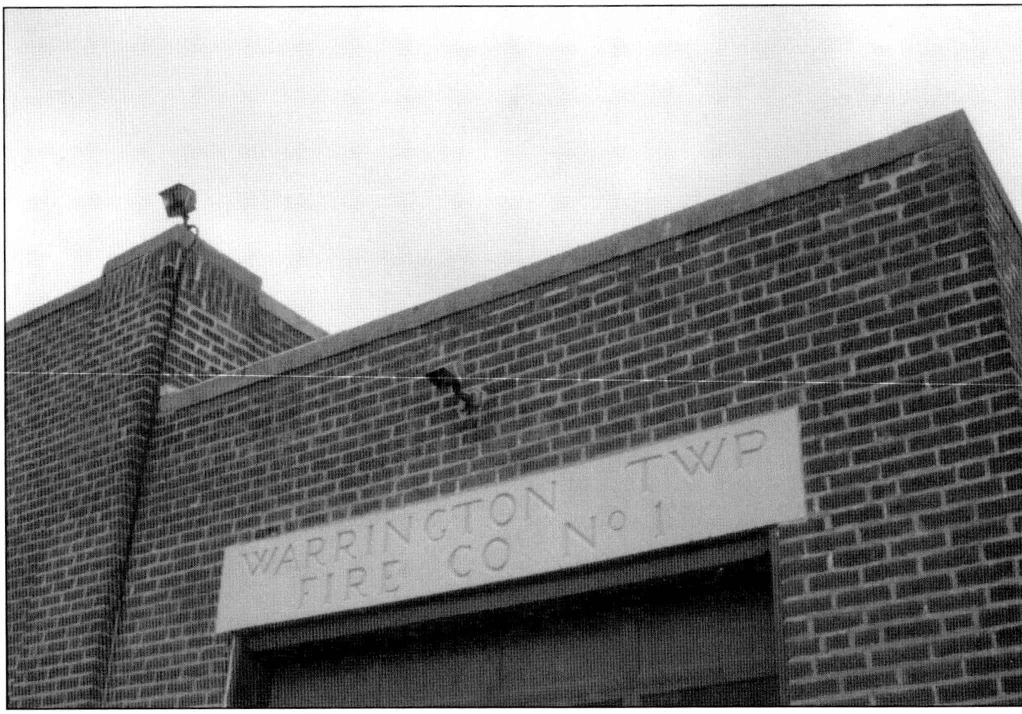

On March 27, 1924, the Warrington Township Fire Company was organized. Harry Woern was chosen as president, and officers were George Tettemer, secretary; Alfred Tettemer, treasurer; Allan Hankle, chairman of the Membership Committee, with Elmer Lewis and Samuel McKinstry assisting. Originally, 22 charter members signed up and paid dues of $1 each.

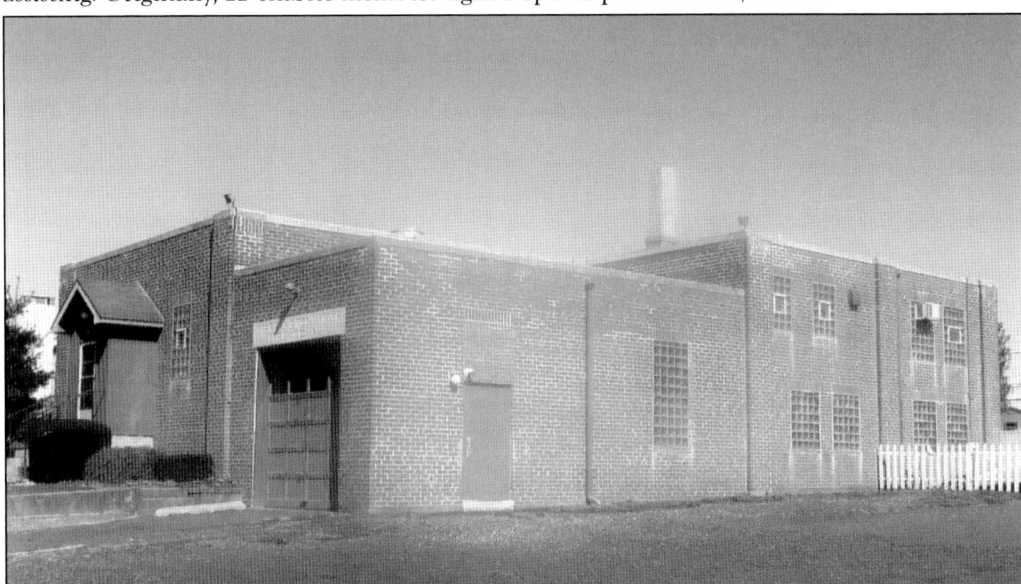

The dedication of the new firehouse on Maple Avenue took place on March 2, 1935. In 1939, A. Oscar Martin drew up plans for an addition to the facility, and R.R. Randall, a builder from Jenkintown, constructed it at a cost of $3,760.99. This was their headquarters until 1977, when a new, larger building was erected at 2310 Freedoms Way.

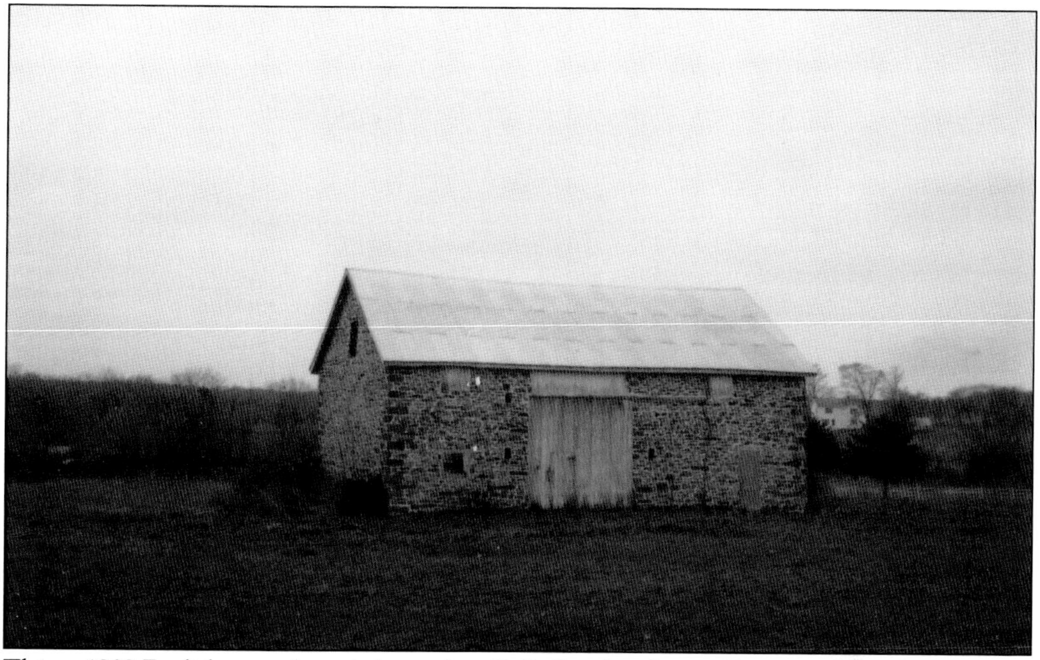

This c. 1802 English stone barn is located on Folly Road in front of Lower Nike Park. This style of barn was replaced by larger Pennsylvania-style bank barns in the early 19th century. There are very few English-style stone barns remaining in Bucks County. An average English barn measured 30 feet by 40 feet and had a large double wagon door on its lateral side.

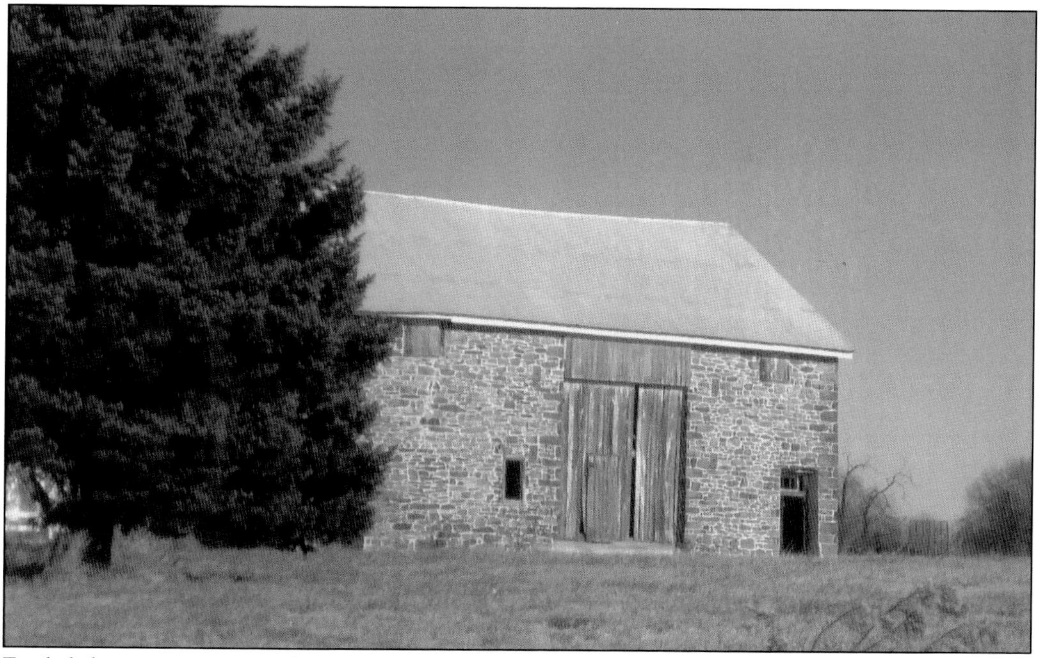

English barns were normally without a basement and stood on level ground. The interiors were characterized by a center driveway that acted as a threshing floor. Livestock were kept on one side, while feed was stored on the other. The historical society is keeping a close eye on this property in the wake of development plans that have been submitted to the township.

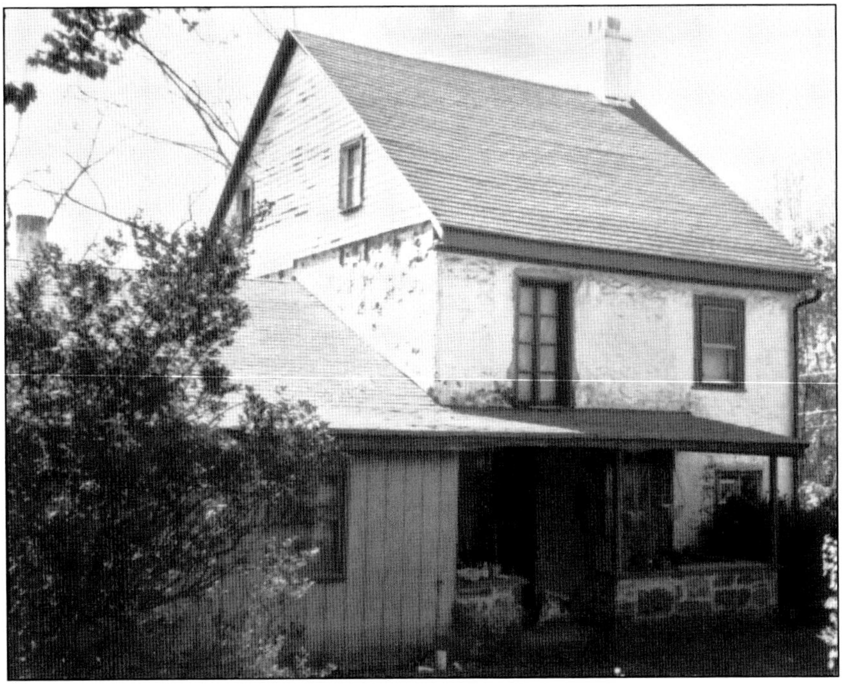

The style and construction methods of this house, located at the corner of County Line Road and Fairmount Avenue, suggest that it was built in the late 1700s. The narrow home's stature shows what many of the houses in the area looked like before additions were placed on them.

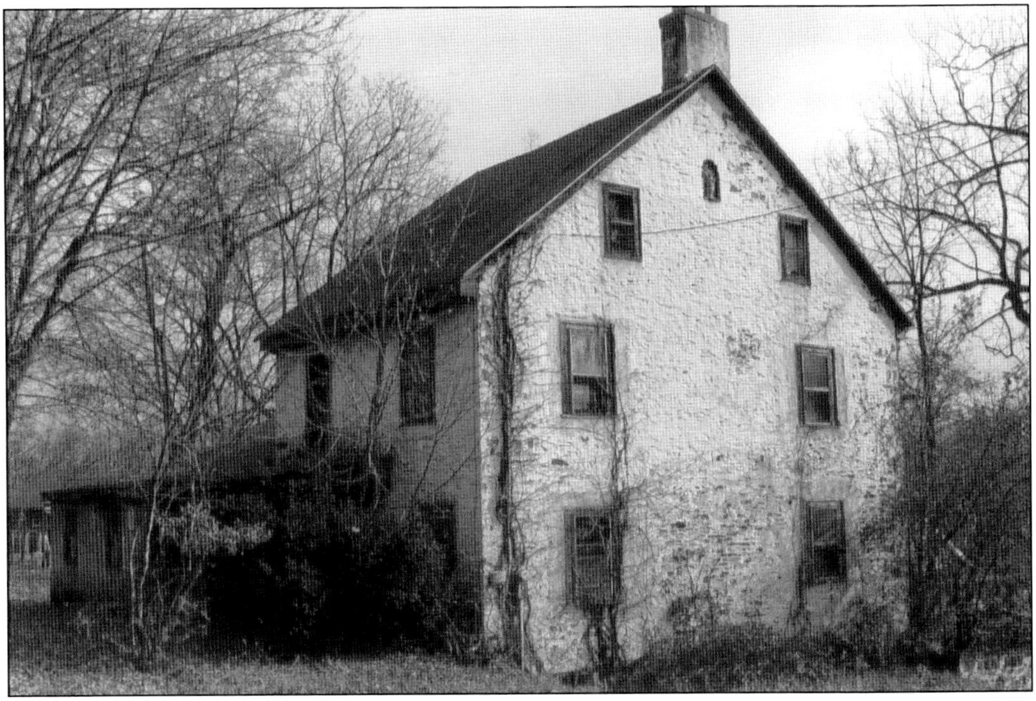

Once owned by James Thompson, this farm consisted of 135 acres and is displayed in J.D. Scott's atlas of Bucks County. The historical society is closely monitoring this property, as the Pennsylvania Department of Transportation has plans to widen County Line Road, which may affect its existence.

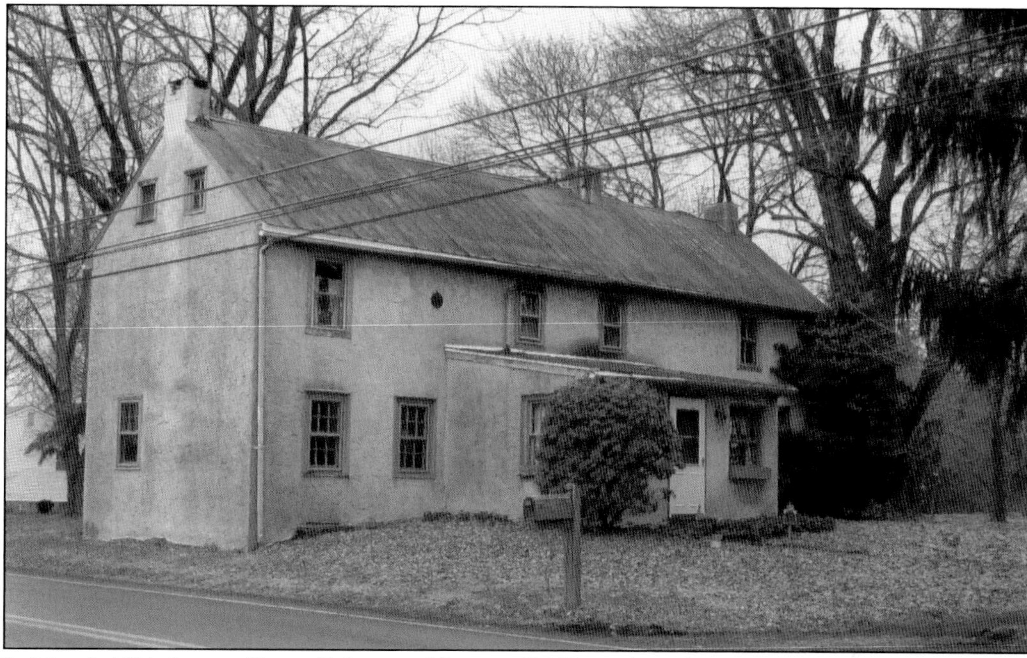

In March 1911, farmer Harry Cohen and his son Wolf purchased 63 acres of land on Street Road. Much of the Cohens' tomato crop was bought by the Campbell Soup Company. Harry first held religious services in this farmhouse on Saturday mornings. On March 26, 1924, Congregation Tiferes B'nai Israel was chartered at a court session of common pleas in Doylestown, Bucks County.

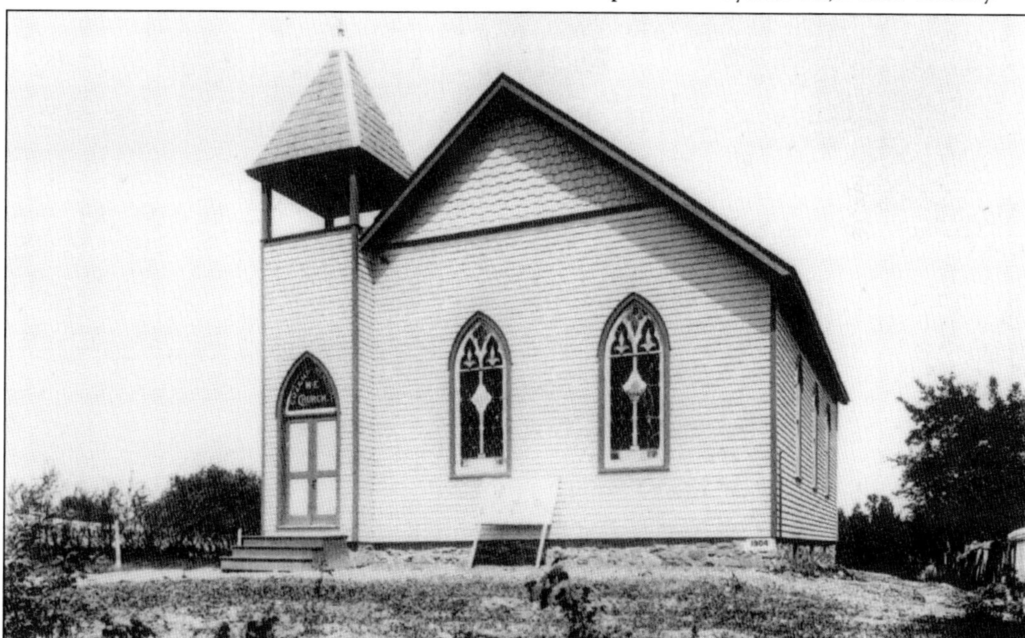

Today the location of Carpet Giant, this structure was built in 1904 and was originally the home of the Neshaminy Methodist Episcopal Church. The building was constructed of wood and had many ornate stained-glass windows. The congregation relocated to a new location within Warrington in 1963.

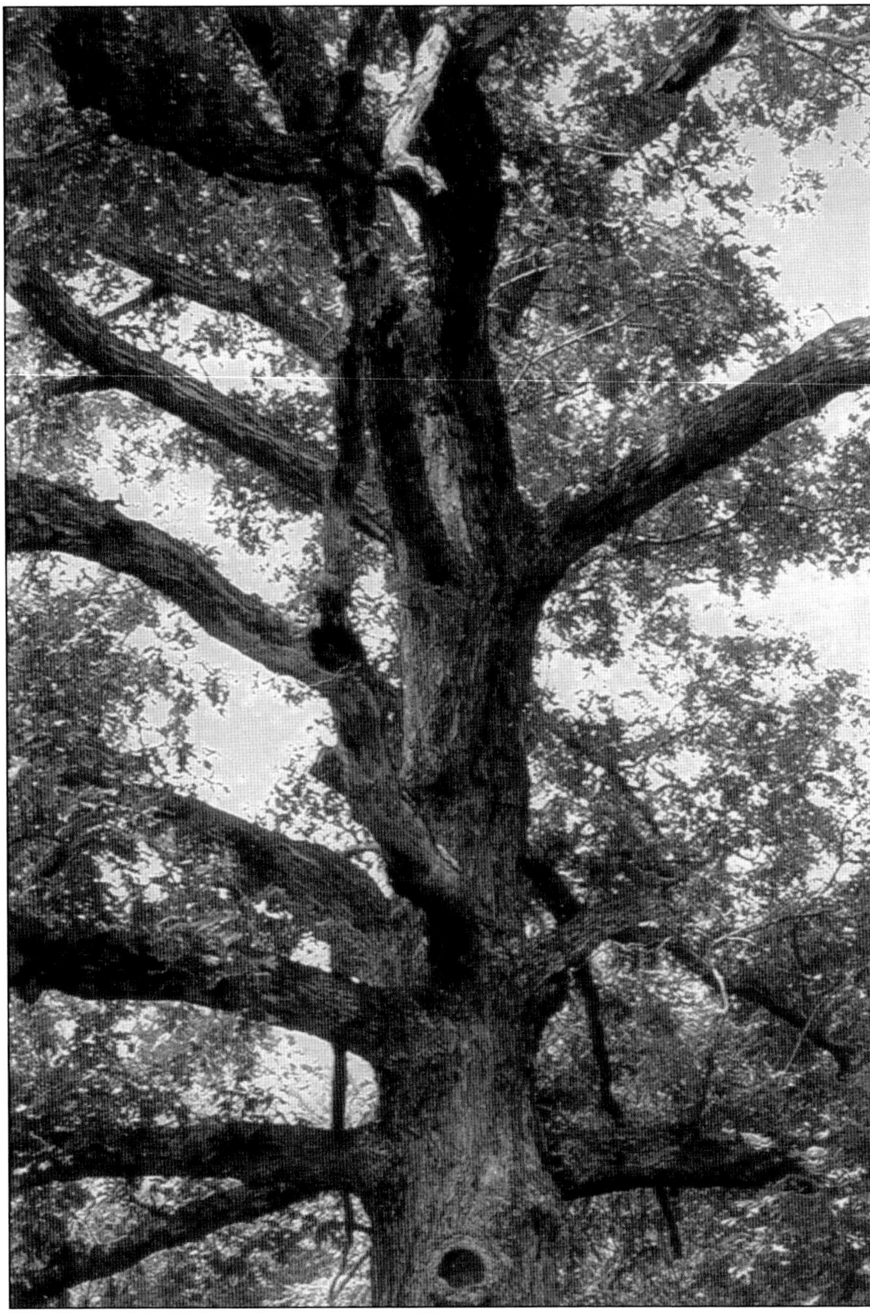

On October 27, 1932, the tree located at the County Line School House was recognized as an authentic William Penn white oak. The tree is estimated to be over 300 years old. During the 19th and early 20th centuries, children who attended the school played under its outstretched limbs. The tree's limbs span over 120 feet, and it has a trunk with a diameter of more than 17 feet. This tree was heavily damaged during a hard downpour the first week of June 2014. Large limbs crashed to the ground, revealing that the main trunk of the tree is greatly hollowed out. In response, the township topped and greatly pruned the tree. Currently, at the time of printing this publication, the tree is still standing, but it is a mere figure of its former grandeur.

Three

Important Structures

The properties mentioned in the following chapter may not have met all of the criteria of the examples in Chapter Two, but they are also important to Warrington Township's heritage. These structures are presently well maintained by their owners and are not currently endangered by township growth or development.

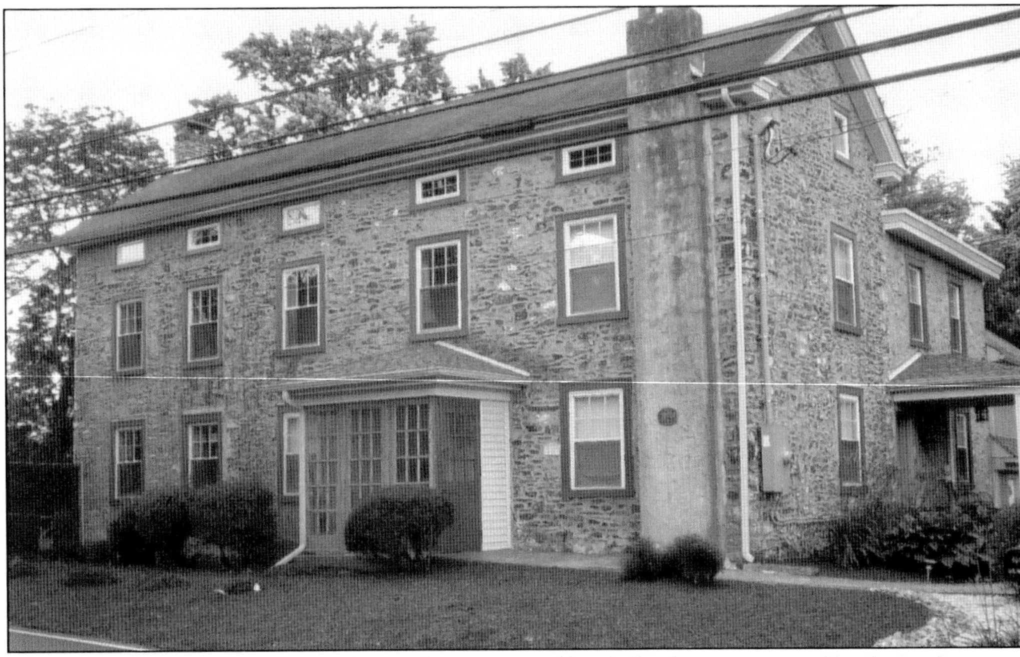

Samuel Garner, born in 1798, inherited a portion of his father's property and built this home on Bristol Road. Samuel's son John took over ownership of the home when his father relocated to Doylestown. John was one of the five who organized the Pleasantville Reformed Church, where he was an elder until the time of his death.

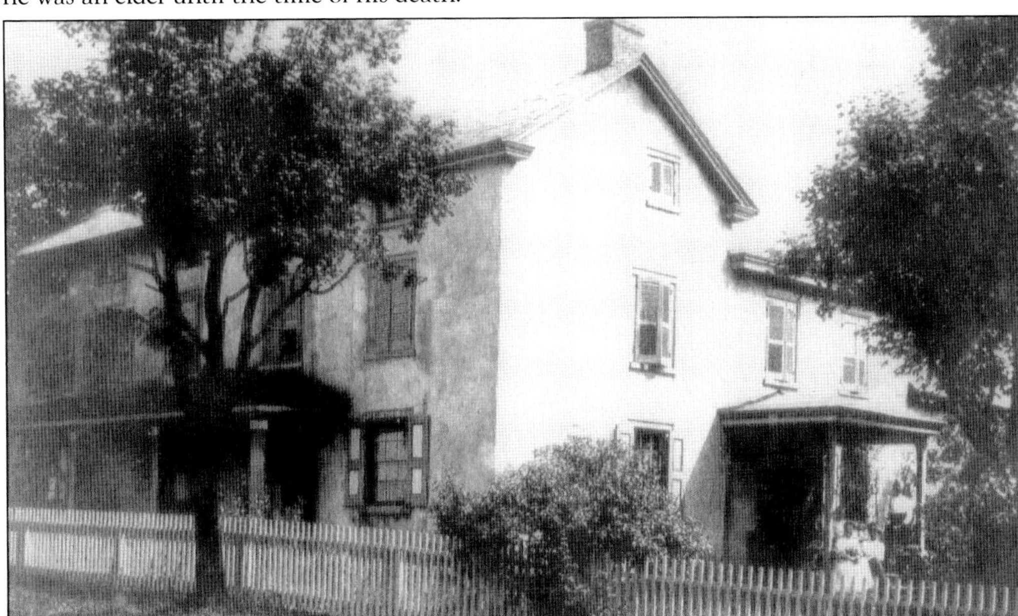

The Garner house, built around 1855, sits very close to Bristol Road. This picture was taken in the late 1800s while Levi M. Garner (youngest son of John) was owner. Levi rented the house upon marrying Emma Wahl in 1862 and took full ownership in 1872 after his father's death. He was one of the first township supervisors when they began meeting in 1906. (Courtesy of the Baniewicz family.)

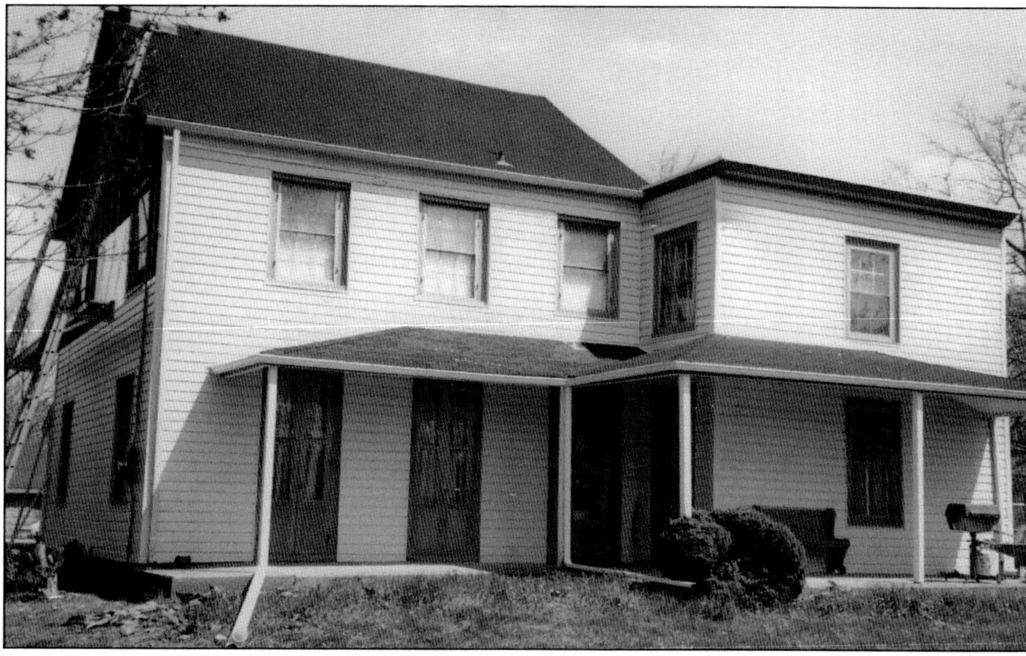

This two-and-a-half-story brick house (now covered in siding) is located off Bristol Road. The home includes a date stone that reads, "D C H 1840." Daniel Harley settled on this property when he married Catherine Grove in 1810. In the late 1800s, when it was owned by J. Dubree, the home was part of a 71-acre parcel.

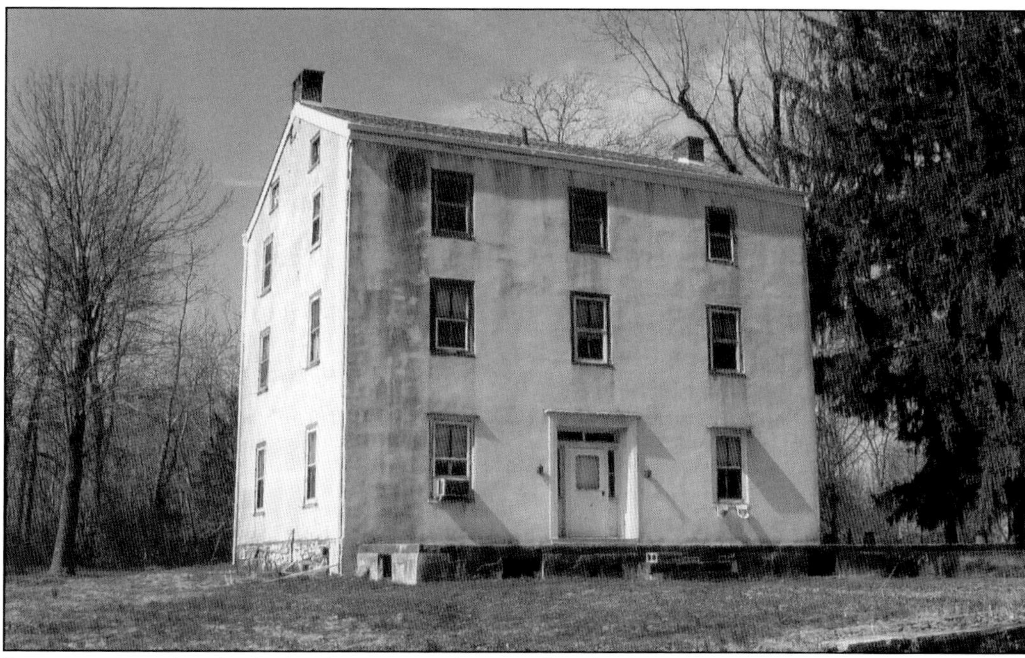

Benjamin Larzelere built this house in 1855. It replaced a house built by James Dunlap that had been on the property since 1749. At one time, this was one of the grandest farms in the township. It consisted of over 300 acres, a large cluster of barns, and other buildings. The farm was displayed in J.D. Scott's 1876 atlas of the area.

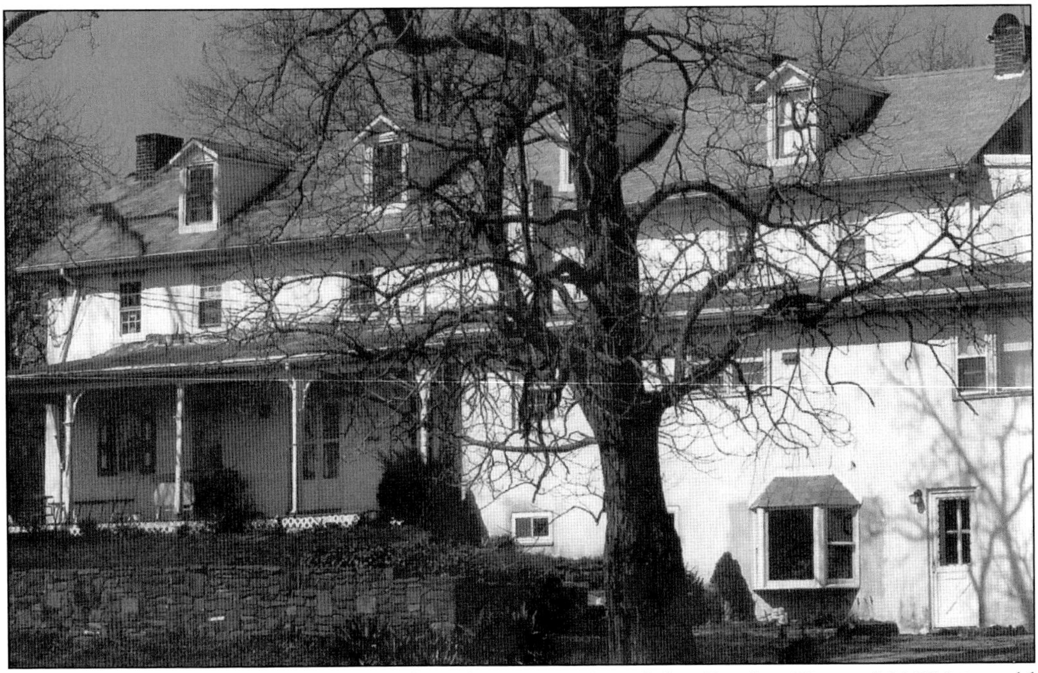

On April 1, 1805, George Walter purchased 131 acres from John Barclay. He paid £1,730 in gold and silver for it. Under the ownership of John B. Walter (George's son), the house was repaired, and a large barn was erected. The farm was considered to be one of the best in the county. Maria F. Walter (John's daughter) married Edward Garges in the early 1890s.

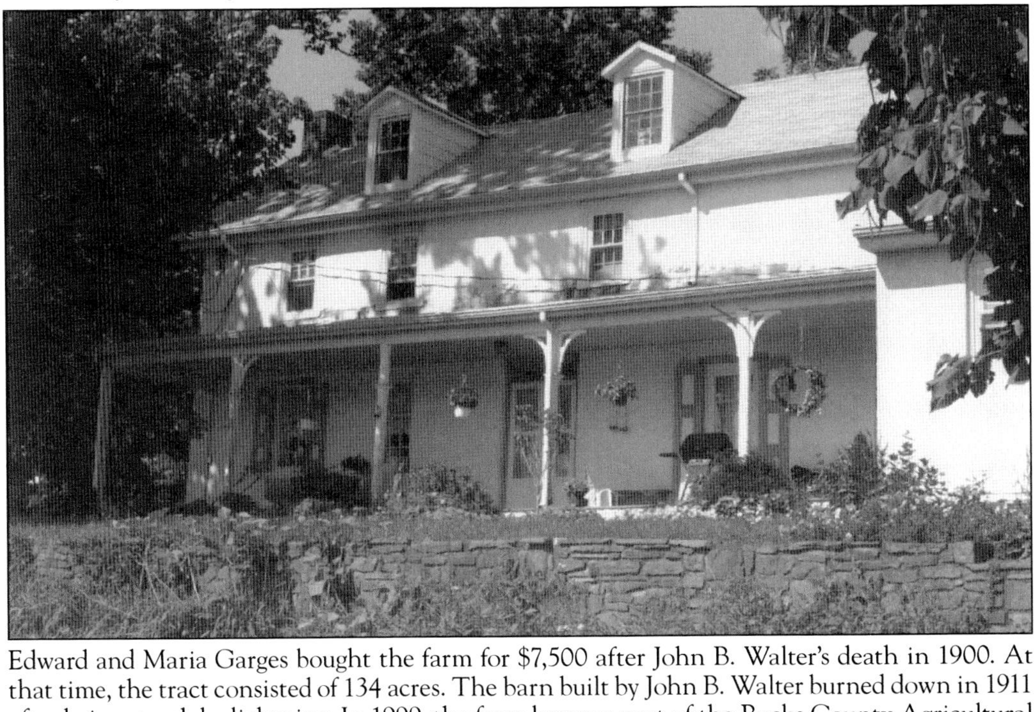

Edward and Maria Garges bought the farm for $7,500 after John B. Walter's death in 1900. At that time, the tract consisted of 134 acres. The barn built by John B. Walter burned down in 1911 after being struck by lightning. In 1999, the farm became part of the Bucks County Agricultural Preservation Program.

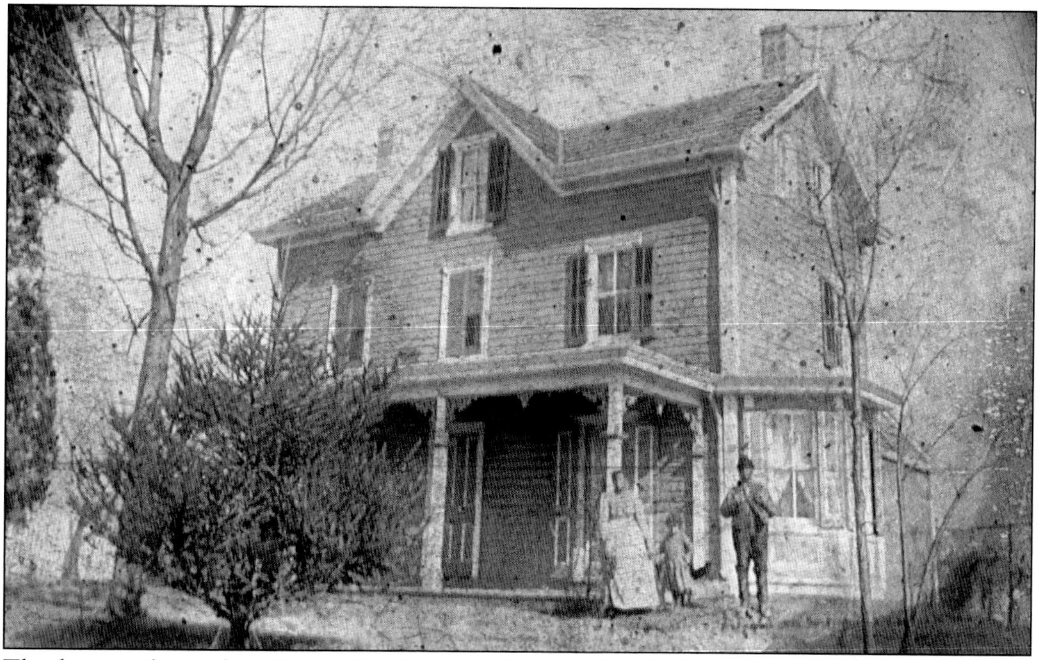

This home is located on Easton Road next to Cozens Church (now Carpet Giant). The Ganges family ran a bed-and-breakfast there called Ganges Homestead. The back of this photograph states the following: "Taken 1899, my father and mother Charles Ganges, Violetta Ganges, Frances Ganges, and rover's tail seen back of mother." (Courtesy of the Ganges family.)

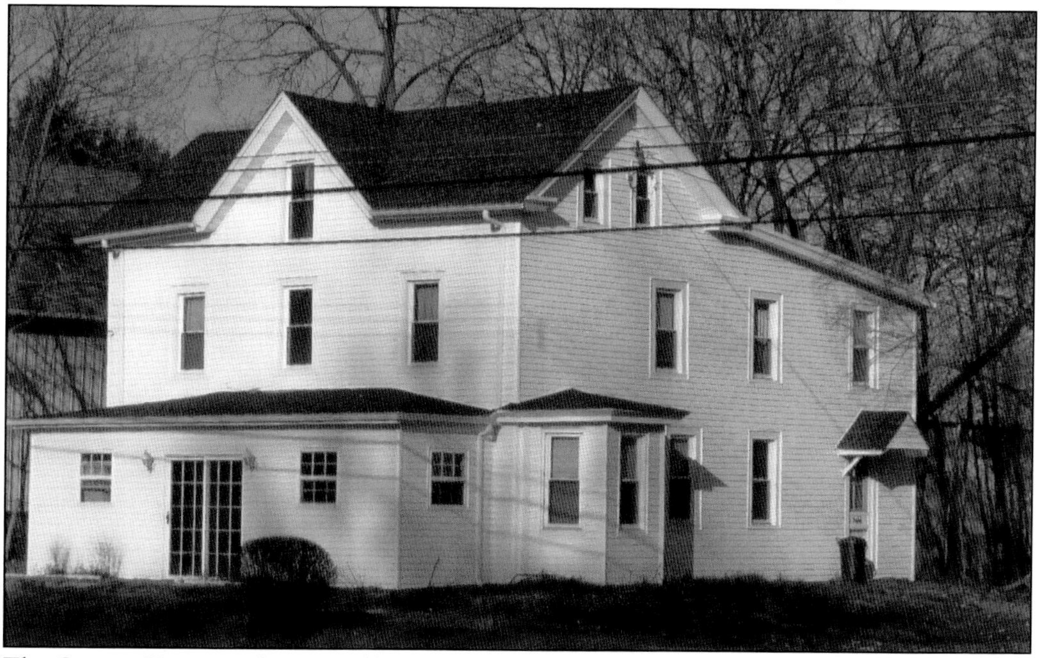

The Ganges Homestead, pictured here a few years ago, still stands on Easton Road. It was built around 1890 and was constructed of wood frame. Like many of the older structures in the township, much of the front yard has been taken for road widening, and the porch with its ornate wooden trim is long gone.

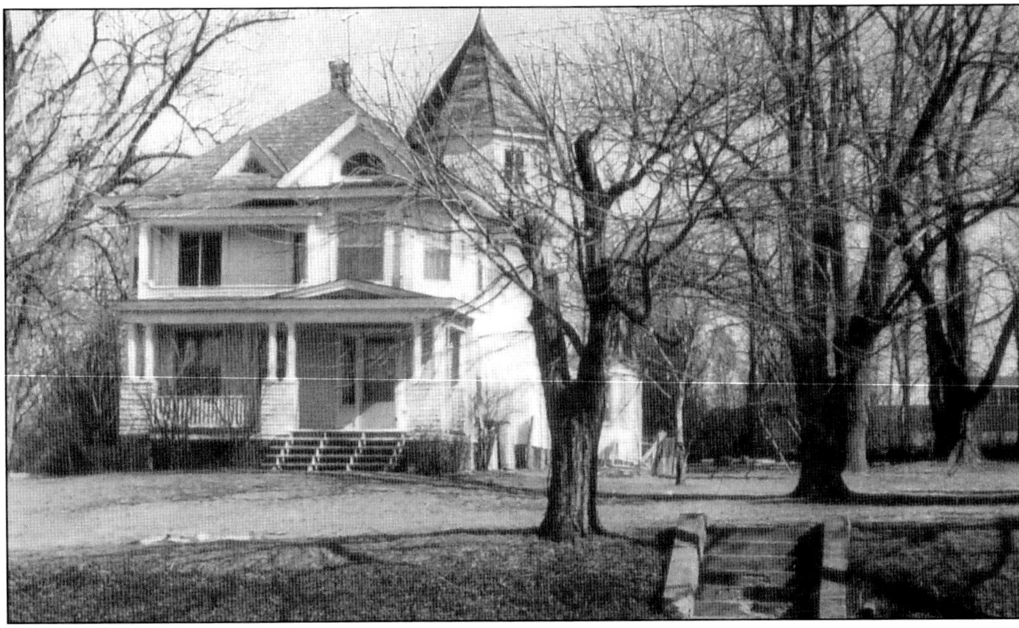

This Queen Anne–style house still sits on Easton Road high atop Warrington Hill. Built around 1895, it was constructed of wood frame and covered in wood siding. It showcased a porch with ornate trim and a hexagon turret topped with a slate roof. Each time Easton Road was widened, the house lost some of its grandeur. (Courtesy of the Lueckel family.)

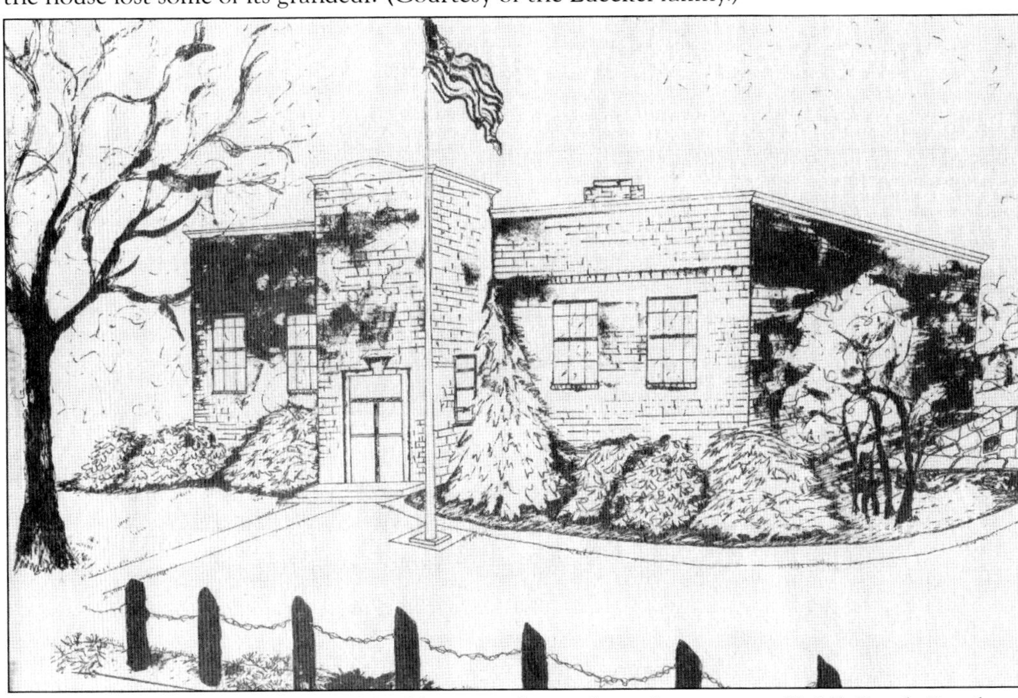

In 1977, the township municipal building was located on the corner of Mill Creek Road and Pickertown Road. This landscaping plan was prepared by Temple University students. Students worked on the proposal, with the five best designs consolidated into this presentation drawing. Municipal offices moved to their current location on Easton Road in 1993.

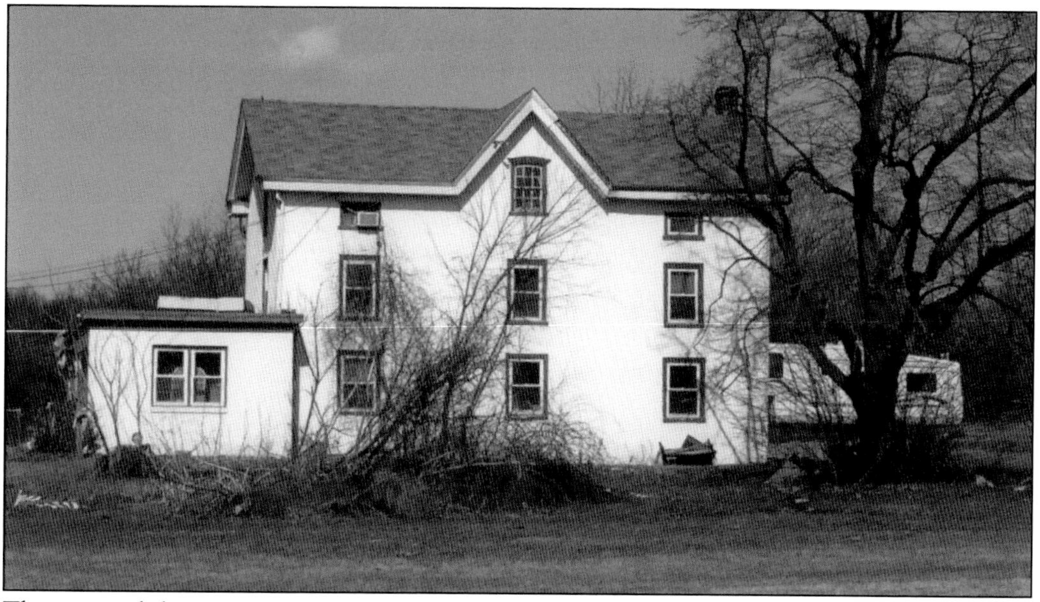

This two-and-three-quarters-story structure, known as the Hoover house, was constructed around 1855 on County Line Road between Limekiln Pike and Lower State Road. In 1902, the Bucks County Gazette reported, "Tilghman A. Hoover, one of the most prominent farmers in the county, died at two o'clock on Saturday morning at his home in Eureka. He was a man of unusual physical vigor prior to the accident." (Courtesy of David Paterson.)

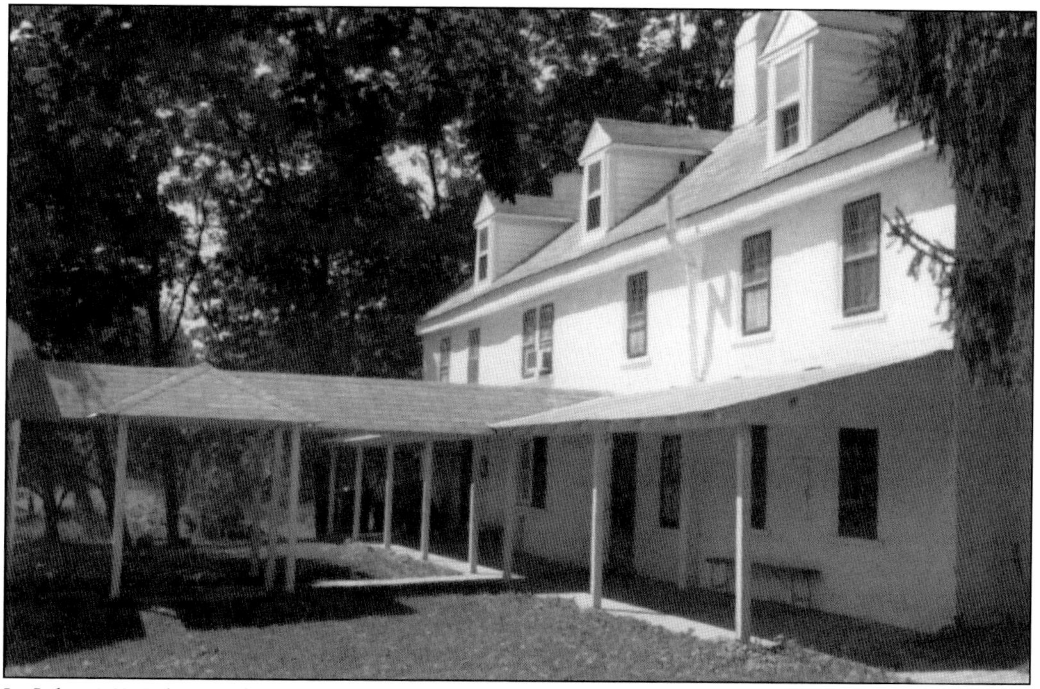

In July 1962, John Rothrock changed the name of this property from Cherry Lane Farm to Red Coat Farm. The house was built in three sections. The first section was a log cabin built around 1810. The second part of the house was a kitchen. The last part was living space. There are three other buildings on the property: a barn, a smokehouse, and a springhouse.

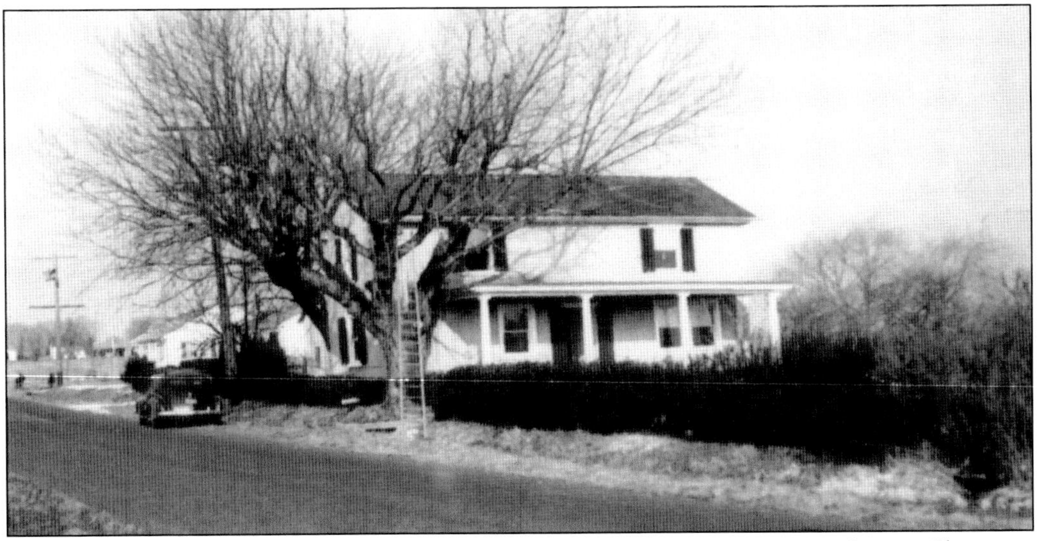

Located on Limekiln Pike just opposite the entrance to the new Warrington Square Shopping Center, this house is believed to have been built in the late 1790s. This picture, taken in 1949, looks north on Route 152/Limekiln Pike. The home is constructed of stone that is covered by stucco. The asymmetrical window positions suggest that it was constructed in two sections. (Courtesy of David Paterson.)

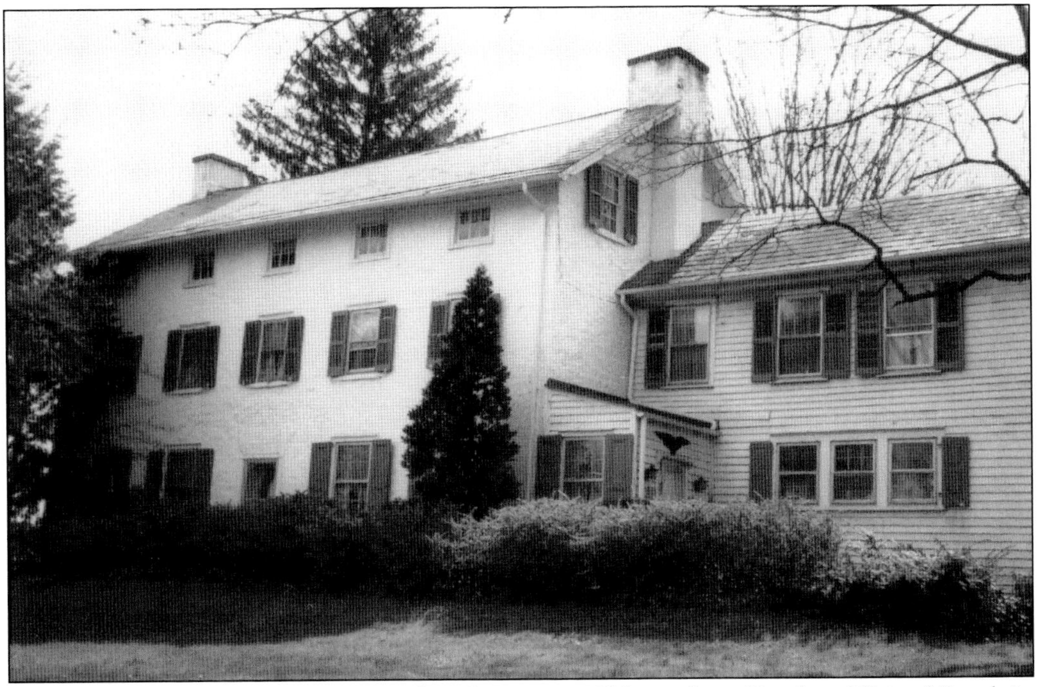

This three-story stone house is located at the corner of Upper State Road and Bristol Road. In 1855, owner John DePrefontaine advertised the home as a "substantial, modern, new stone house." The property included 60 acres, a large stone cellar barn, a wagon house, a carriage house, and a springhouse with an icehouse attached. DePrefontaine sold the property to George G. Mill in 1856 for $5,100.

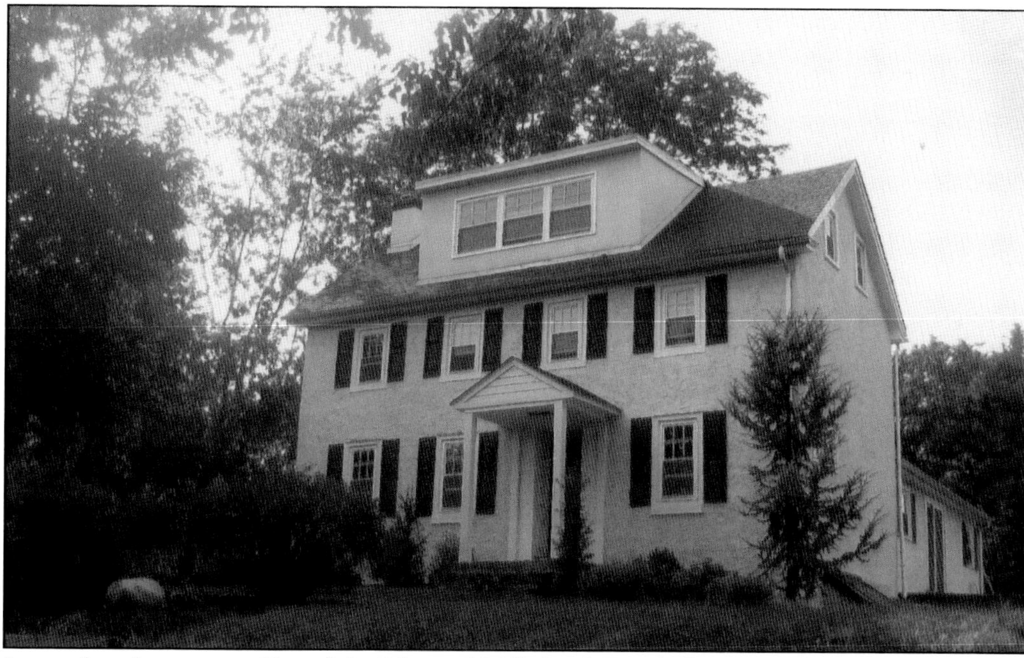

Located at the corner of Limekiln Pike and Mill Creek Road, the original stone portion of this house (facing Mill Creek Road) was built around 1796. The wood-frame addition was constructed around 1820. H. Clymer is documented as being the owner in 1890, while Benjamin Larzelere is documented as being the owner in 1876 and 1891, when the property consisted of 50 acres.

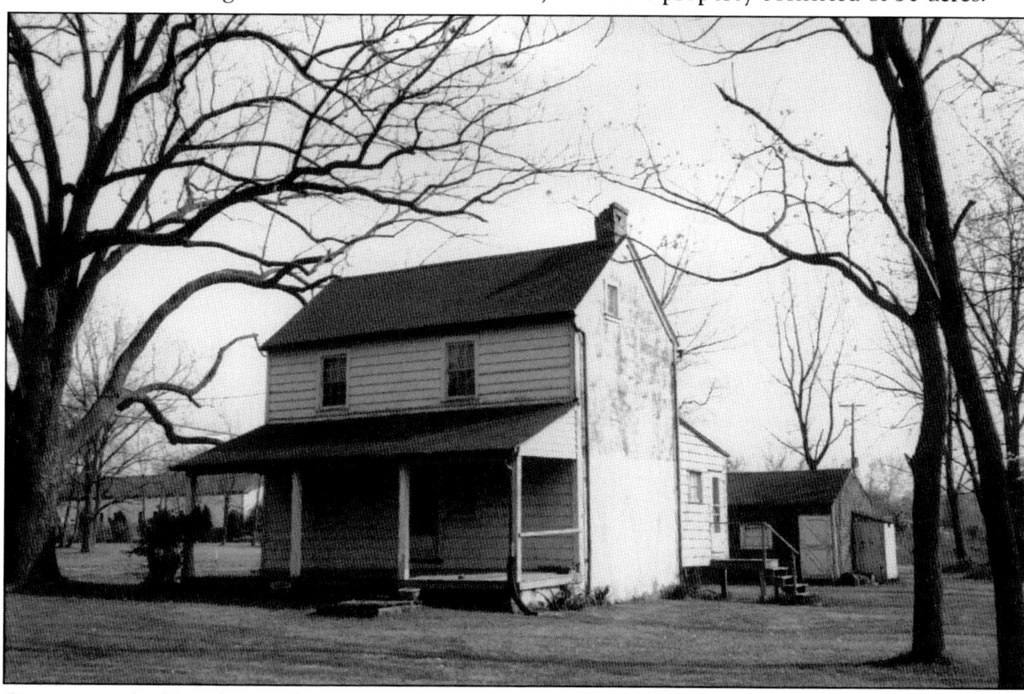

Constructed of local stone between 1800 and 1810, this home is located at the corner of Bristol Road and Cooper Lane. Parts of the exterior were covered in stucco and other parts in wood siding. While owned by A. Copper in the 1870s, the home sat on a 38-acre parcel.

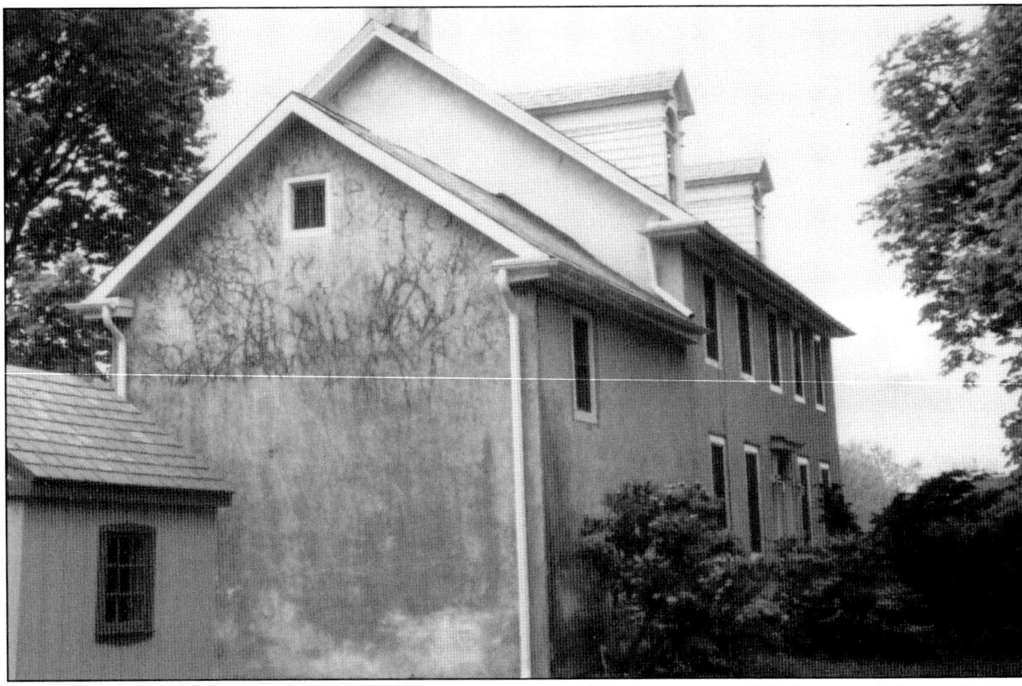

Prior to Stuckert's ownership, the property was owned by Benjamin Walton and, later, Robert Walker. As of 1811, Henry Stuckert lived on 215 acres off what is today known as Stuckert Road. Stuckert built this two-and-a-half-story Federal-style home around 1830. After his death in 1843, the home was advertised as a large stone mansion built in modern style.

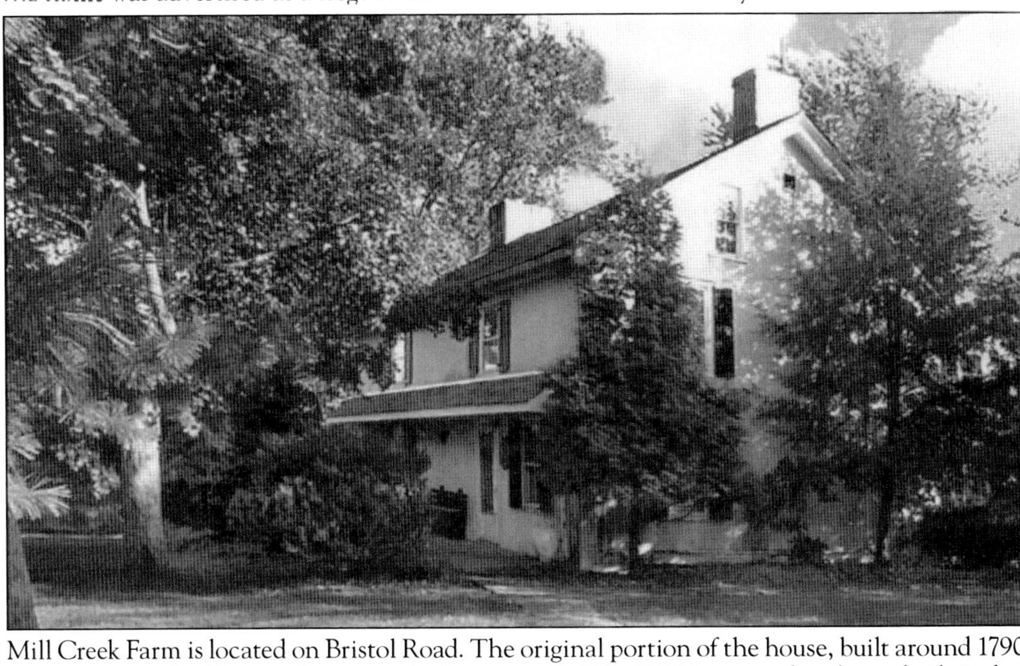

Mill Creek Farm is located on Bristol Road. The original portion of the house, built around 1790, was constructed of logs and consisted of two rooms. The 3,000-square-foot barn, built in late 1800s after a previous barn burned to the ground, still stands today. Philip Burner (assessor of the township) owned the home and 78 acres during the latter half of the 1800s.

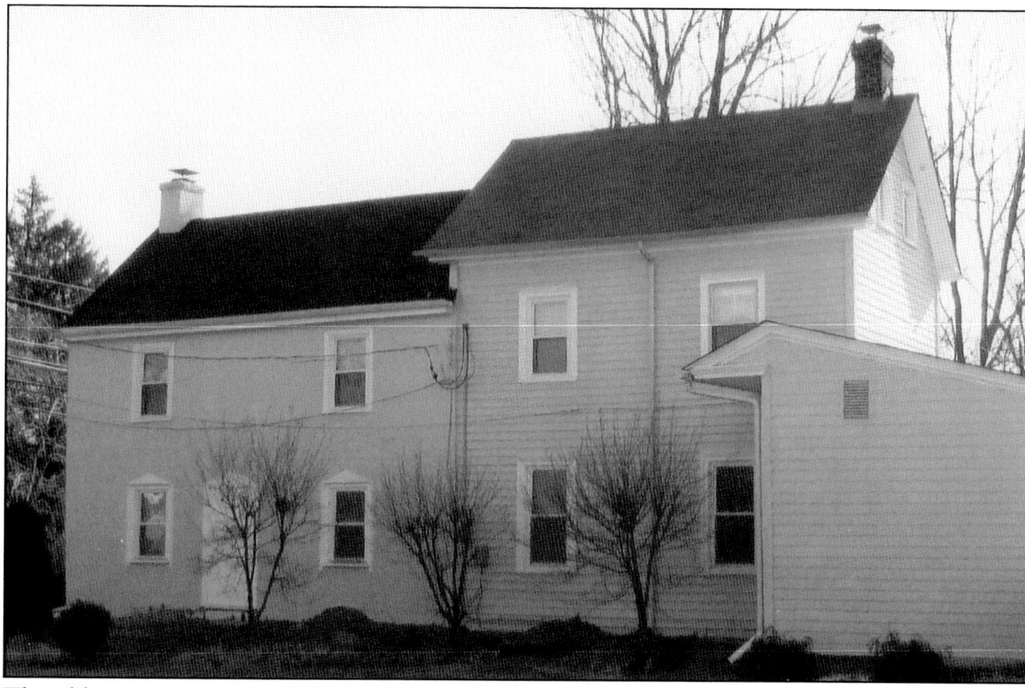

The older, stone portion of this home located at Bristol Road and Holly Road was built around 1770. The larger wood-frame addition was built around 1820. Documents show that Andrew Long sold this parcel and the dwelling in 1775. Joseph Selser is documented as the owner in the mid-1800s, when the property consisted of 30 acres.

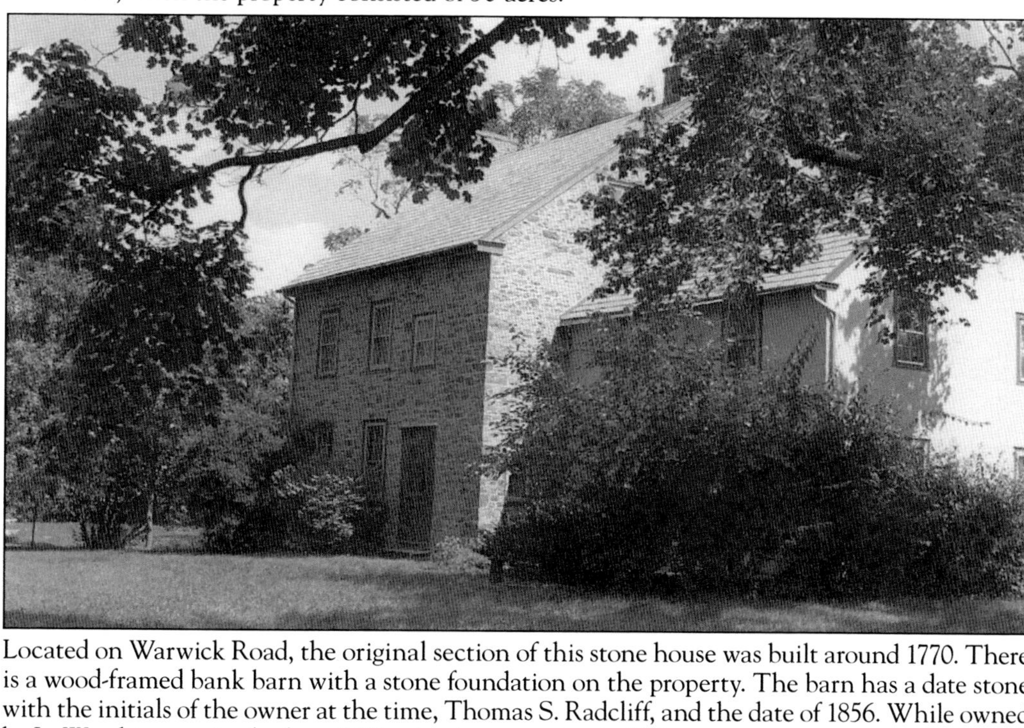

Located on Warwick Road, the original section of this stone house was built around 1770. There is a wood-framed bank barn with a stone foundation on the property. The barn has a date stone with the initials of the owner at the time, Thomas S. Radcliff, and the date of 1856. While owned by L. Worthington in the late 1800s, the farm consisted of 70 acres.

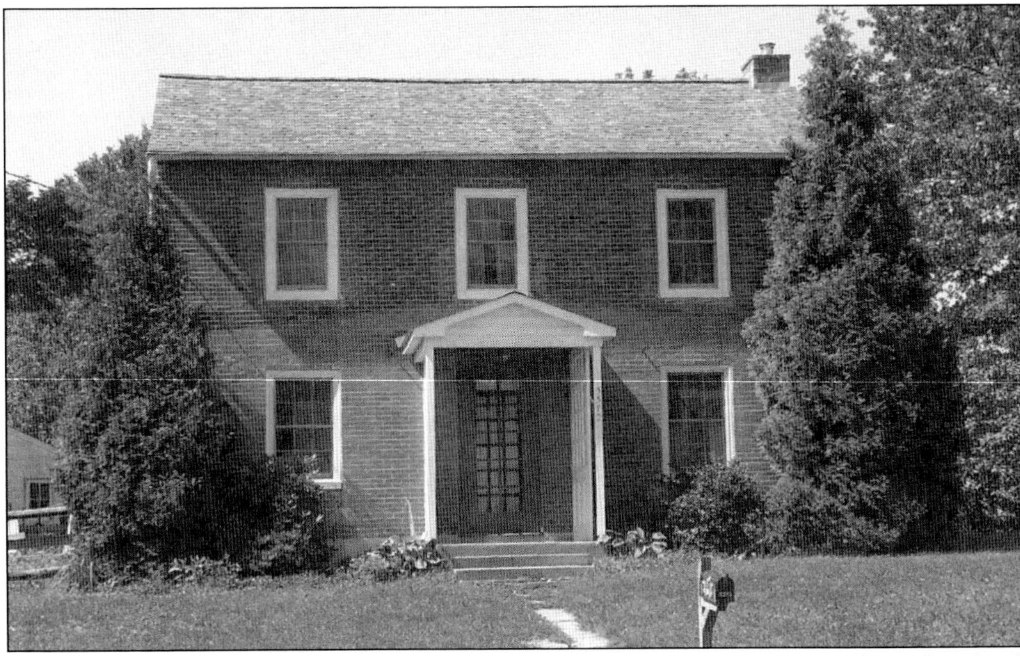

Known as the Haldeman–McNair house, this home was built around 1780. It is the earliest brick-constructed house in the township. Marks on the front of the structure show where there was once a large hip-roofed porch. Irvin McNair, Warrington's justice of the peace and lifelong resident, lived here. While owned by the McNairs, the home was part of an 11-acre parcel.

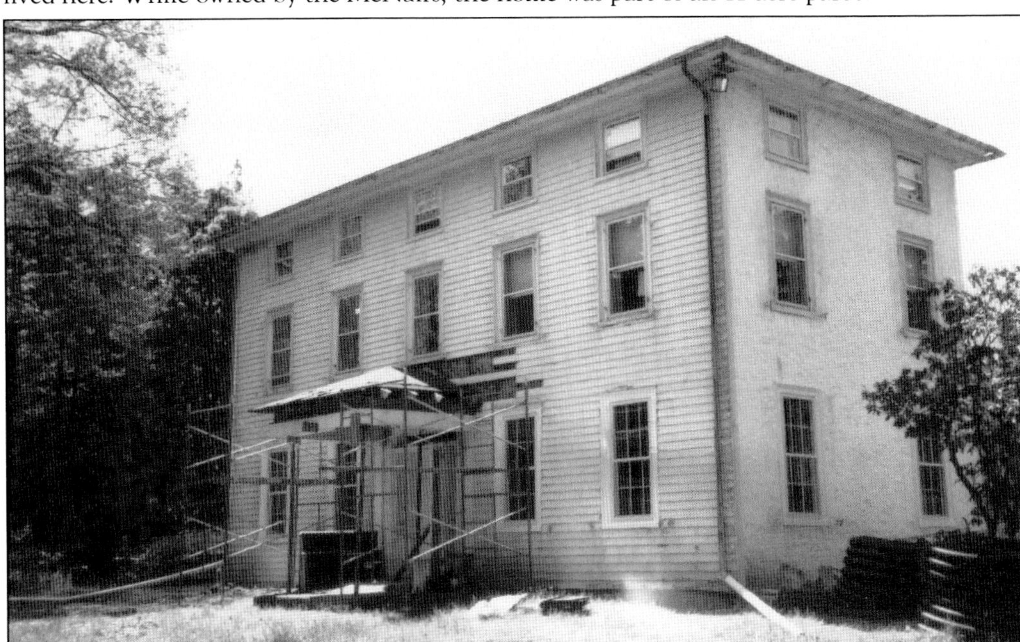

This two-and-three-quarters-story house, built around 1840 on Harvard Drive, is constructed of local stone. It has a hip roof that is covered in slate. Some of the building was covered with wood German siding, which has since been removed in favor of exposed stone. In the late 1800s, the home was part of a 134-acre parcel and was owned by William B. Graham.

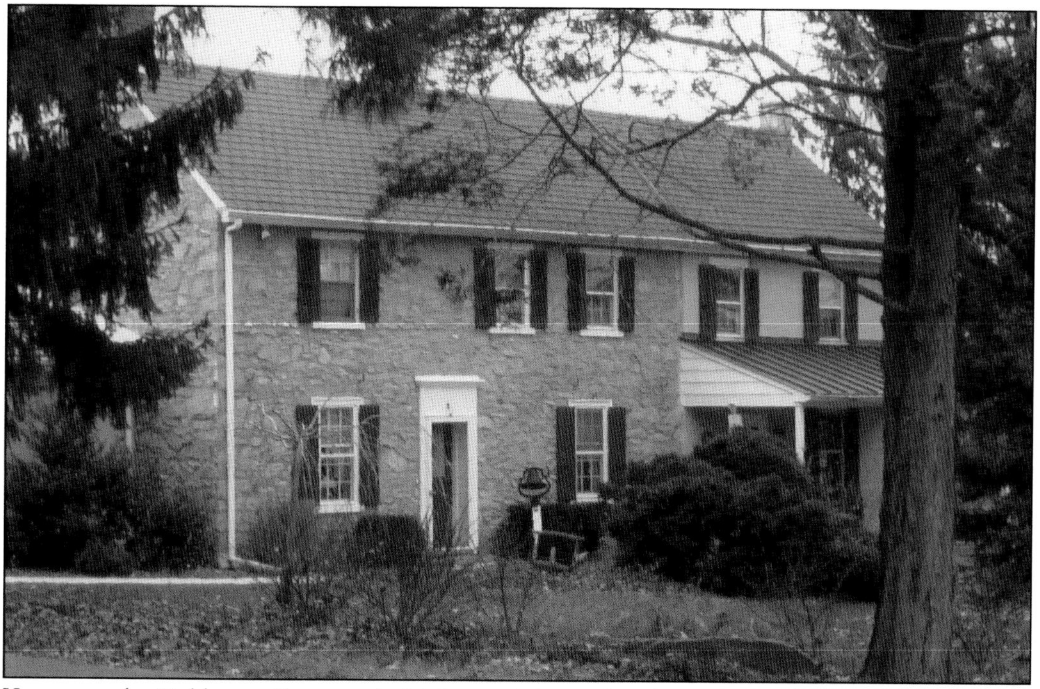

Known as the Haldeman Farmstead, this house is located at the corner of Stump and Pickertown Roads. The property consists of a dwelling, corncrib, hog house, and large bank barn. The original section of the home is constructed of uncovered rubble stone. During the late 1800s, three Haldeman farms made up the entire length of Stump Road between Pickertown Road and Bristol Road.

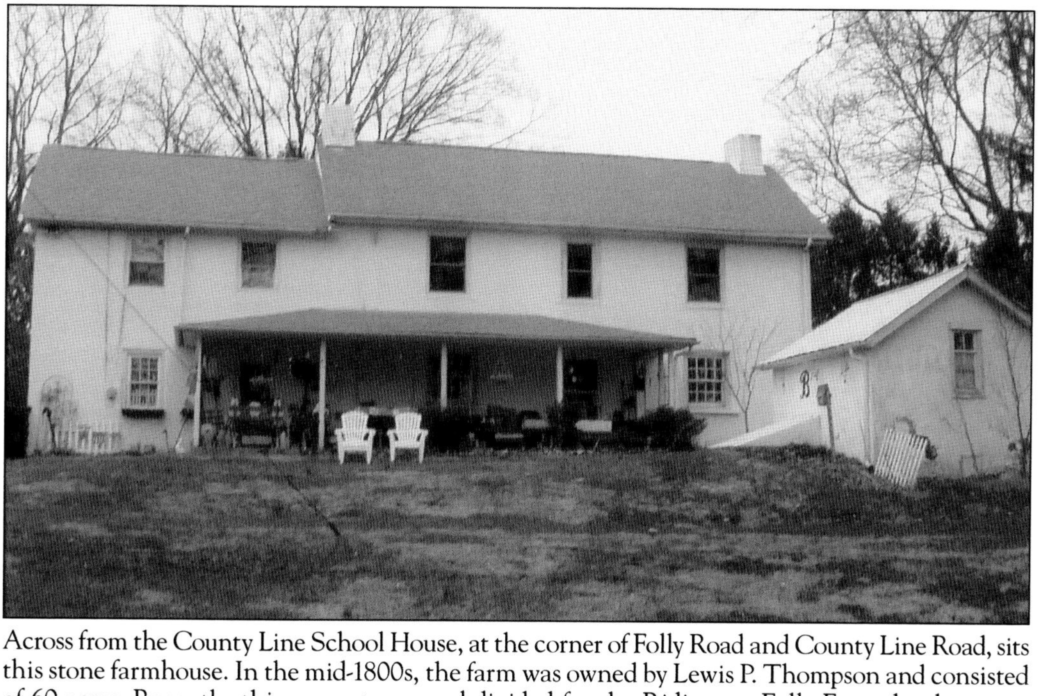

Across from the County Line School House, at the corner of Folly Road and County Line Road, sits this stone farmhouse. In the mid-1800s, the farm was owned by Lewis P. Thompson and consisted of 60 acres. Recently, this property was subdivided for the Ridings at Folly Farm development. The home and farm buildings are still present on a smaller lot.

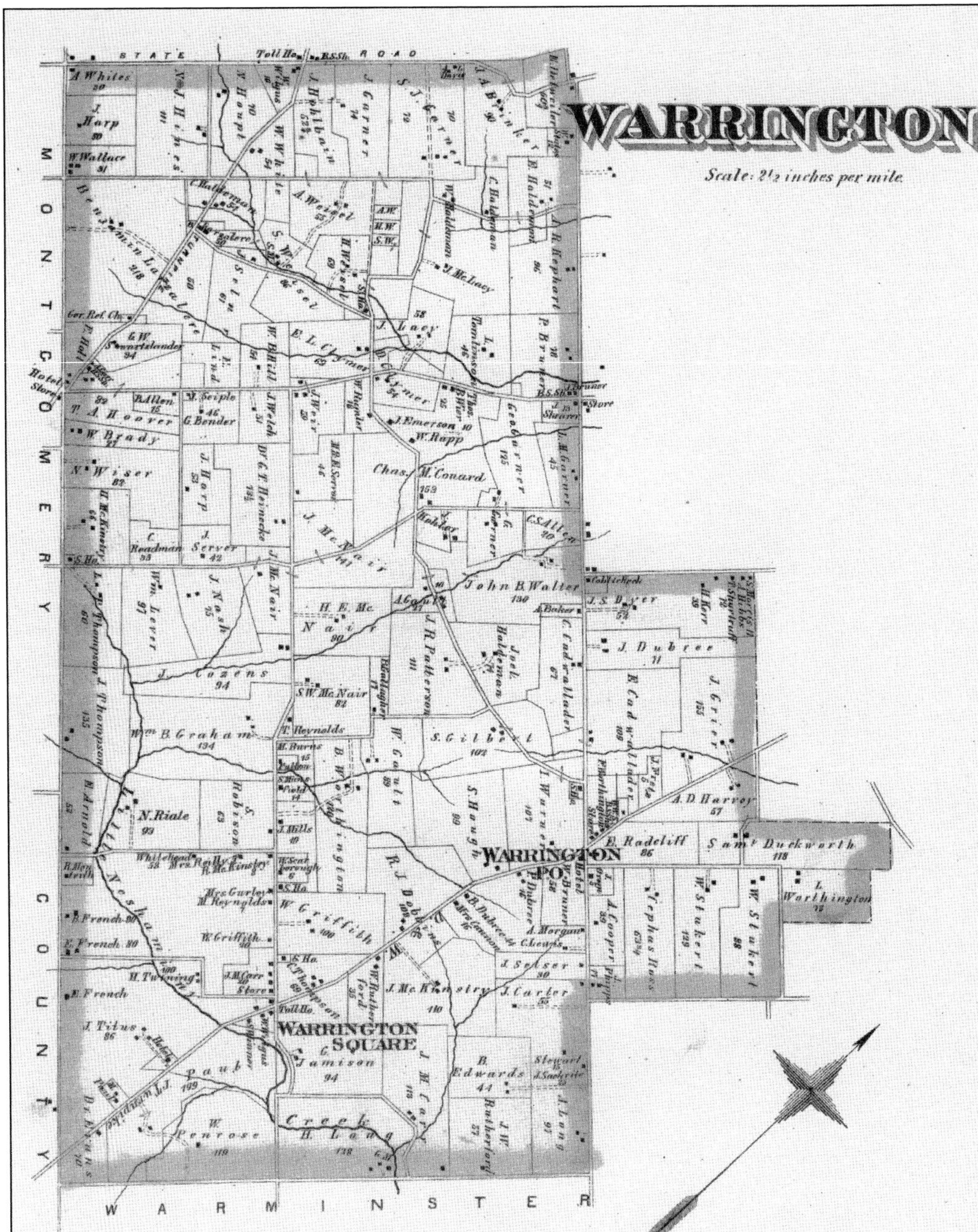

This is a map of Warrington Township from the *Atlas of Bucks Co, Pa.* by J.D. Scott in 1876. This atlas was a well-known publication during its time of printing. The maps included names of current land/business owners and the amount of land under their ownership. In addition, a directory of local businesses and drawings of a selected few well-off properties were also between the covers.

Four

Roads, Bridges, and Transportation

William Watts Hart Davis wrote in his book *The History of Bucks County Pennsylvania*, published in 1876, the following:

> Prior to Penn's arrival there was little use for roads. Earlier settlers lived on the river and along the creeks that emptied into it, and traveled by boat. There were no wheeled carriages to require open roads. With the English came vehicles, creating a necessity for roads so that they could travel through the wilderness. William Penn wanted to have a liberal and uniform system of roads in this county. In the original survey, there was an allowance for them of six acres in every hundred. He envisioned a series of highways on northwest lines parallel to each other and running back from the Delaware into the interior, intersected by others at as nearly a right angle as circumstances would permit. Before 1695, County Line, Street, and Bristol Roads, as well as a number of others, were projected on this plan. But his plans were interfered with. Because the early settlers enclosed their lands before the roads were laid out, they were encroached upon by the fences and the system could not be carried out. This gradually led to the county becoming covered with a network of crooked roads.

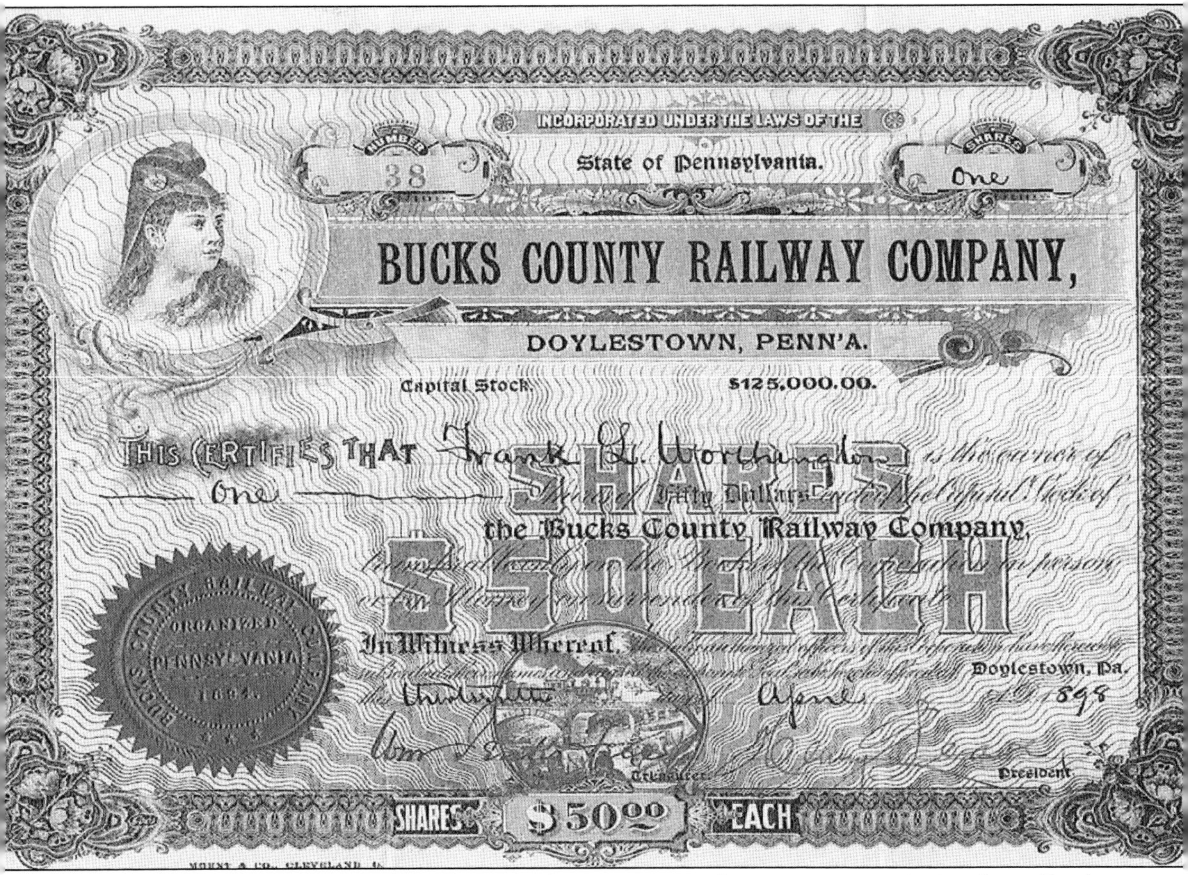

On May 26, 1898, the Bucks County Railway Company began to run a 12.18-mile trolley line on the Doylestown and Willow Grove Turnpike/Easton Road. It ran from Doylestown to Willow Grove on the northbound side of the road. According to the 1904 McGraw Electric Train Manual, *The Red Book of American Street Railways Investments*, the Bucks County Railway Company was chartered on August 3, 1894. In April 1897, the construction of the line had commenced. In order to build their infrastructure (including a powerhouse), company stock was sold to raise needed funds. This certificate, dated April 13, 1898, was purchased by Frank L. Worthington, a resident of the Neshaminy Village. The powerhouse, seen at the top of page 88, has a date stone on it that reads, "Bucks Co. Railway Powerhouse Paul Valley Erected 1897."

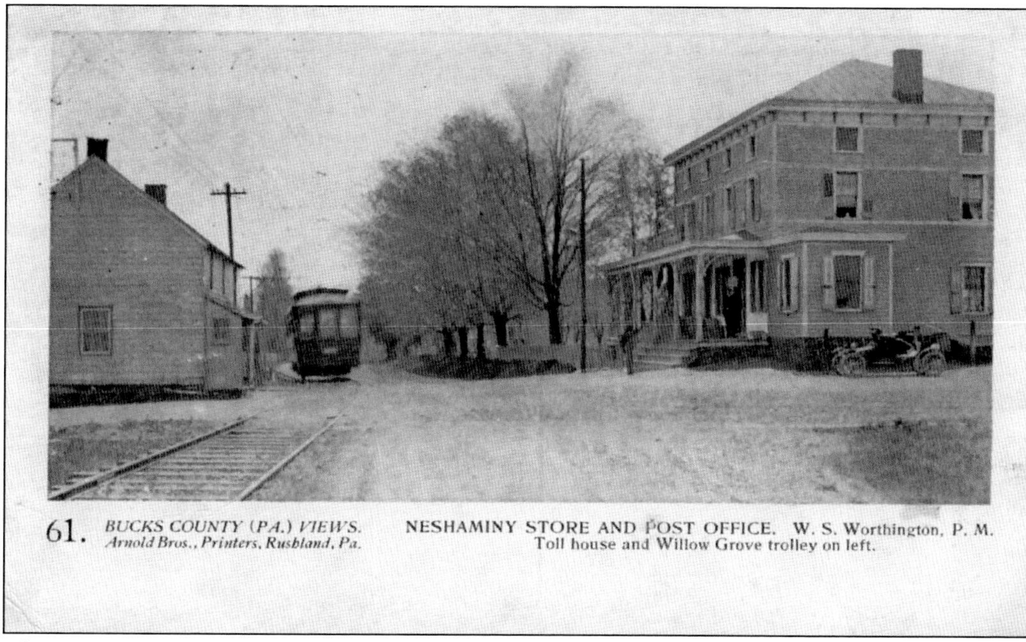

This c. 1910 postcard shows the Neshaminy Village at Easton Road and Street Road, looking south toward Willow Grove. Pictured from left to right are the old tollhouse, the Philadelphia Rapid Transit Company trolley and tracks, and Worthington's General Store/post office. (Postcard published by Arnold Brothers.)

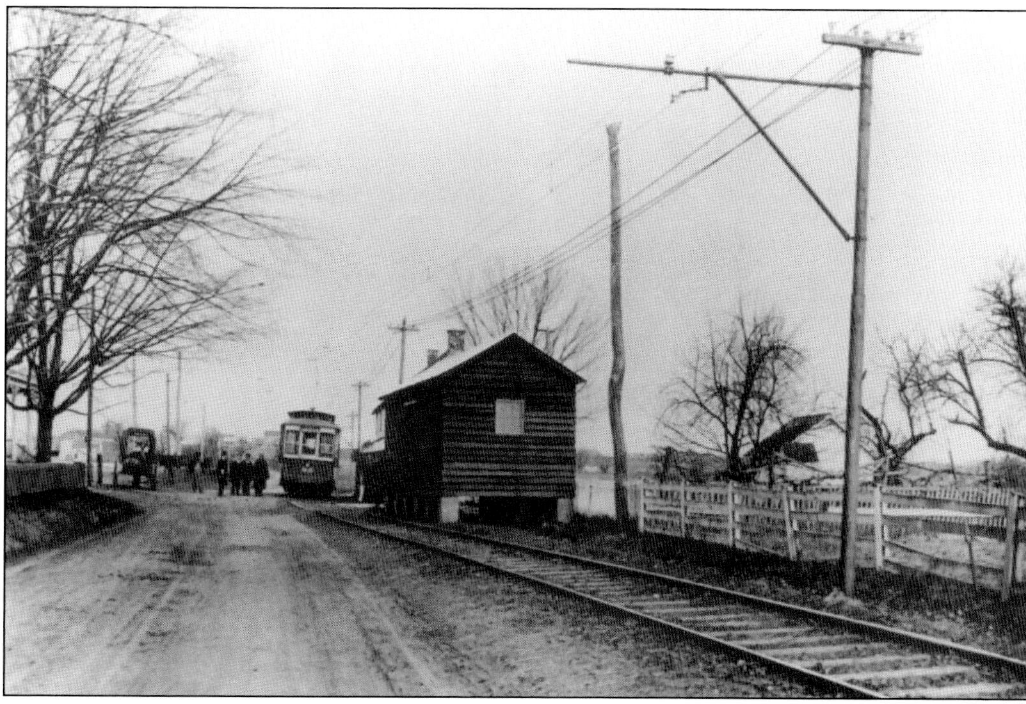

This photograph shows the same location on Easton Road as the above, this time looking north toward Doylestown. Pictured from left to right are the Worthington's General Store/post office, the Philadelphia Rapid Transit Company trolley tracks, and the old tollhouse.

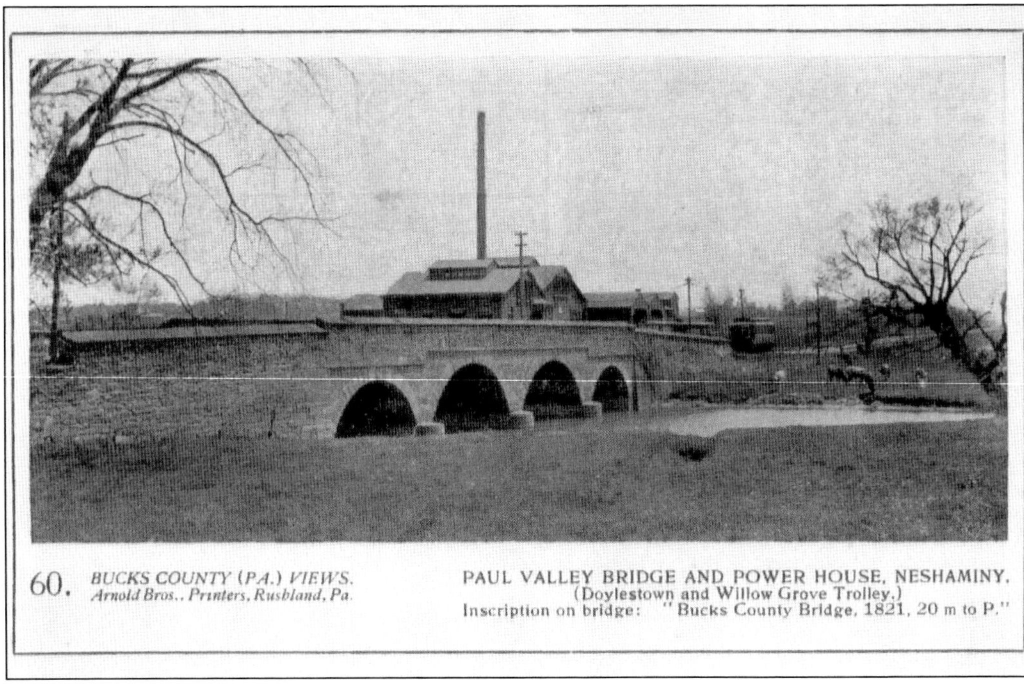

Later, the Doylestown and Willow Grove Railroad Company ran the line, followed by the Philadelphia Rapid Transit Company. On July 1, 1903, Easton Road was leased to the Philadelphia Rapid Transit Company for 999 years. This postcard is a view of the Paul Valley Bridge built in 1821. (Postcard published by Arnold Brothers.)

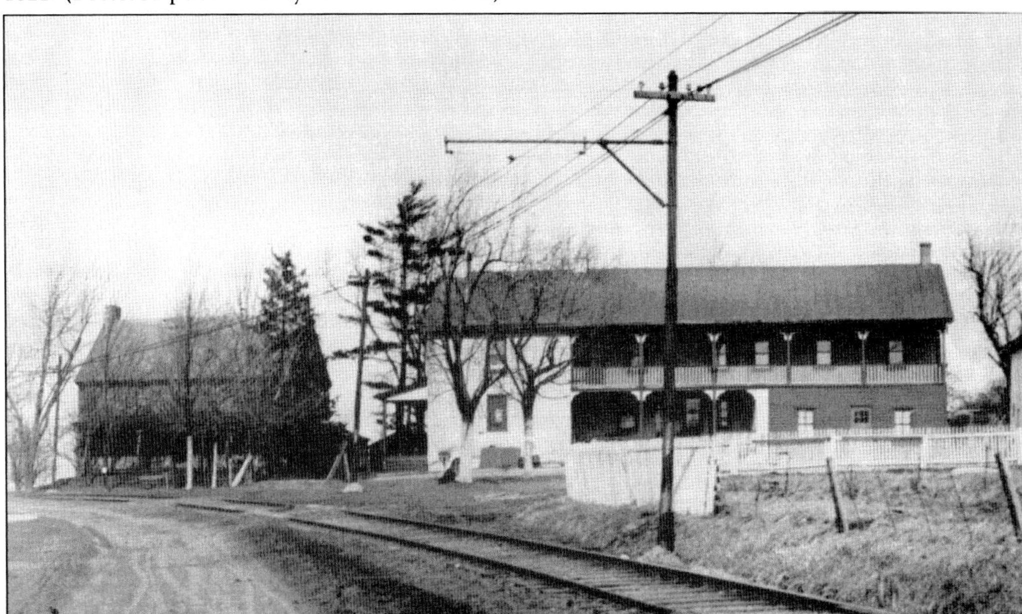

This view from about 1915 shows the trolley tracks traveling north along Easton Road prior to being paved. The Barclay house, shaded behind many trees, is seen in this image. At this point in time, the tall pine tree that had been a landmark at this corner had been removed. To the right is the Warrington Inn.

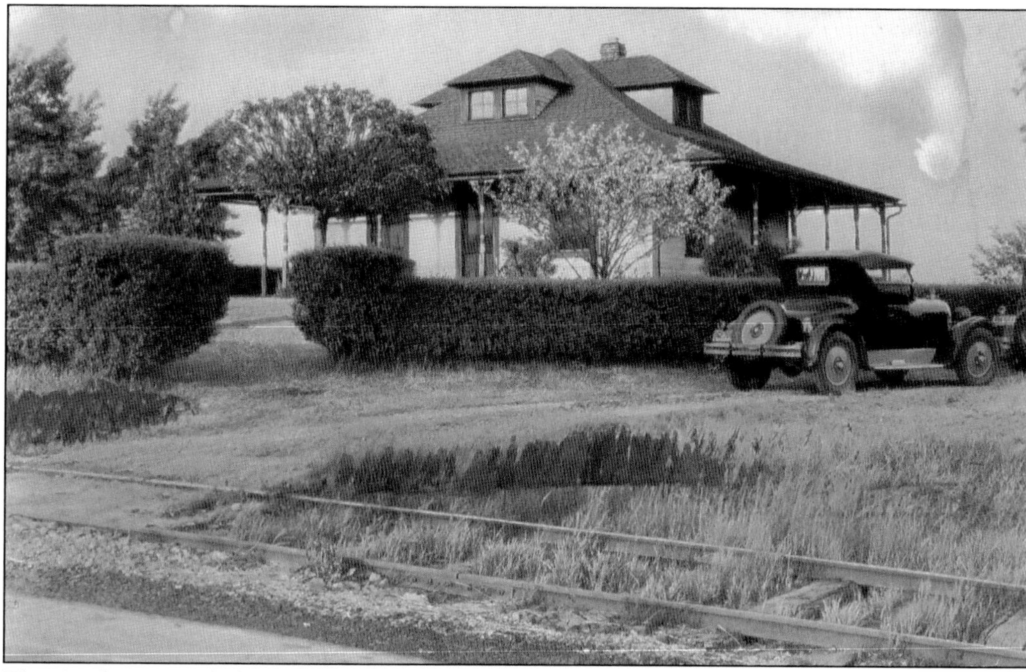

The Craftsman-style bungalow pictured here still stands on Easton Road between Hilltop Lane and Georges Lane. This photograph, taken in the mid-1920s, shows the house shortly after being built. The trolley tracks can be seen running along Easton Road. Many of the houses built in the area during this time period were used as summer residences by families from Philadelphia. (Courtesy of Frank Knight.)

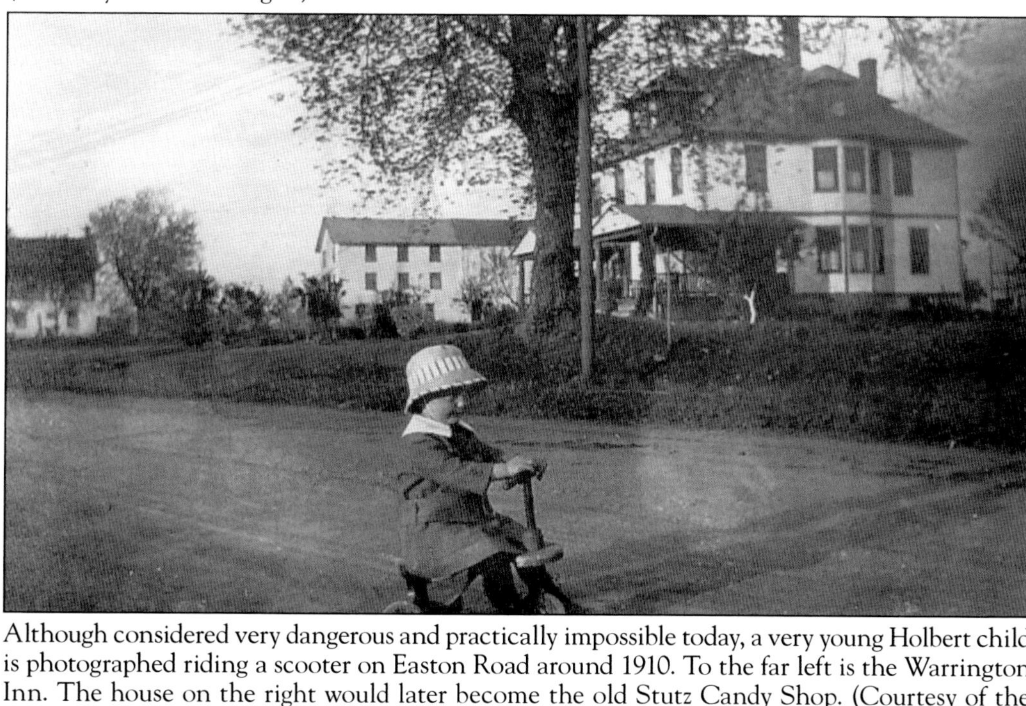

Although considered very dangerous and practically impossible today, a very young Holbert child is photographed riding a scooter on Easton Road around 1910. To the far left is the Warrington Inn. The house on the right would later become the old Stutz Candy Shop. (Courtesy of the Holbert family.)

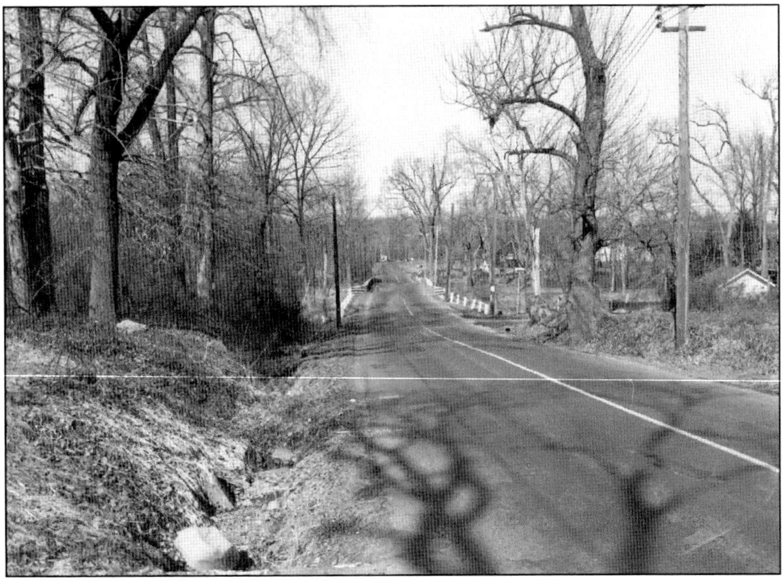

Today, when traveling on Street Road between Valley and Easton Roads, one would never know that the road's path followed a different curved route prior to 1960. The road was straightened and widened in the early 1960s. Brinkworth Avenue is seen on the right, followed by the three-arch stone bridge.

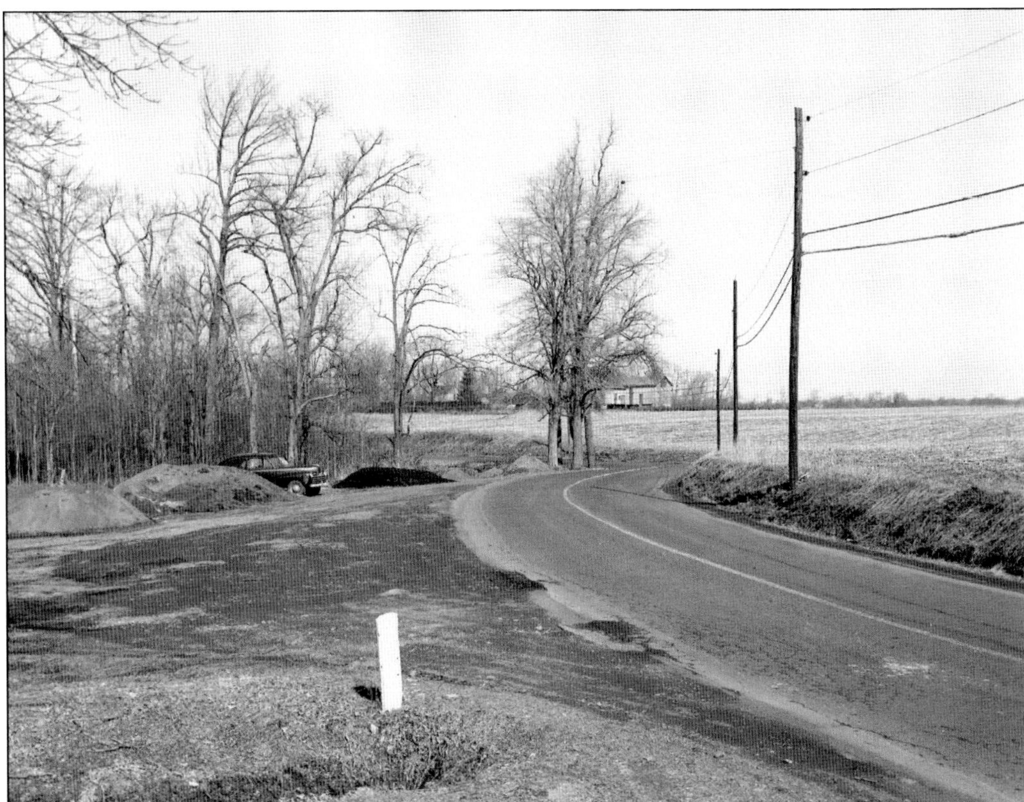

At one time, the old Street Road had a large curve. The Neshaminy Creek, which can be seen to the left, was actually redirected about 100 feet so that the road could be straightened. The Army Corps of Engineers and the Pennsylvania Department of Transportation worked together to accomplish this enormous feat.

Seen here is the old Street Road route as it exited the curve. To the left is the current location of the Street Road entrance to the Valley Square Shopping Center. The small cement-slab bridge in this picture still exists, now abandoned and surrounded by trees in the woods by the corner of Street Road and Valley Square Boulevard.

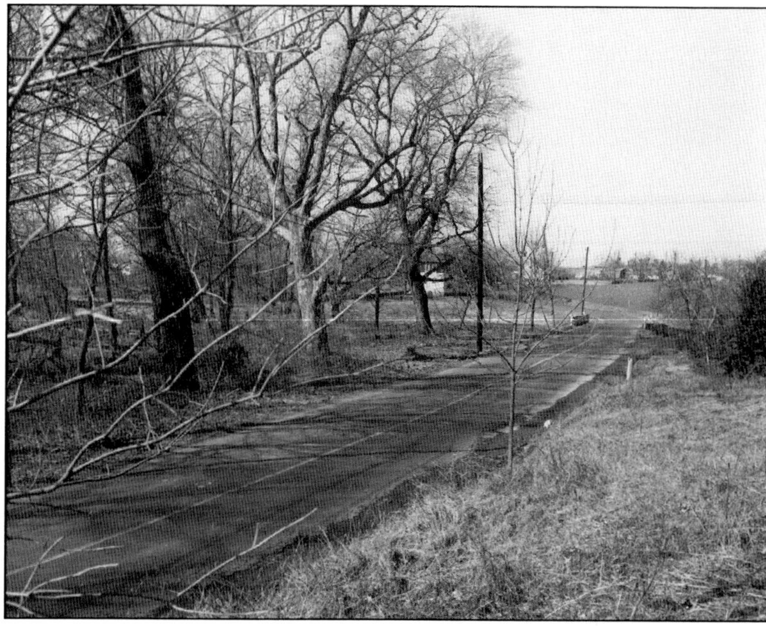

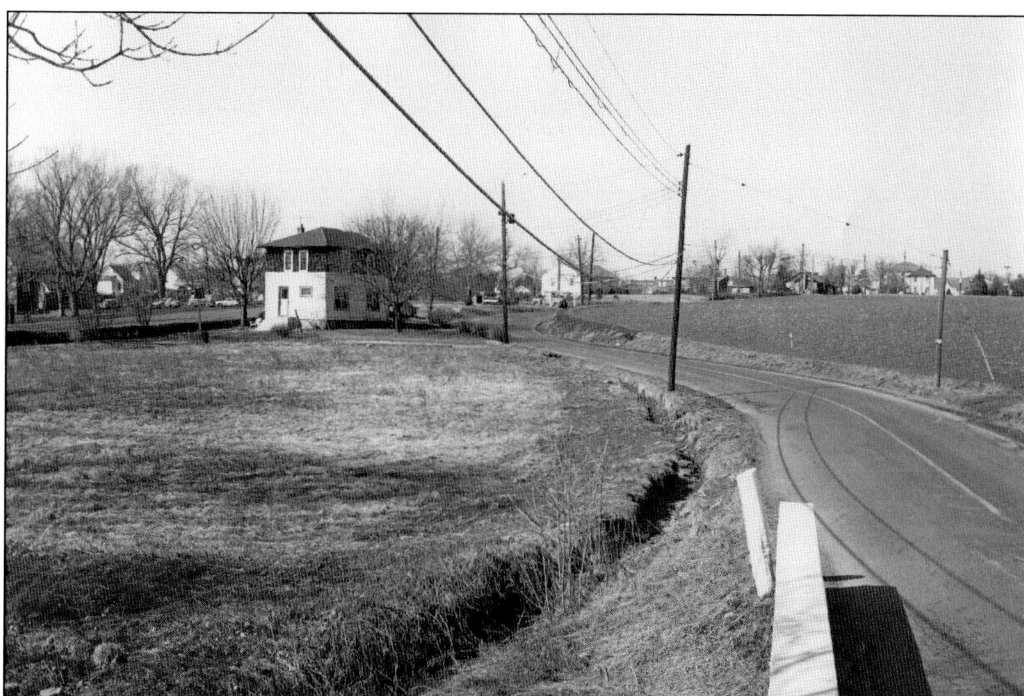

Coming out of the curve and back onto straight pavement, the intersection of Street Road and Easton Road can be seen. The Neshaminy School, Cozens Church, the Warrington Fire House, Worthington's General Stove, and the tollhouse/post office are just a few of the structures that are visible in the background of this image.

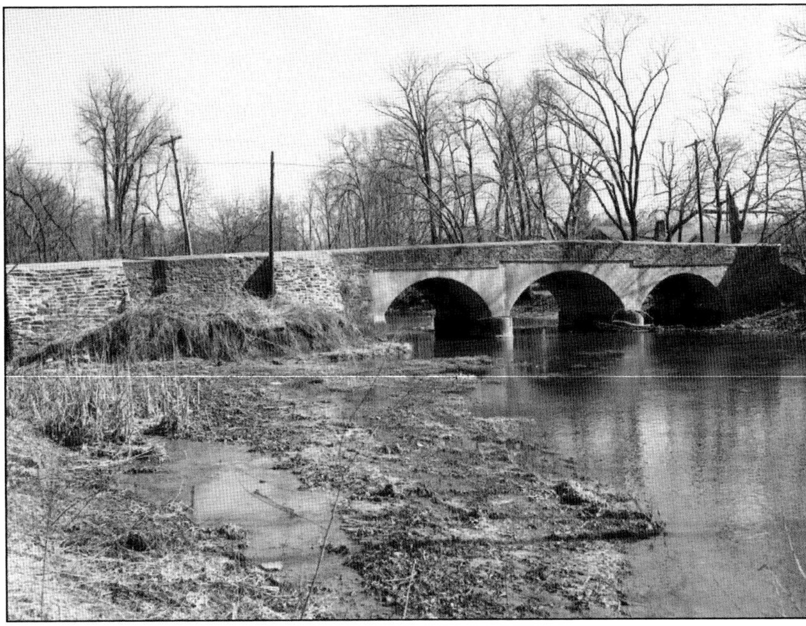

Seen here at creek level is the three-arch stone bridge that was located on Street Road between Brinkworth Avenue and Neshaminy Avenue. The bridge had a span of 170 feet and was replaced by a modern structure in 1960, around the same time Street Road was straightened and widened.

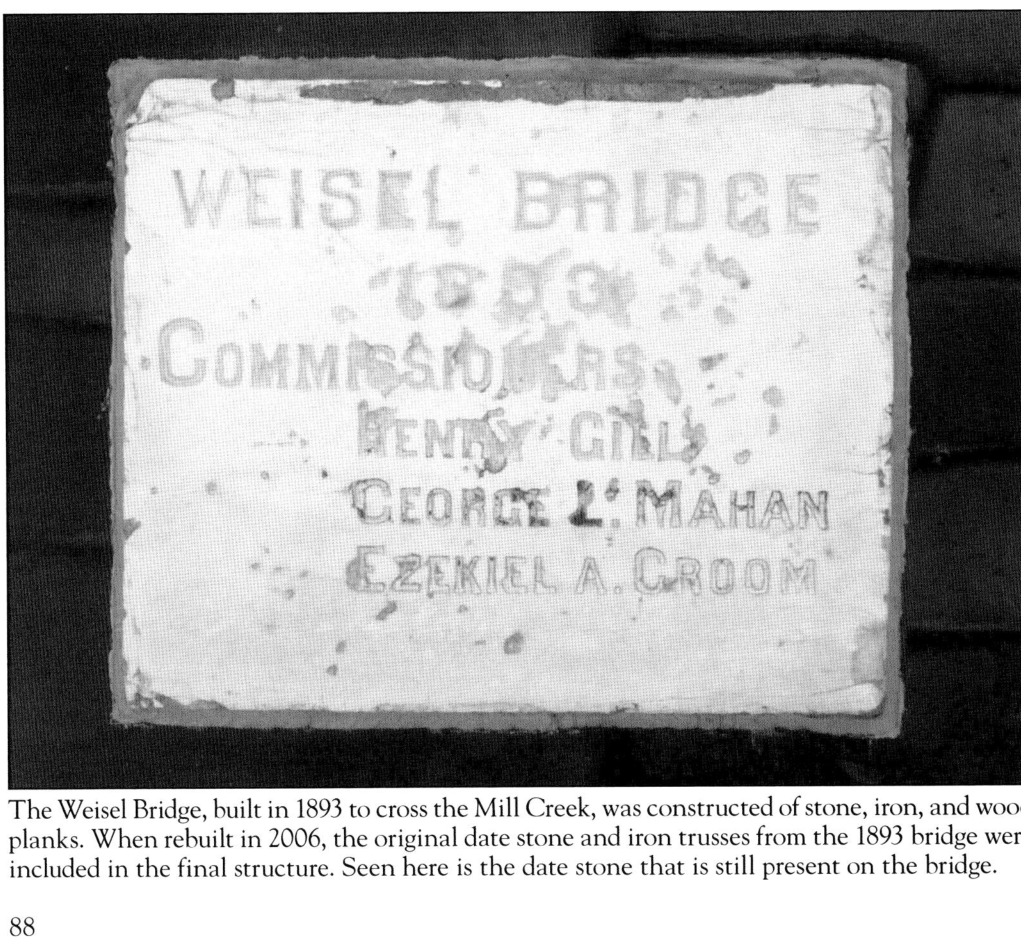

The Weisel Bridge, built in 1893 to cross the Mill Creek, was constructed of stone, iron, and wood planks. When rebuilt in 2006, the original date stone and iron trusses from the 1893 bridge were included in the final structure. Seen here is the date stone that is still present on the bridge.

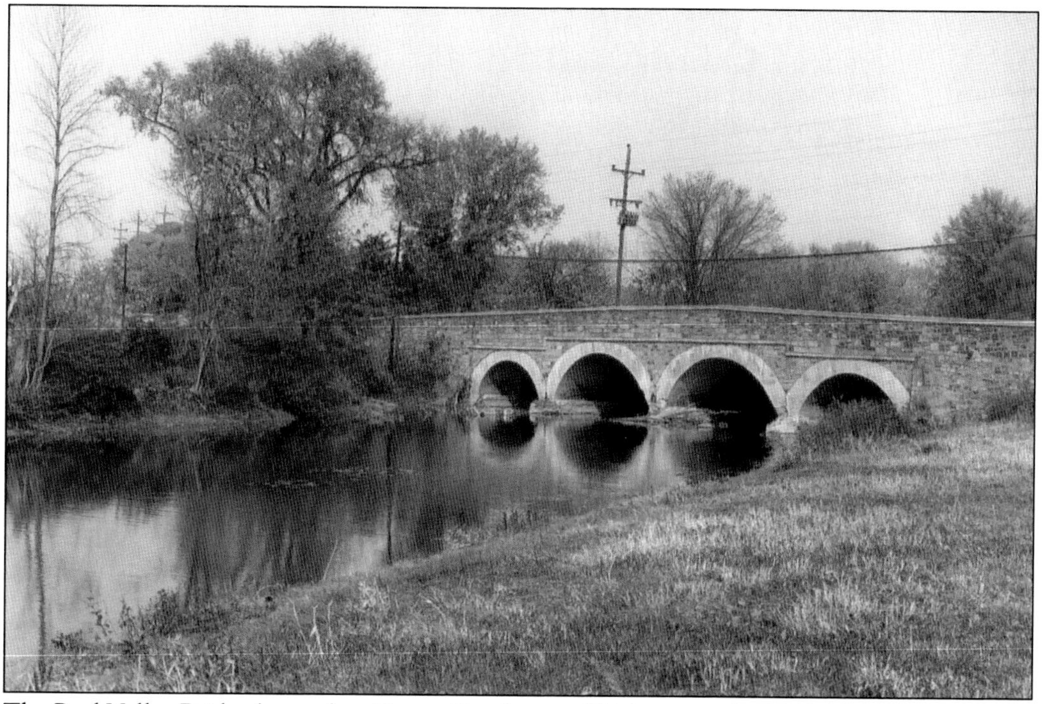

The Paul Valley Bridge located on Easton Road spans 104 feet over the Neshaminy Creek. It was constructed of stone and had four arches. Built in 1821, it replaced a wooden bridge that dated to before 1795. The bridge carried the trolley tracks on the east side, and the other lane was used mostly for horses and buggies and, later, automobiles.

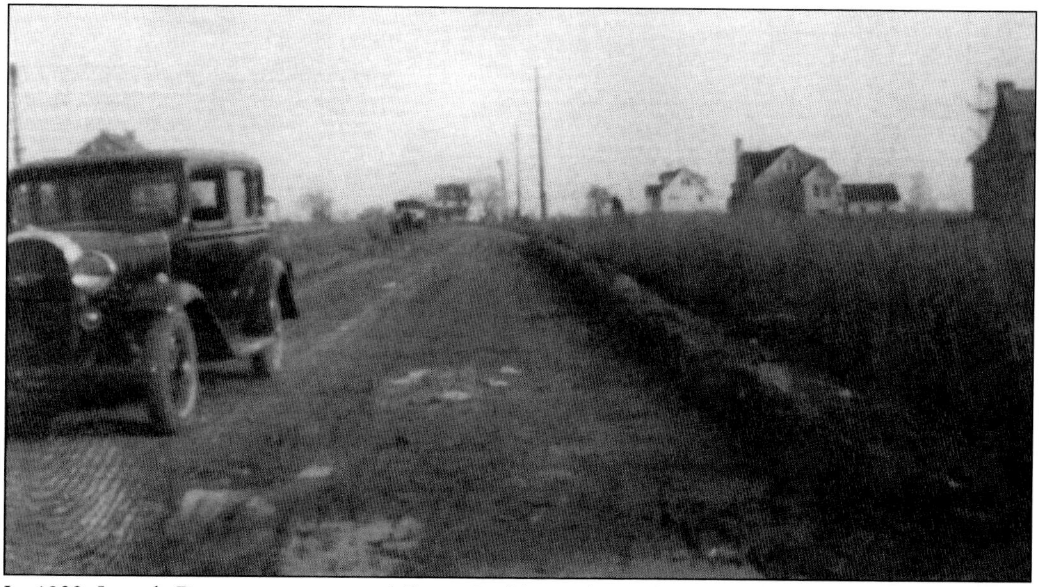

In 1933, Joseph Barness constructed Cape Cod bungalows that were described as follows: "Five rooms and bath, shower, heat, electric, laundry trays, hot and cold water, open fireplace, Artesian well, garage, and one acre of land. All for the price of $3,990.00." Pictured here around 1940 is Park Road heading toward Easton Road while Barness homes were being constructed. (Courtesy of the Barness family.)

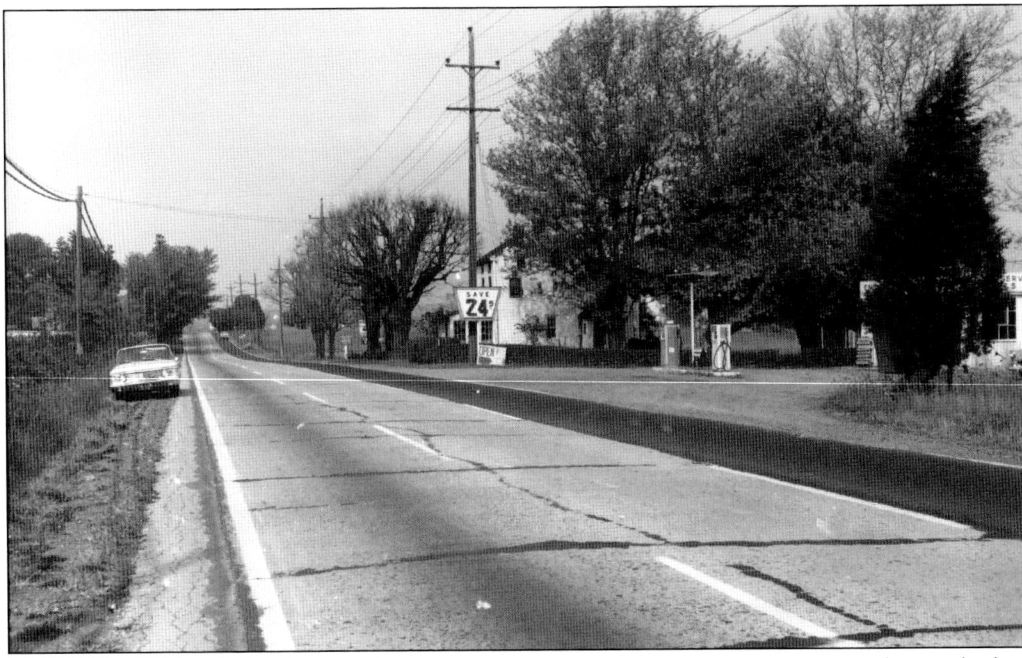

This is a northward view of Easton Road prior to the modernization and widening that took place in 1962. This photograph was taken just after crossing County Line Road. To the left is where the entrance to the Regal Movie Theater currently exists. To the right is the old Neshaminy Service Station, where Pete's Car Wash and Enterprise Car Rentals are now located.

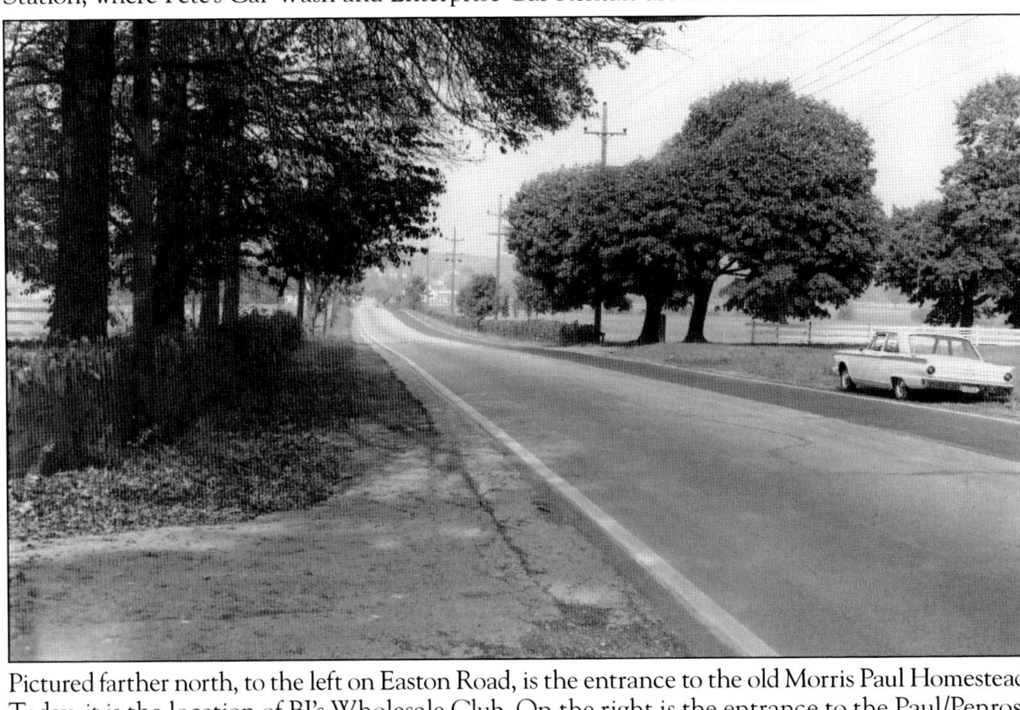

Pictured farther north, to the left on Easton Road, is the entrance to the old Morris Paul Homestead. Today, it is the location of BJ's Wholesale Club. On the right is the entrance to the Paul/Penrose Farm that is now under development. The road during this time was paved with cement. The darker asphalt pavement to the right was installed when the trolley tracks were removed.

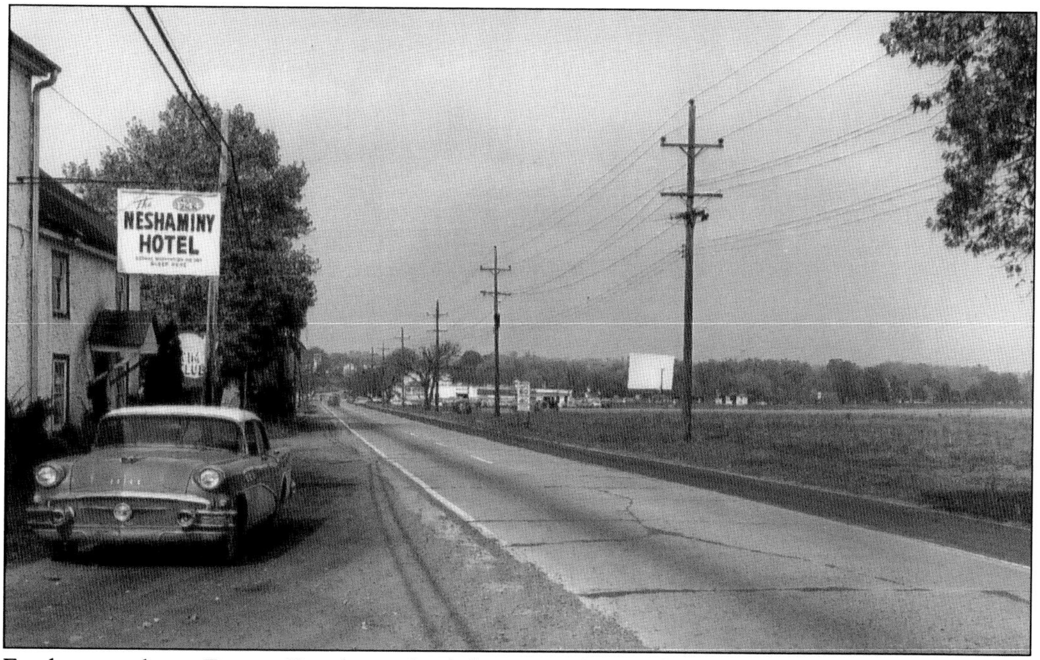

Farther north on Easton Road, on the left, is a 1956 Buick Century parked in front of the Neshaminy Hotel. To the right is part of the Paul/Penrose farm and the entrance to the Bucks County Drive-In. The Neshaminy Hotel (later the Neshaminy Inn) was razed in 2013, and the drive-in is now the location of Lowe's and Target.

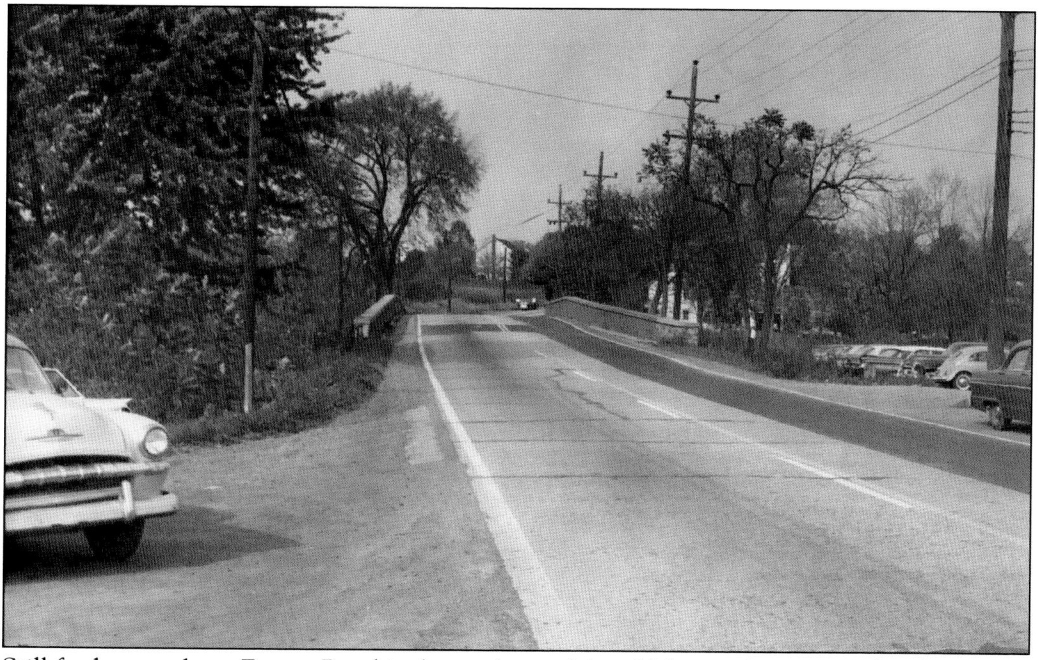

Still farther north on Easton Road is the roadway of the old four-arch stone Paul Valley Bridge that crossed over the Neshaminy Creek. This bridge, built in 1821, would soon be replaced as a result of the modernization and widening of Easton Road. Out of view to the right are the trolley barns and powerhouse for the trolley line.

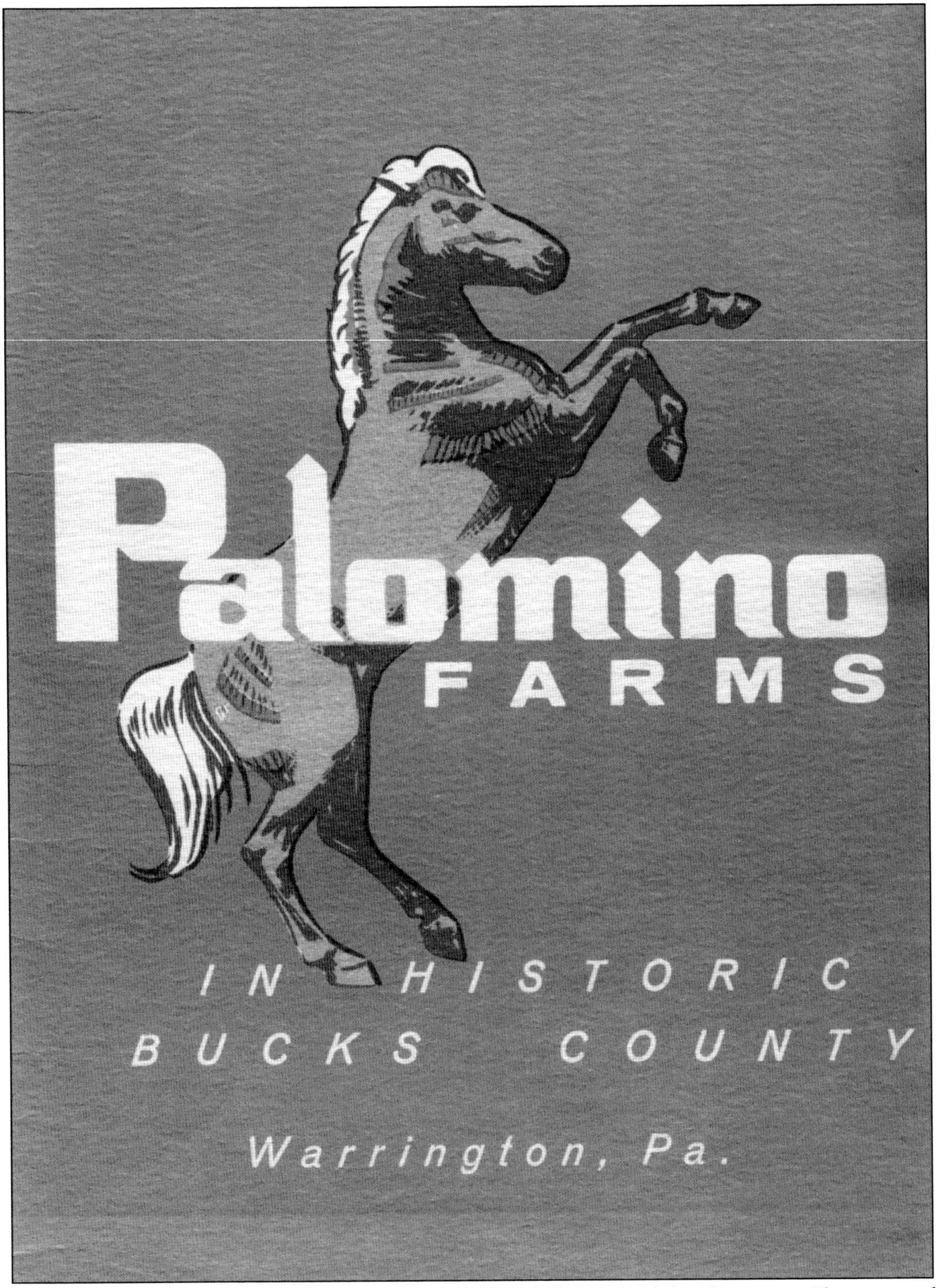

As the township grew, there was a need for single-family homes and developments. Phase one of Palomino Farms was started in 1963. Sale brochures described the development as a "beautiful community for the utmost in safety with wide winding streets both for appearance and to keep traffic at a slow pace" and noted, "Along its borders are bridle paths for those who enjoy riding."

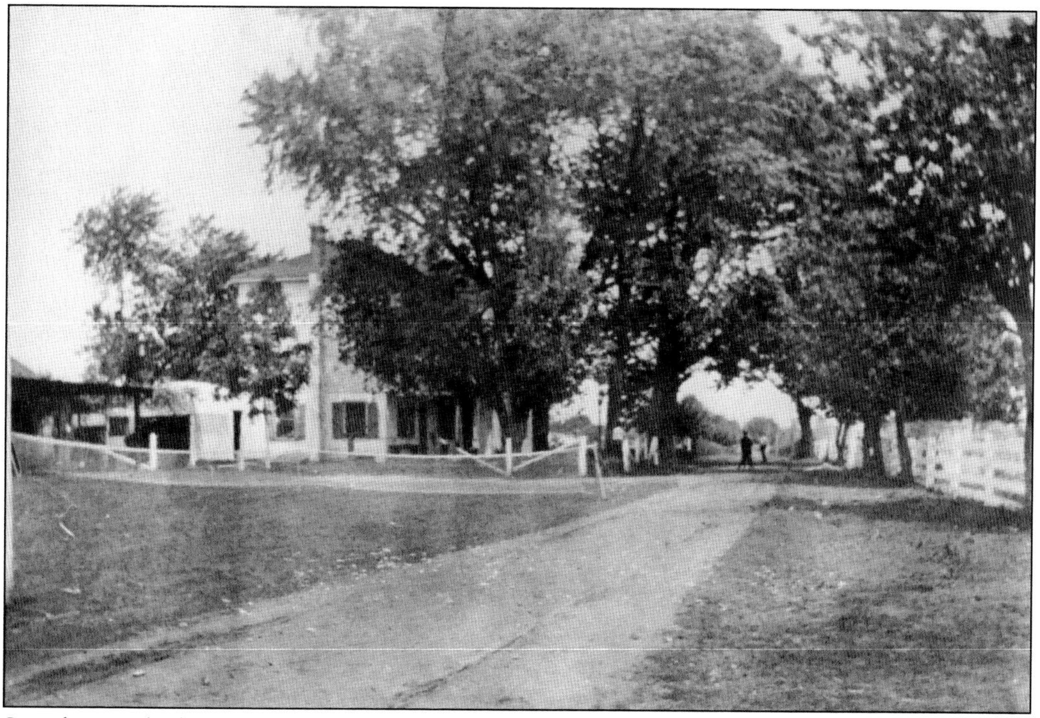

Seen here is the lane from the Titus Homestead looking toward Easton Road. Jacob Titus bought these 137 acres off Easton Road in 1852. The house and outbuildings were built in 1855. One of Jacob and Elizabeth's children, Oliver, married Florence Dobbins and purchased the family farm in 1899. Florence D. Titus is the namesake of Titus Elementary School. (Courtesy of Alberta Titus Mininger and Charles Titus.)

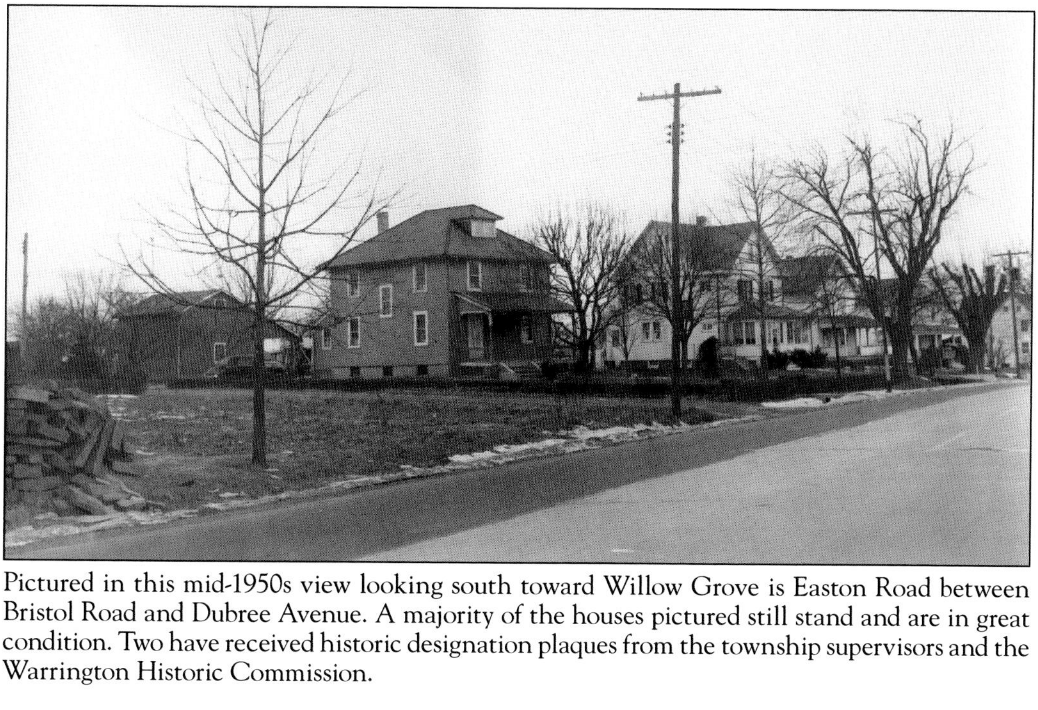

Pictured in this mid-1950s view looking south toward Willow Grove is Easton Road between Bristol Road and Dubree Avenue. A majority of the houses pictured still stand and are in great condition. Two have received historic designation plaques from the township supervisors and the Warrington Historic Commission.

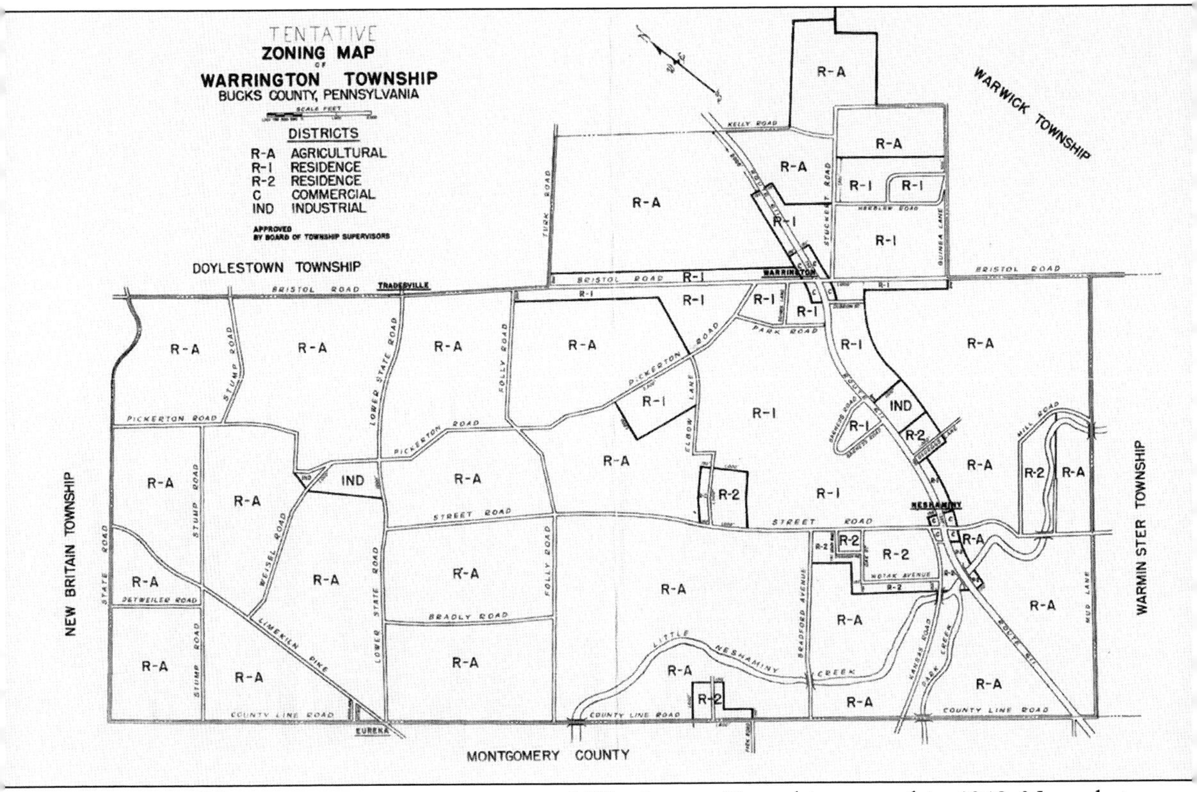

Presented here is a tentative zoning map of Warrington Township created in 1948. Note that there is very little commercial and industrial zoning on this map.

Five

Clubs, Township Events, and Daily Happenings

Once individuals and families moved within the township's borders, groups and clubs were formed to create a better sense of community. One of the first service groups in the township was Warrington Lodge No. 447 of the Independent Order of Odd Fellows. Formed in 1851, they met at a building located next to Craig's Tavern. The Woman's Club, fire department, Ladies Auxiliary for the fire department, Junior Woman's Club, Lions Club, Rotary Club, Jaycees, and Warrington Athletic Association are just a few of the groups that have also made a difference in the lives of local residents. From these organizations have come memorable fundraising events: the Lions Club horse show, Warrington Day, community carnivals, and parades. The following images show a time when Warrington Township was a much smaller place where everyone was known by name.

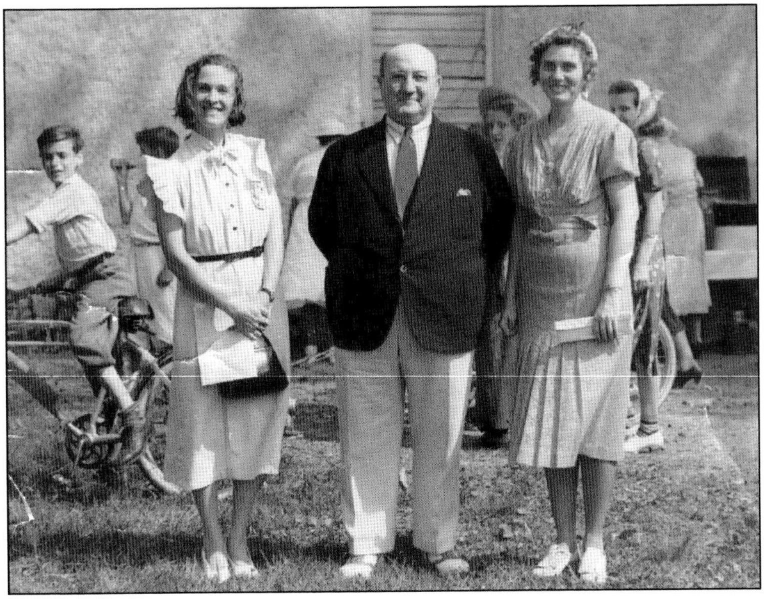

The first documented Warrington Township Community Day was held on July 10, 1937. The early community days were sponsored by the Warrington Junior Women's Club, and activities were centered at the Warrington School House on Bristol Road. Pictured here on June 25, 1938, are, from left to right, Ethel Klein (cochair), Dr. Calvin Althouse (guest speaker), and Jane Tufts (cochair).

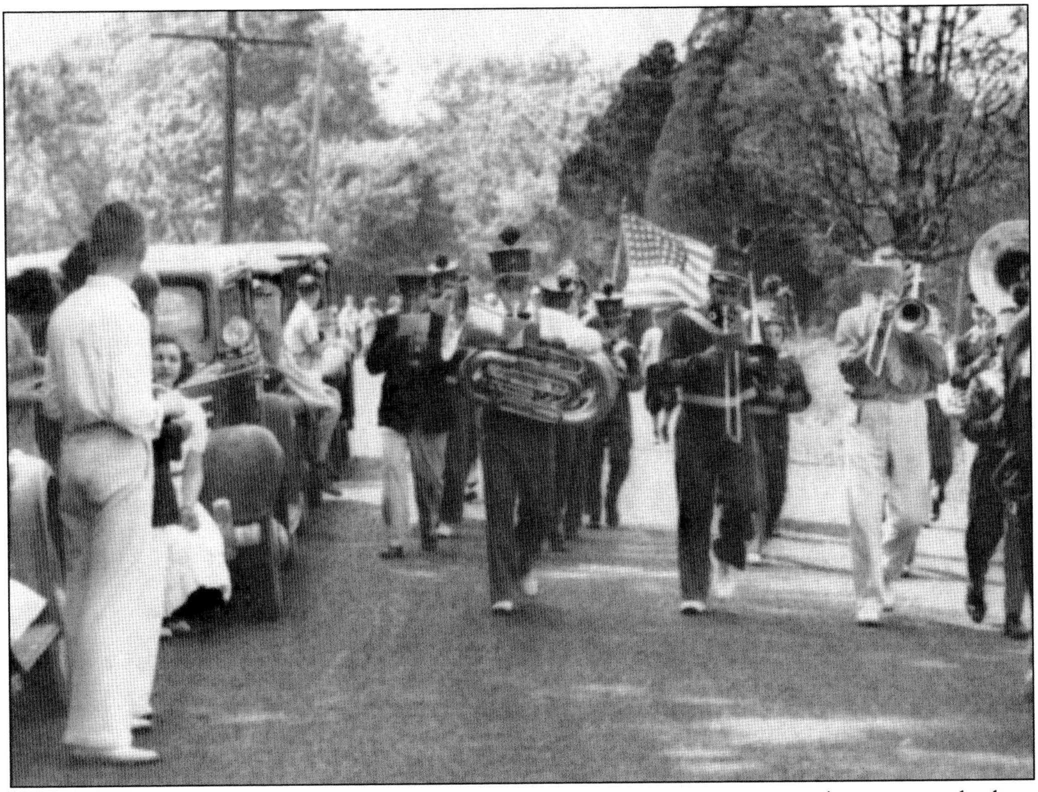

In the late 1940s, community days were held at different locations. In 1947, the event took place at the old ball field (where the Warrington Shopping Center is located today at Easton Road and Bristol Road). In 1948, it was held at the Center House Picnic Grounds (where the current firehouse on Easton Road is located today). Seen here is a parade marching along Bristol Road.

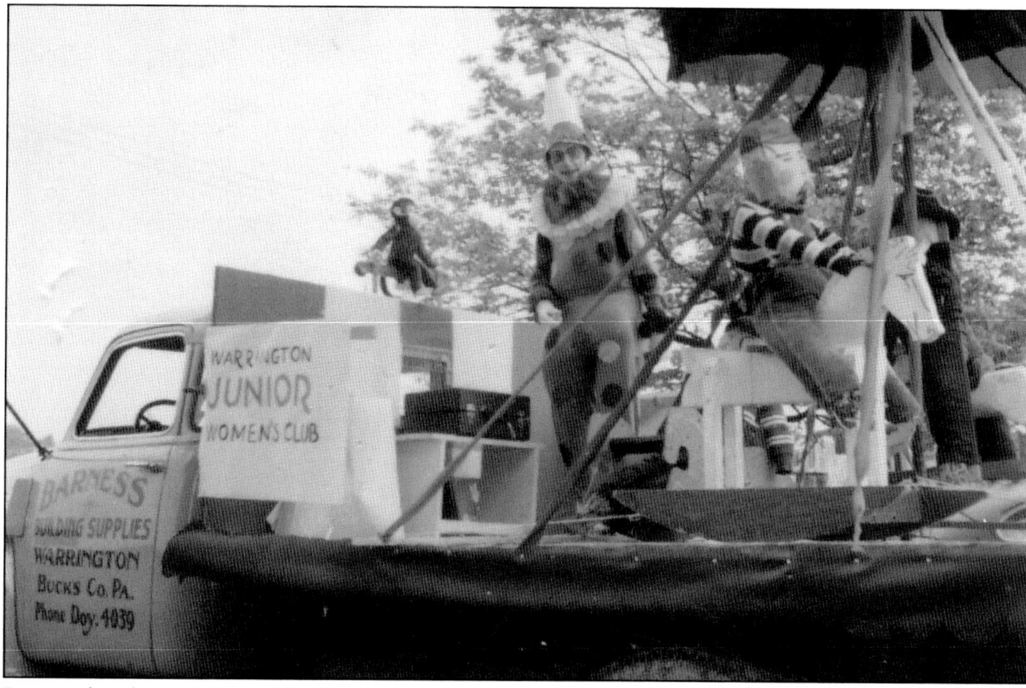

Pictured is the Warrington Junior Women's Club parade float for Warrington Day in the summer of 1950. Note that the float is on the back of a Barness Building Supplies flatbed truck. The purpose of the celebration was to allow neighbors to become better acquainted and to promote good fellowship within the township.

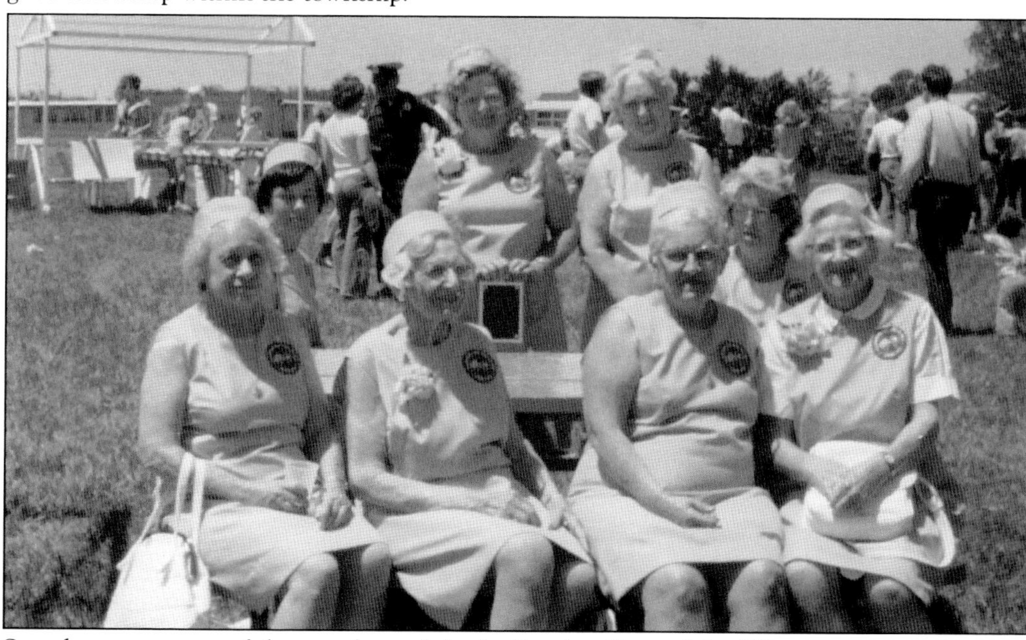

Seen here are many of the members of the Ladies Auxiliary of the Warrington Township Fire Department at Warrington Day in June 1977. From left to right, they are (first row) Bertha Yowell, Anna Murray, Dot Price, and Lenola Emerson; (second row) Marilyn Konsowitz, Betty Feriod, Mae Krapt Regenhard, and Mary Cantwell.

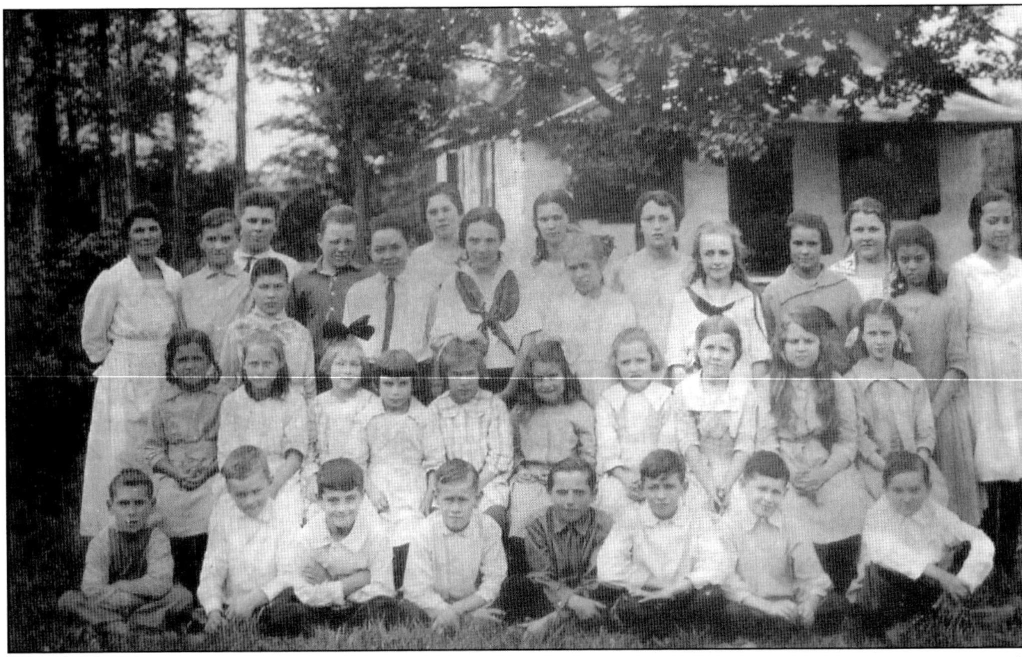

Flora Clymer McNair is the teacher in this Mill Creek School class picture from approximately 1912. The deed to the schoolhouse was written by John Dubois in September 1864. When proposals to build a new facility were reviewed, the only bids received were from mason James Cozens and carpenter Joseph Garner. They agreed to build it for $1,290.

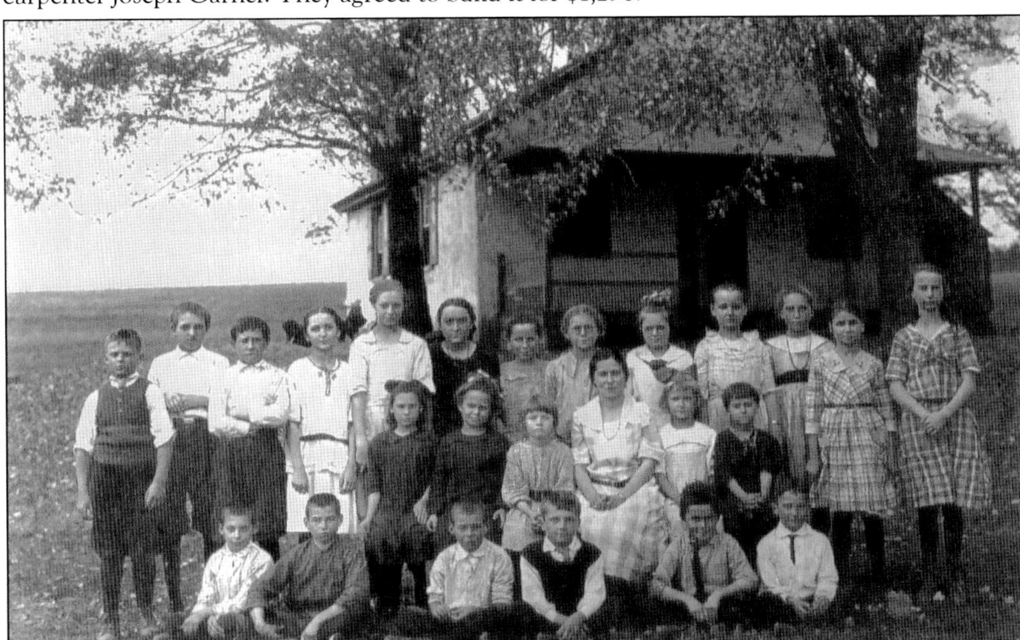

The teacher in this 1923 County Line School class picture was Mariem Frankenfield. A red tin roof was most likely placed over the original wood shingles in 1872 or 1873 after a fire. The locals referred to the school as "Red Top College" because of the new red tin roof. (Courtesy of David Paterson.)

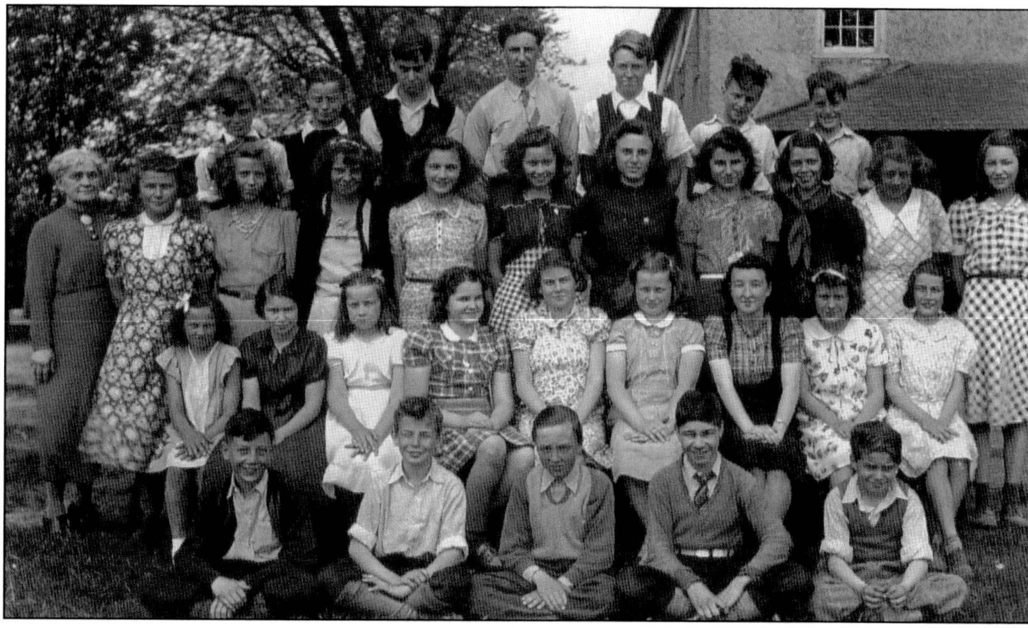

Here is Warrington School's fifth-through-eighth-grade 1940 class picture with teacher Miss Haldeman. In 1929, Warrington Township School Board meeting minutes read, "It was decided from a reliable electrician an estimate of the cost of wiring the Warrington School House for the installation of electrical lights. Complaints have been made by the patrons that on dull or cloudy days pupils could not study for the lack of sufficient light." (Courtesy of David Paterson.)

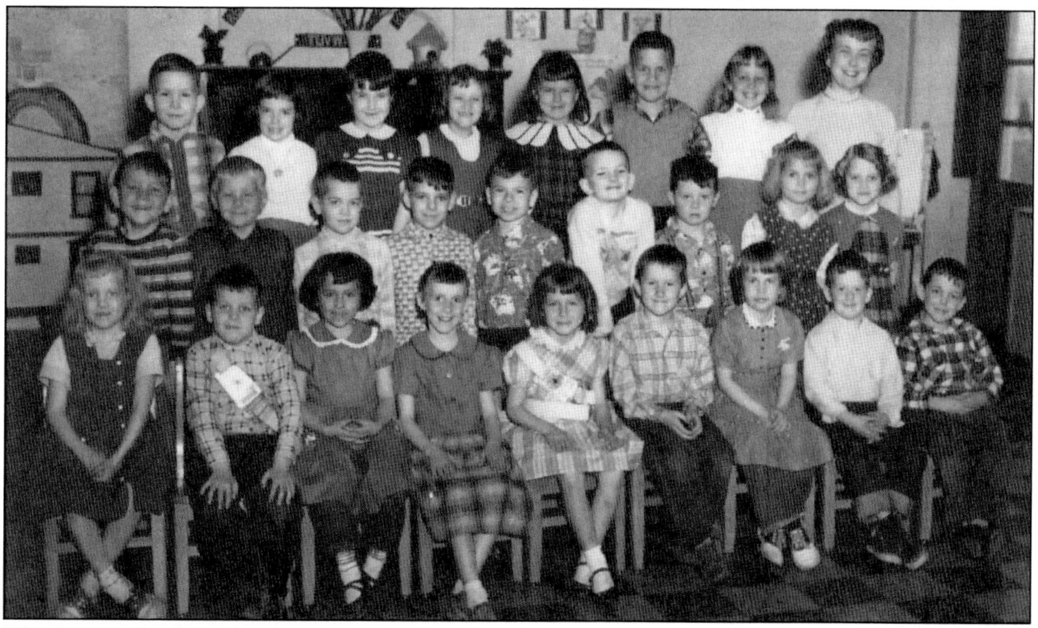

The first grade class of 1955 at Warrington Elementary (renamed the Florence D. Titus Elementary School after Florence Dobbins Titus) had Miss Urick as its teacher. The Warrington and Neshaminy schoolhouses were closed and were consolidated when the new six-room Warrington Elementary School was opened (at a cost of $188,200). The new school was dedicated on September 9, 1951. (Courtesy of the Barness family.)

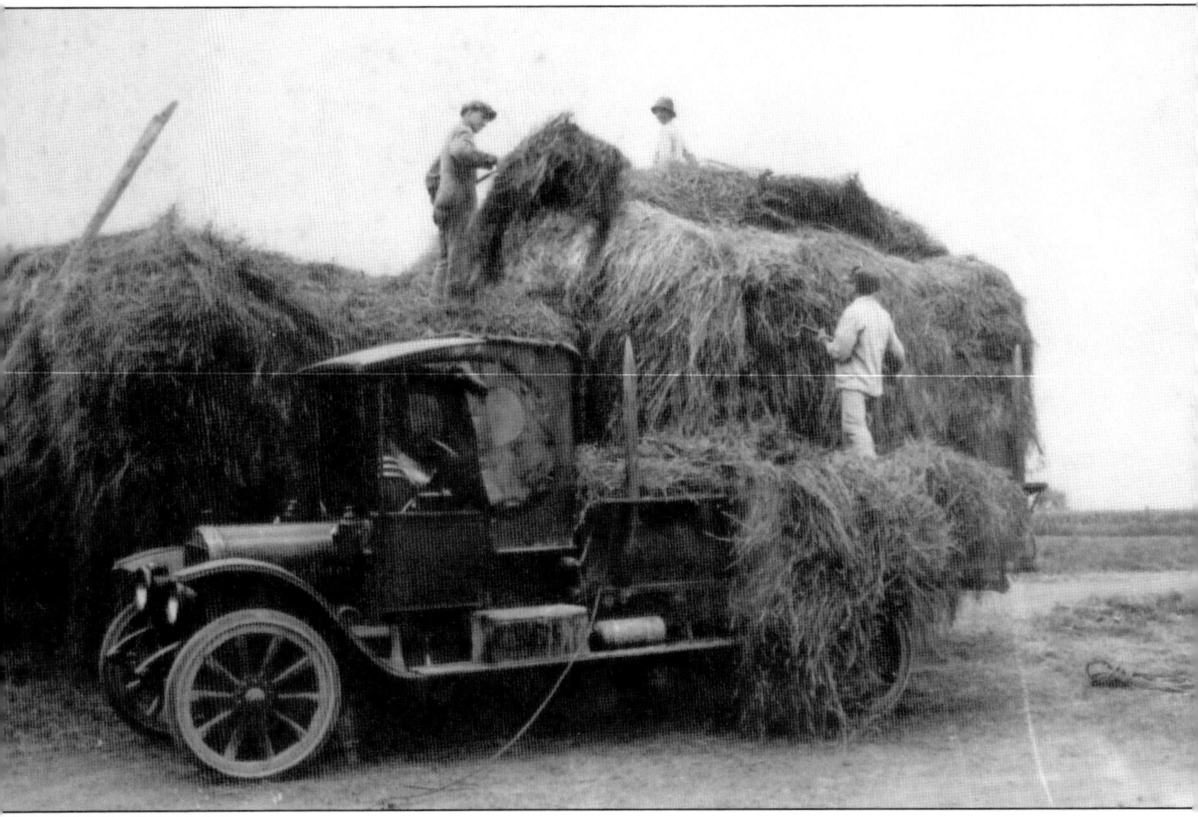

During William and Jennie Kohler's ownership of 3263 County Line Road (around the time of World War I), hay was grown as one of the main crops. At harvest time, overloaded horse-drawn wagons and, later, White motor trucks would line County Line Road. (Courtesy of Bob and Jane Henderson.)

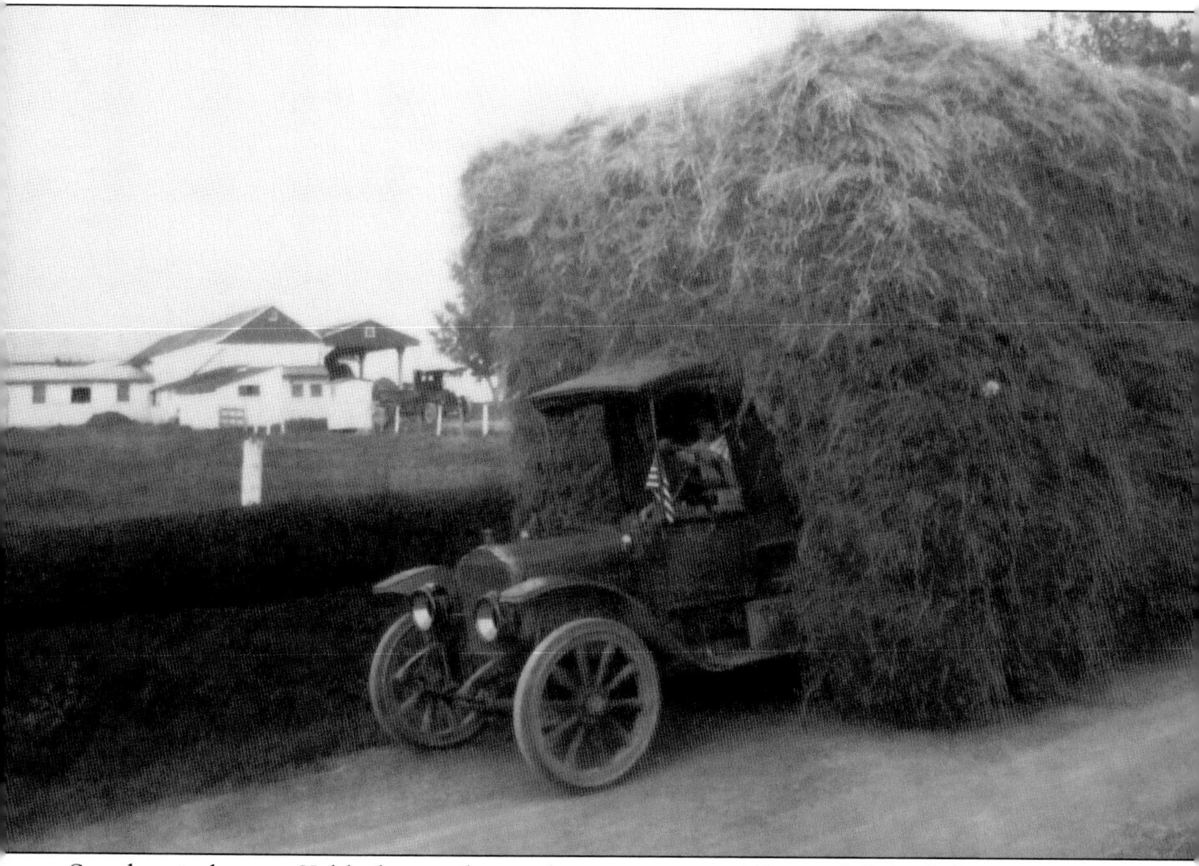

Seen here is the same Kohler hay truck as in the image on page 100; now fully loaded, it is ready to bring the crop to market. The Kohlers provided the City of Philadelphia stables and the Abbott's Dairy stables (among others) with hay. The farm was at its largest and most profitable during this time. (Courtesy of Bob and Jane Henderson.)

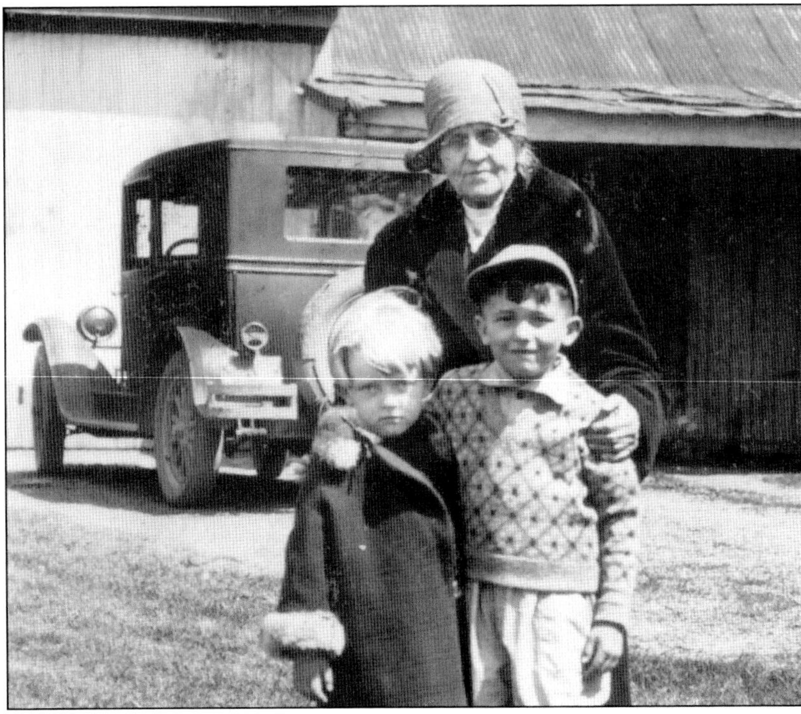

The Titus family lived on an 86-acre farm located behind the Neshaminy Inn. Pictured here around 1928 are Sarah Jenkins Dobbins (mother of Florence D. Titus, a township school board president for many years) and two of her great-grandchildren, cousins Jean and Joe Titus, on the family farm. (Courtesy of Alberta Titus Mininger and Charles Titus.)

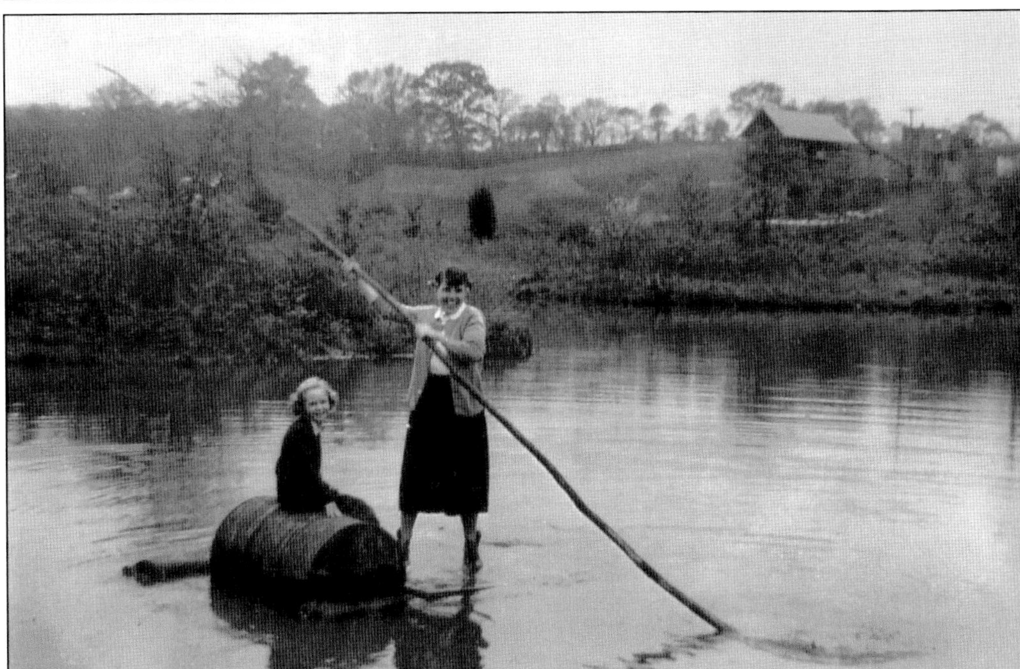

Anna Cornell DeHart and her niece Susan Cornell Hoy row on a homemade raft at the quarry located behind the Cornell family farm and airfield on Bristol Road. Anna attended the Mill Creek School located on Pickertown Road and Mill Creek Road. After her schooling, she spent some time as a substitute teacher at the Warrington School House located on Bristol Road. (Courtesy of Anna Cornell DeHart.)

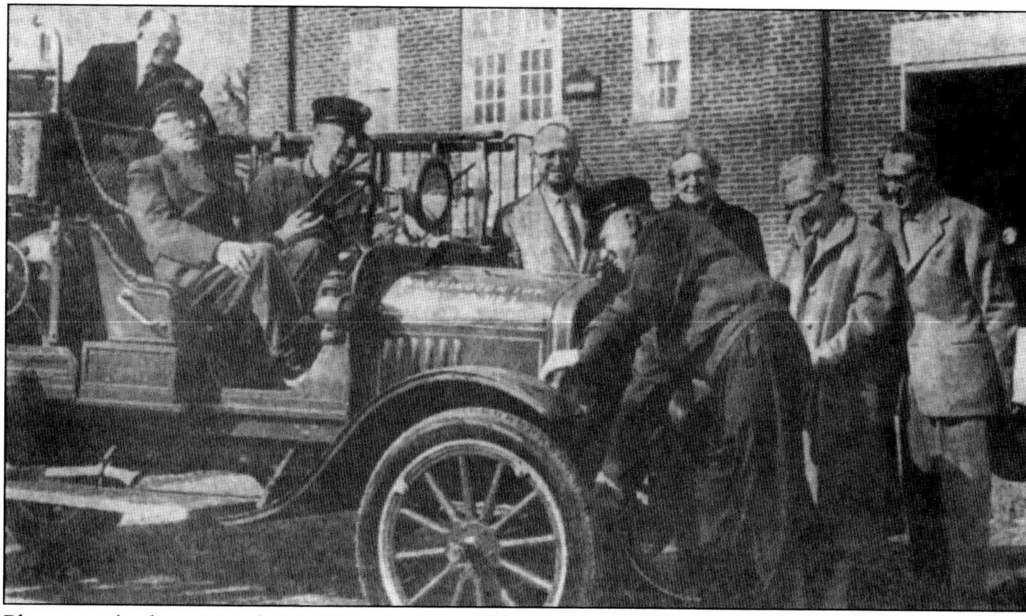

Photographed on March 24, 1964, Stephen Kunstl (front of the truck) is cheered on by other charter members and some of the Women's Auxiliary. Joseph Penrose, who owned the 1925 Ford Model TT American La France Chemical Fire Truck, is at the wheel, with Charles Loux alongside and James Speakman in the rear. Standing from left to right are C. Leroy Murray; his wife, Anna; Lenola Emerson; and her husband, Irvin.

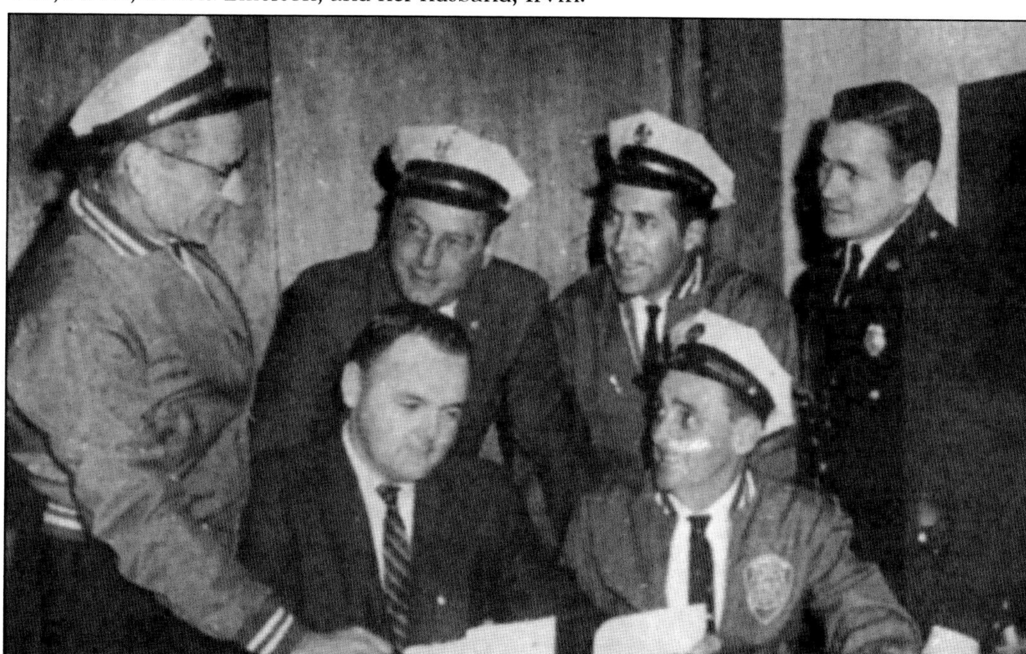

In 1964, a photograph of the Warrington Township Fire Company No. 1 officers was taken. Pictured from left to right are (seated) Daniel Gallagher (president of the fire company) and Joseph Gallen (fire chief); (standing) Herman Blair (assistant chief), Donald Riley (constable of Warrington Township), John Rossetti (assistant chief), and Kenneth Reiff (captain of the fire police).

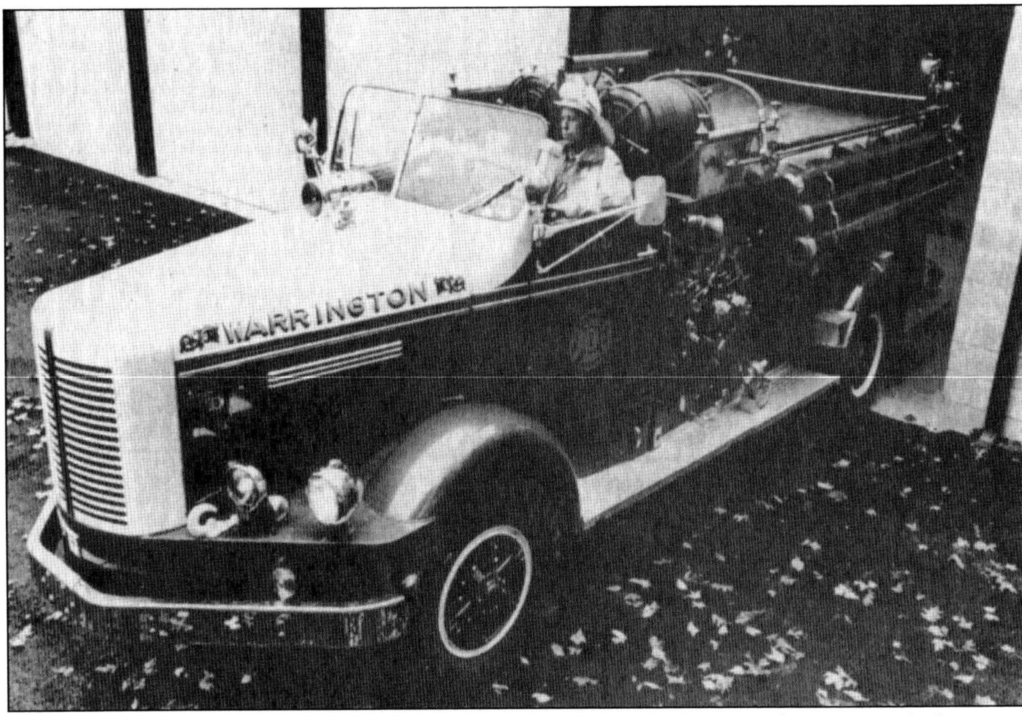

Assistant fire chief John Kincade parks a fire truck at the new township garage (substation) behind the municipal building (the old Mill Creek School built in 1927) located on the corner of Mill Creek Road and Pickertown Road in 1974. This new location was needed to ensure the protection on the northwestern end of the township.

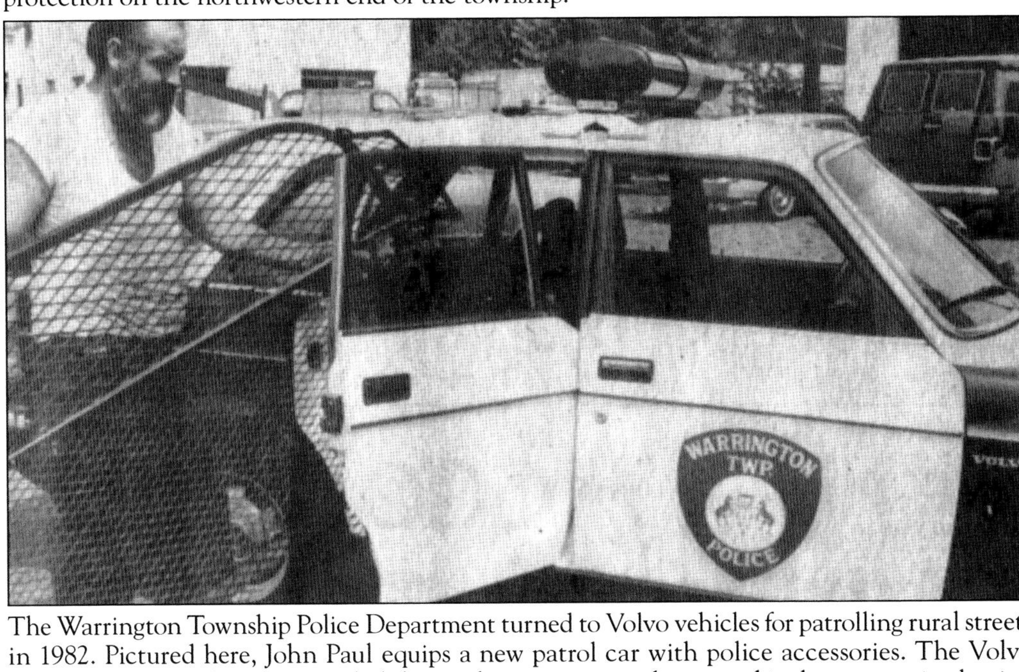

The Warrington Township Police Department turned to Volvo vehicles for patrolling rural streets in 1982. Pictured here, John Paul equips a new patrol car with police accessories. The Volvo was chosen for use because its reliability and superior gas mileage, and its less-expensive leasing opportunities made it a more cost-effective option.

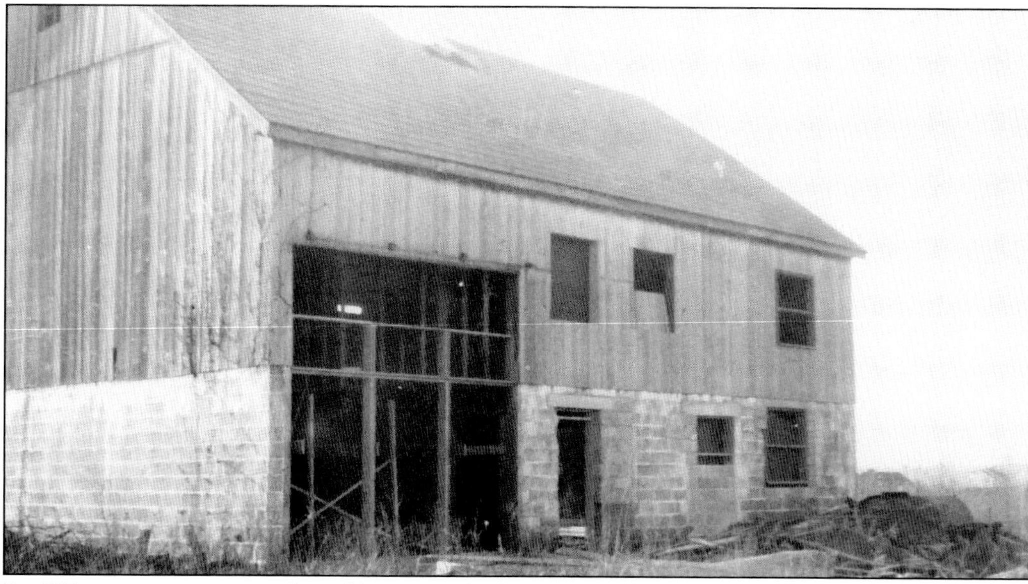

Paul Keene was an artist who told stories of African Americans through imagery that combined ancient cultural traditions with a distinctly modern, urban point of a view. In 1955, Keene and his family moved to Warrington. With help from an architect friend, they remodeled a barn on Bristol Road that was given to Keene by his parents. Pictured here is the barn prior to remodeling. (Courtesy of Laura Keene.)

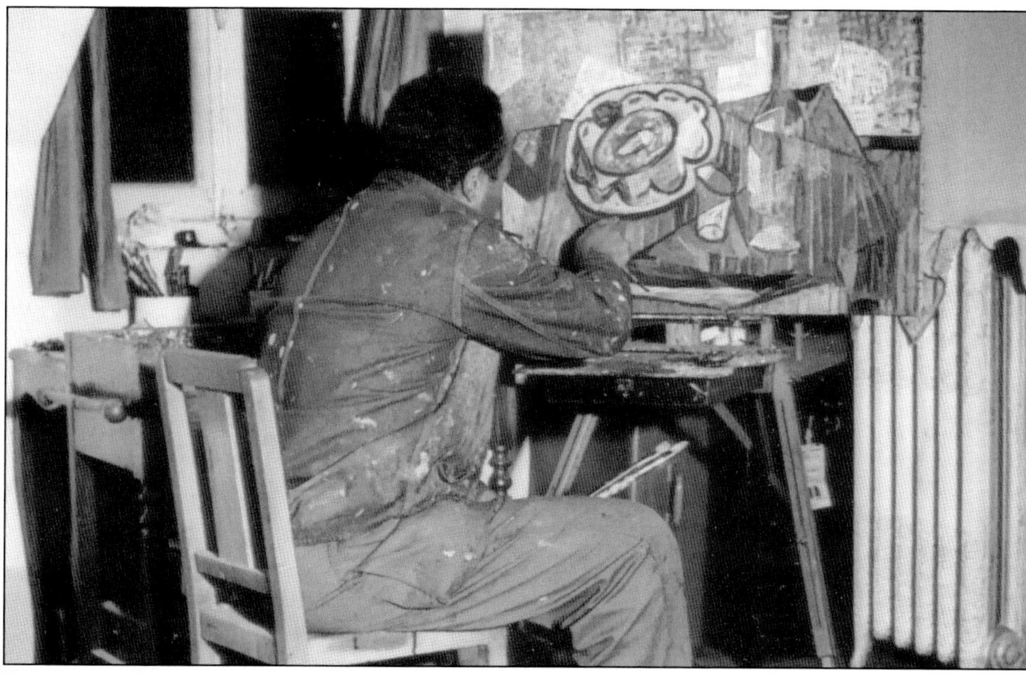

During World War II, Paul Keene began painting and drawing illustrations while serving with the Tuskegee Airmen. After his service, Keene finished his education and received his bachelor of fine arts and master of fine arts from Tyler School of Art, Temple University. Keene taught at the Philadelphia Museum School of Art from 1964 to 1968 and at the Bucks County Community College from 1968 through 1985. (Courtesy of Laura Keene.)

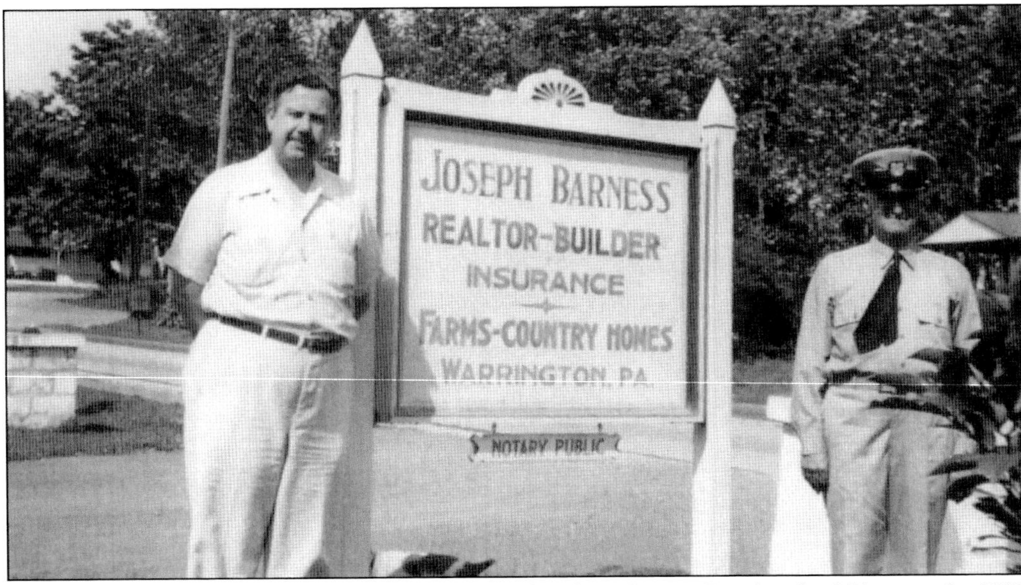

Joseph and Mary Barness purchased 80 acres of land on Easton Road to build homes. In 1925, Joseph formed the Barness Organization. Later, his son Herbert Barness ran the business and greatly expanded it. Herbert's daughter Lynda Barness eventually took over, and the Barness Organization was sold to developer Deluca Homes of Yardley in 2005. Pictured are Pete Crouthamel (left) and Herbert Barness (right). (Courtesy of the Barness family.)

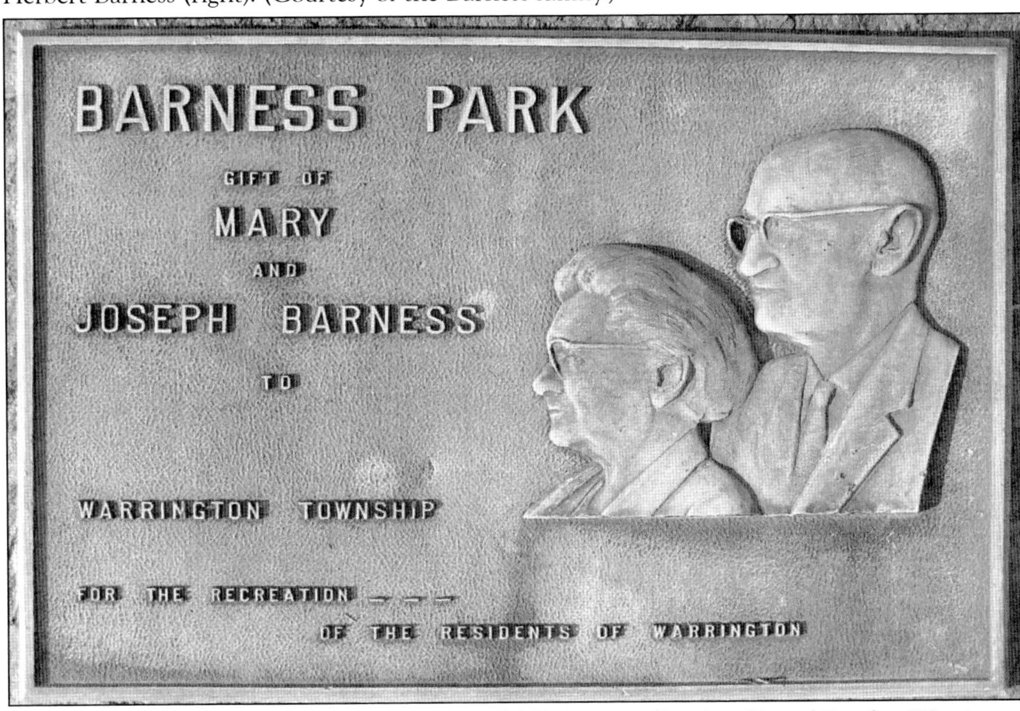

On January 1, 1962, Joseph and Mary Barness sold 22.8 acres of land on Bristol Road to Warrington Township for $1. This eventually became Barness Park, now the home of the Warrington Athletic Association. This monument, located at Barness Park, honors the Barnesses' dedication to Warrington Township.

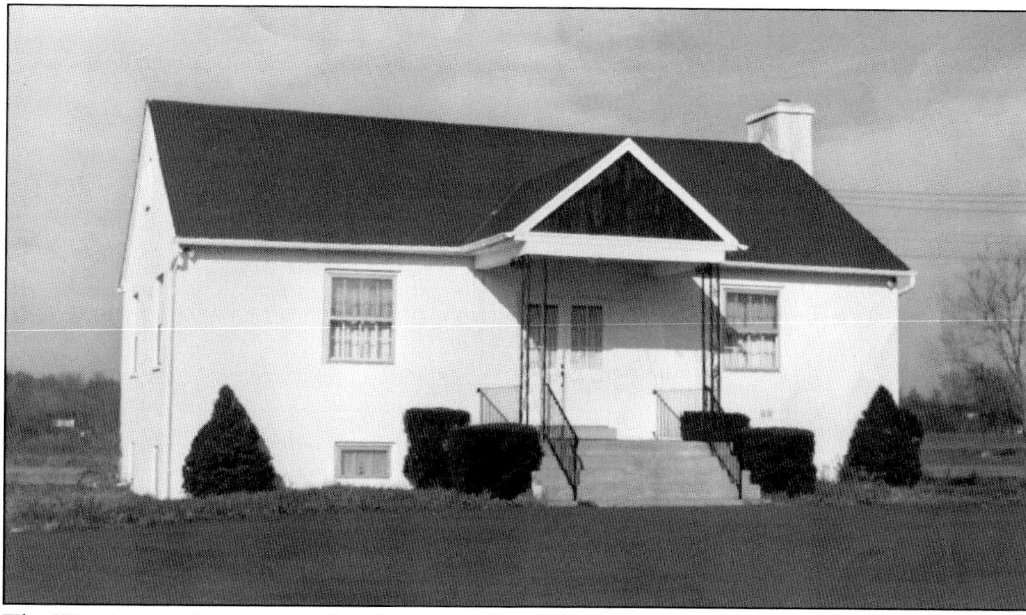

The Warrington Community Building, once located at 1248 Easton Road, was dedicated by the Lions and Women's Clubs in 1952. The building was mainly constructed and paid for by club members, and many other township groups used it as a meeting place. For a short time—from April 1960 to May 1962—the Warrington/Neshaminy Post Office rented space here. (Courtesy of the Lueckel family.)

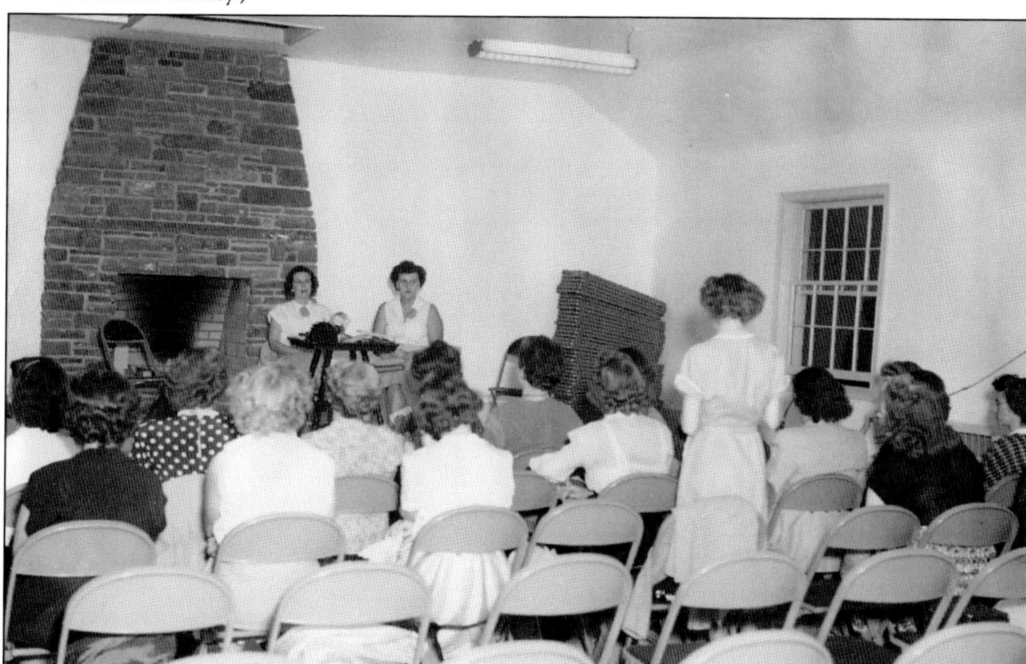

Warrington's chapter of the Junior Women's Club was founded in 1934. Pictured here is a meeting of the club inside the newly completed Warrington Community Building in late 1951. On the stage are clubs president Maxine Amelung (left) and vice president Mary Wieland (right). The woman standing to address them is the corresponding secretary, Sally Tettemer.

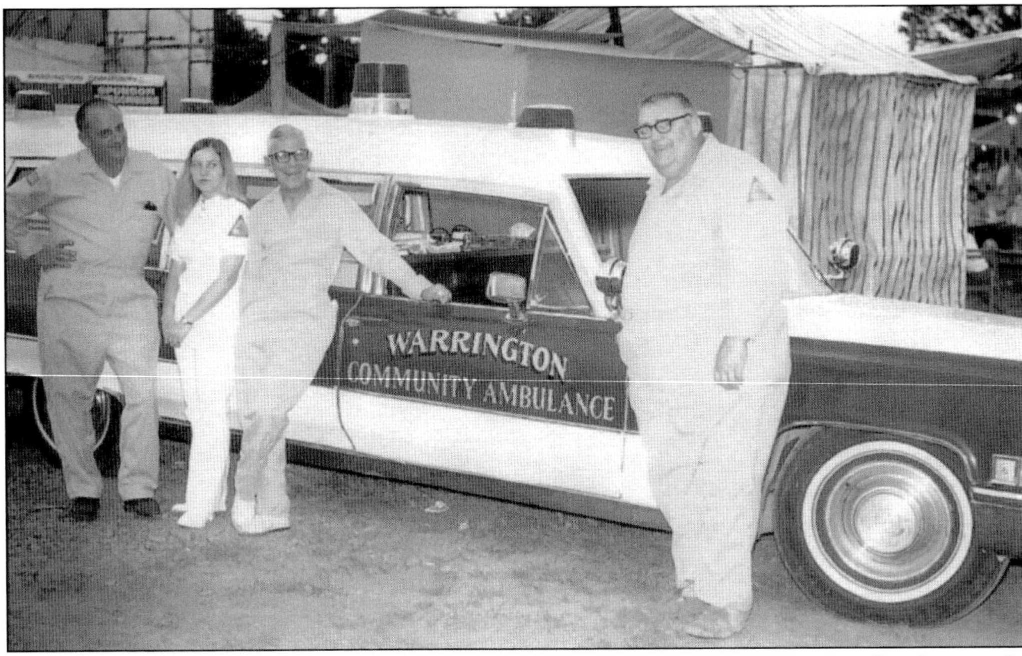

Members of the Warrington Community Ambulance Corporation are on standby duty at the community carnival with their 1969 Cadillac. In October 1974, the Cadillac was replaced with a Dodge van for improved reliability. The new building and the need for a new ambulance put great financial strain on the corporation.

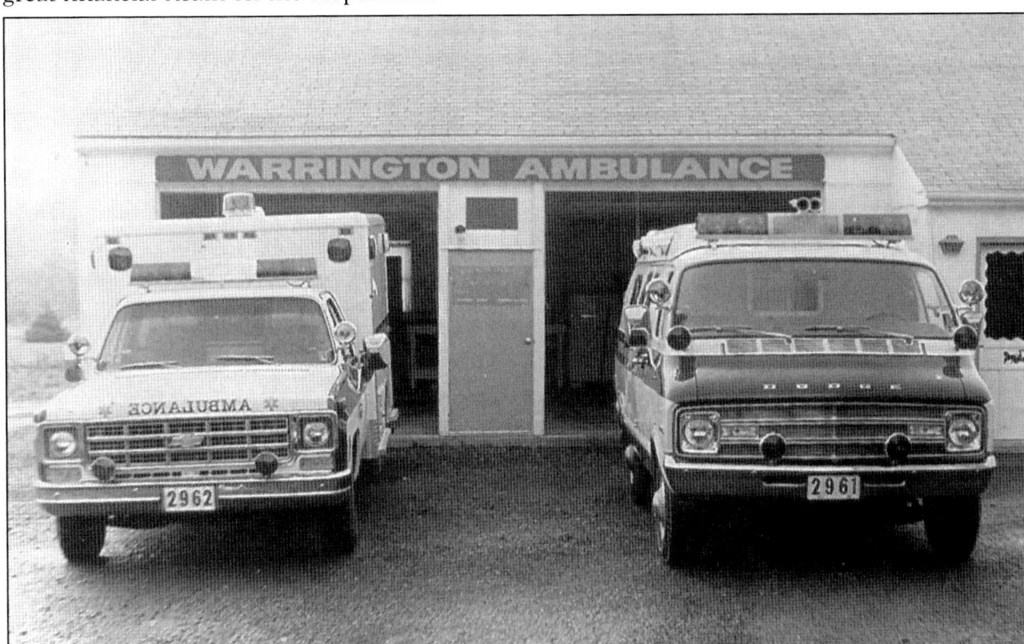

A building to house the Warrington Community Ambulance Corporation was dedicated on January 26, 1974, in the memory of Joseph Barness. This structure, located at 1248 Easton Road behind the Warrington Community Building, housed two ambulances, an office, and a training/ready room. Pictured here in 1978 is the most modern and advanced equipment available.

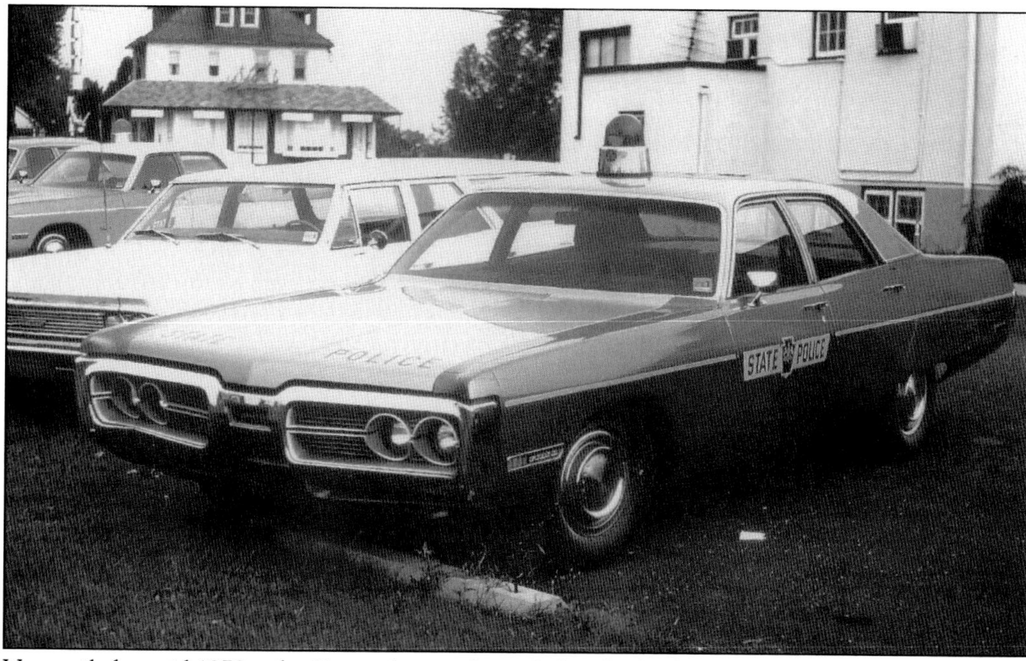

Up until the mid-1970s, the Pennsylvania State Police had a barracks located on Easton Road at the Barness Building. Seen here is a 1972 Plymouth Fury parked in their lot. The new color combination of blue and gold on this car was only used for one year. Across the street, the old Stutz Candy Shop, which later burned down, can be seen. (Courtesy of Everett Goff and Steven Furlong.)

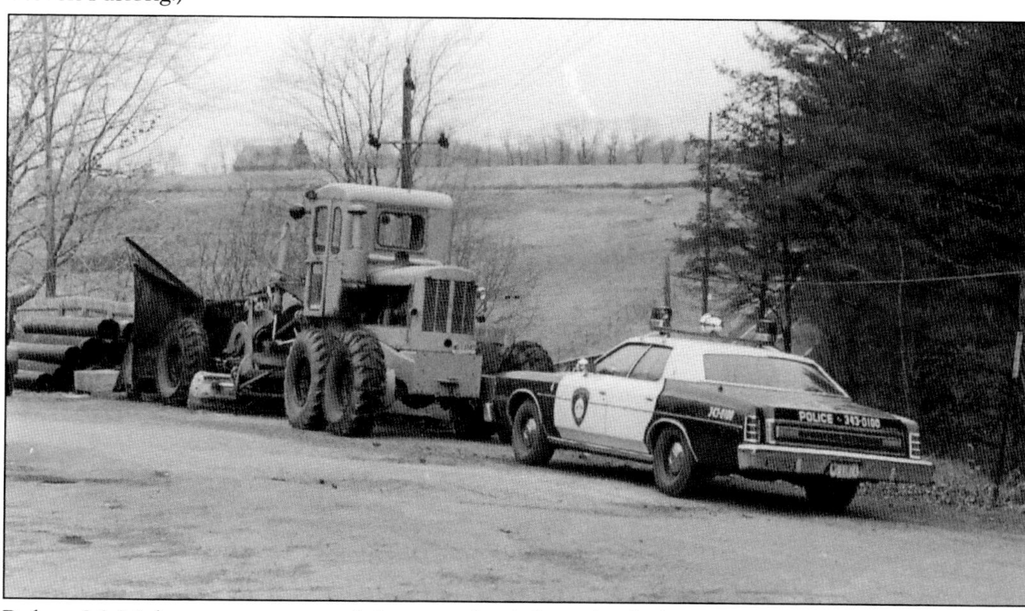

Robert McMahon was appointed the township's first chief of police by the board of supervisors on April 2, 1971. On May 8 of the same year, four part-time policemen were hired. John Bonargo was appointed the township's second chief of police in 1980, followed by James Miller as the third police chief in 1998. Seen here is a patrol car parked behind the old municipal building on Mill Creek Road.

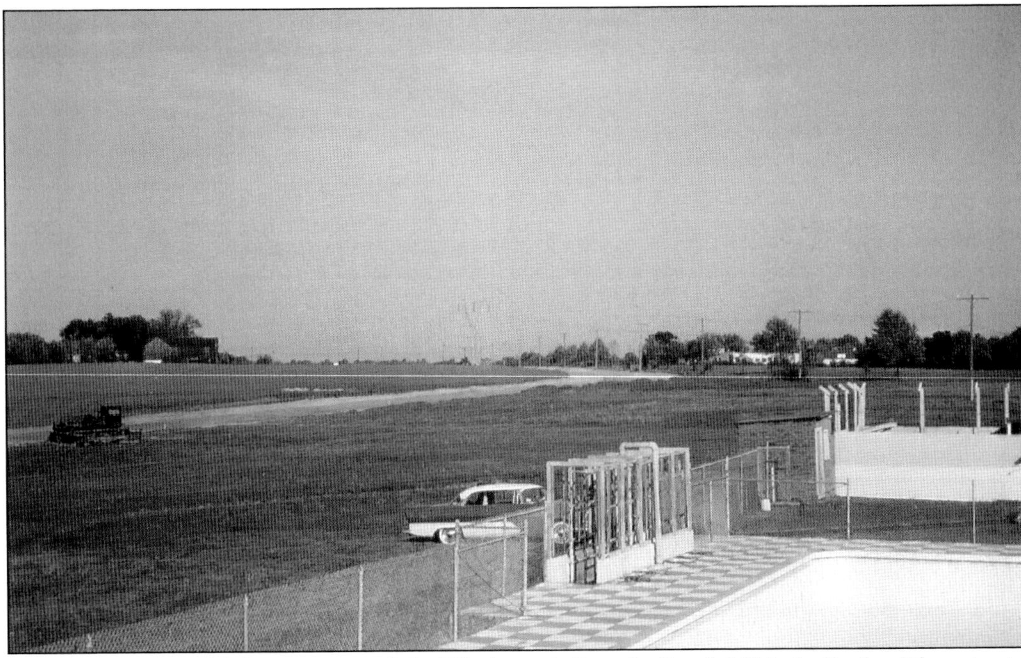

In 1939, the Philadelphia District of the Workman's Benefit Fund, USA, built the Olympic-size pool that is today located at 2501 Freedoms Way. During World War II, the US Navy took over management of the pool complex and the picnic grounds. This picture shows the entrance showers and part of the original changing rooms. (Courtesy of the Mich Michner.)

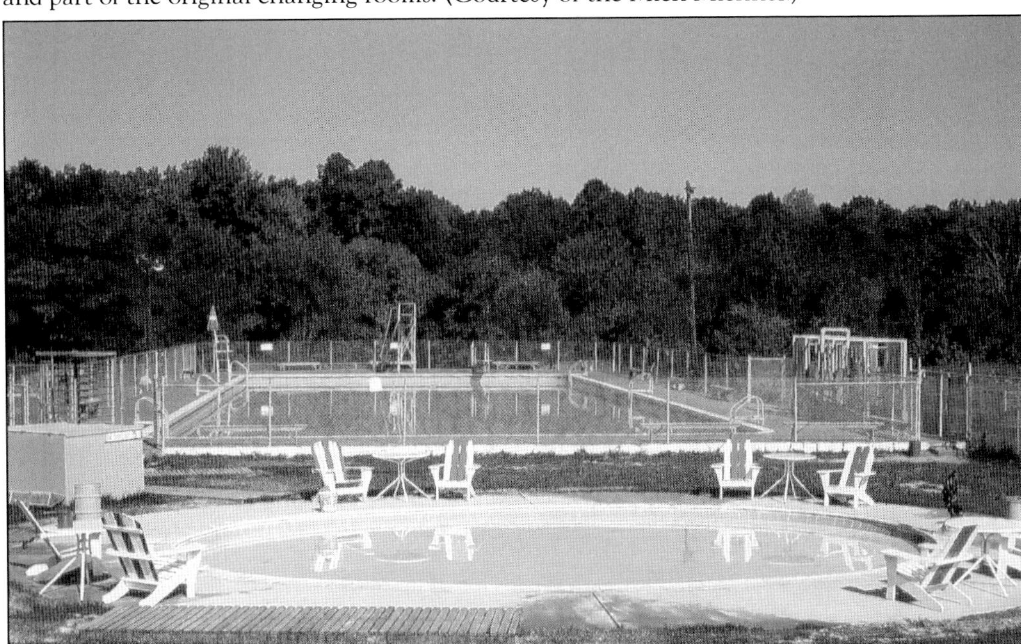

The pools were given to the township after the Barness Organization bought and developed the property, which was later renamed the Mary Barness Tennis and Swim Club. The dance hall and outhouses behind the picnic groves were torn down to make room for the development. (Courtesy of the Mich Michner.)

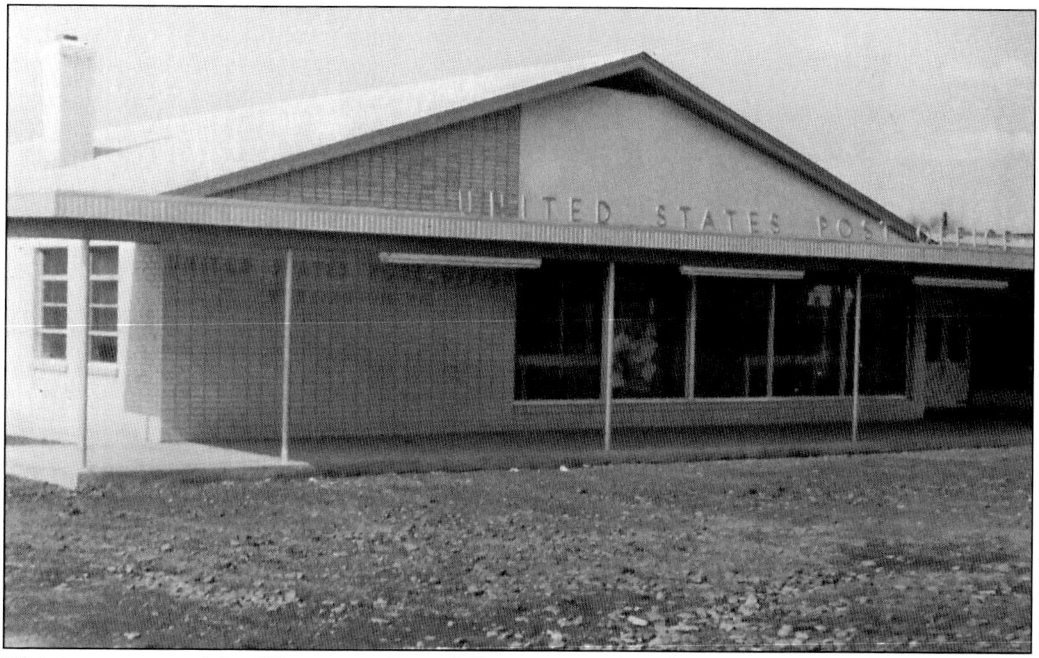

This is a picture of the Warrington Post Office prior to the official dedication. The presence of the Color Guard from the Nike Base at the opening on May 5, 1962, added to the fanfare. Lester Gordon was the first postmaster of this new location. (Courtesy of the Lueckel family.)

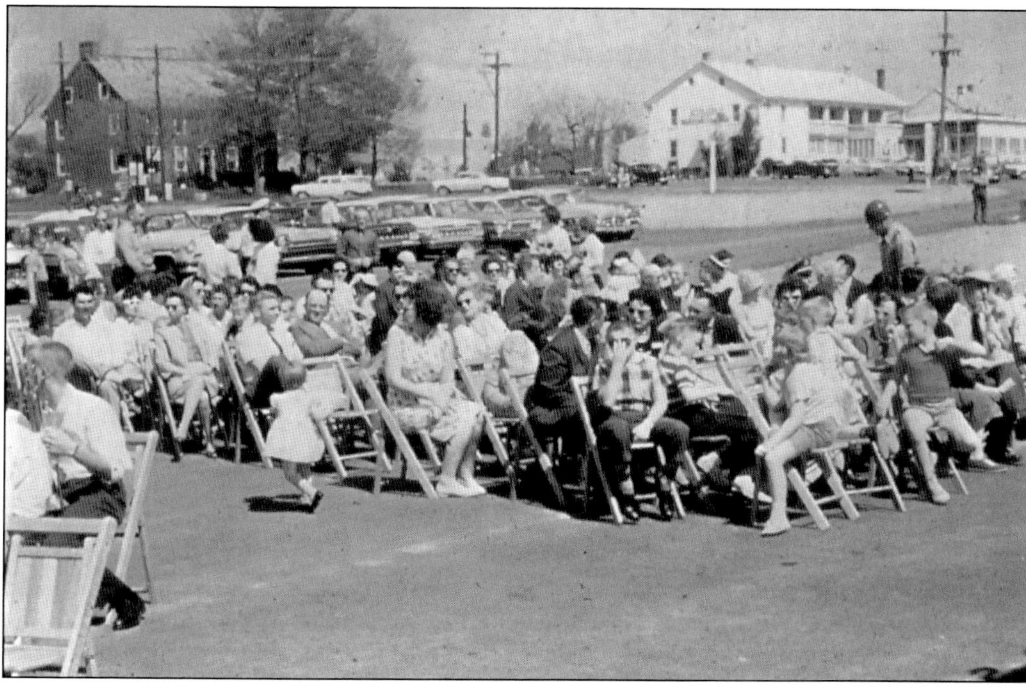

This photograph shows the audience at the Warrington Post Office dedication. In the background, the intersection of Easton Road and Bristol Road can be seen. To the left is the Barclay house (prior to modifications that made it a bank), and to the right is Vincent's Warrington Inn. (Courtesy of the Lueckel family.)

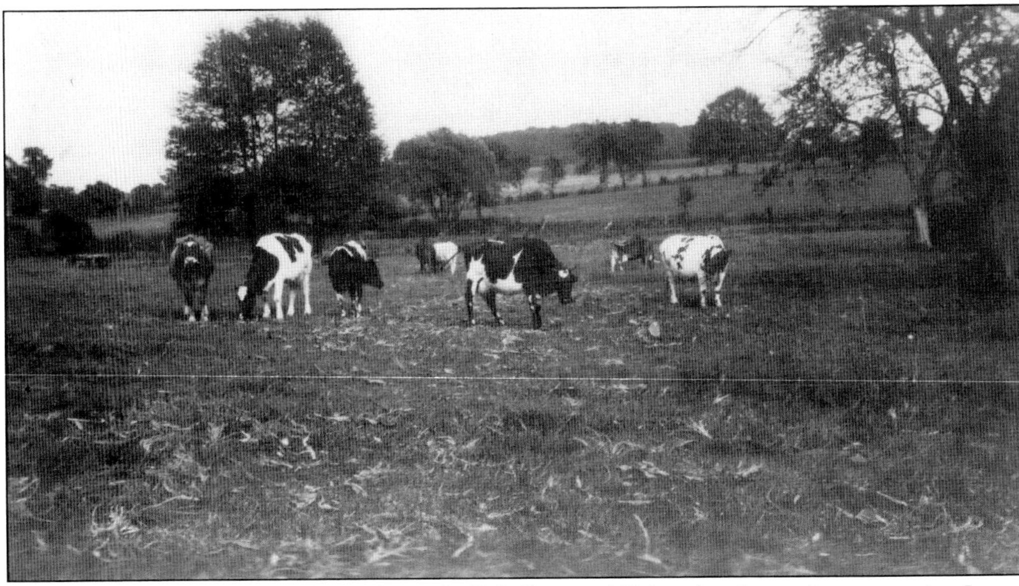

After graduating from Franklin and Marshall College in 1926 with a degree in economics, Joseph Penrose returned to his family's farm, where he tended 35 cows. He sold the milk to Abbott's and Scott Powell Dairies in Philadelphia, and he also grew oats, corn, barley, and hay on the property. (Courtesy of the Penrose family.)

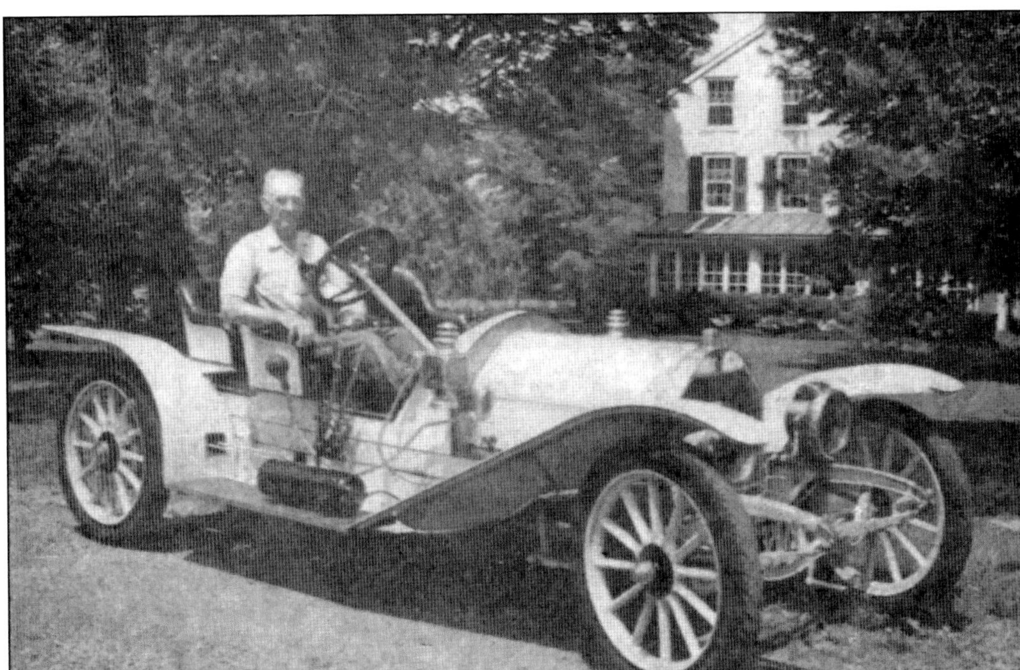

Joseph Penrose Sr. is pictured in 1974 with the family's 1910 Otto. The Otto was originally bought by William Penrose Jr. in 1910. Later, his half brother Joseph Penrose Sr. owned the car, and it was then passed to Joseph Penrose Jr. In 2009, the Otto left Warrington Township for good when Joseph Penrose Jr. donated the car to the Antique Automobile Club of America Museum, located in Hershey, Pennsylvania.

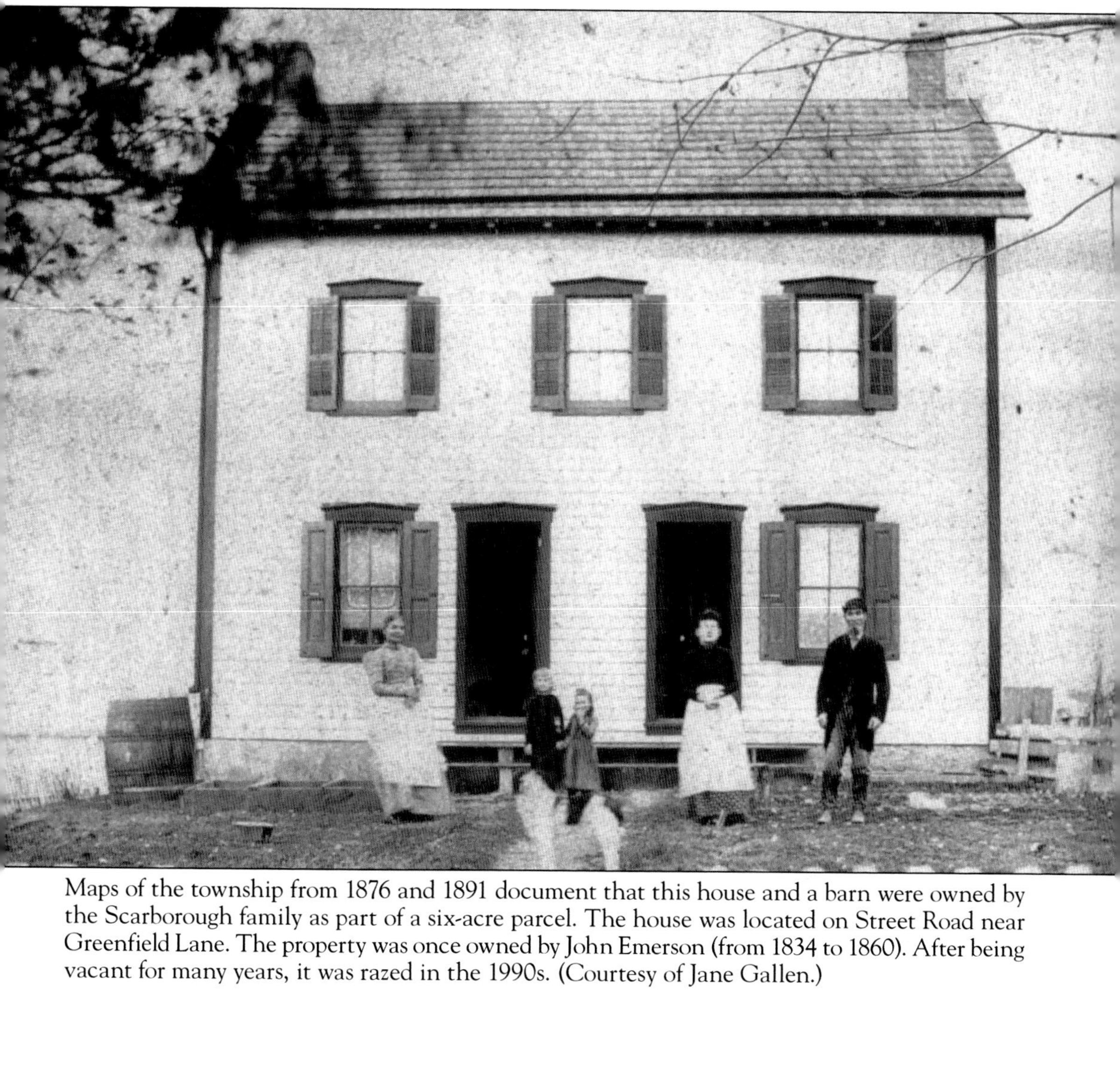

Maps of the township from 1876 and 1891 document that this house and a barn were owned by the Scarborough family as part of a six-acre parcel. The house was located on Street Road near Greenfield Lane. The property was once owned by John Emerson (from 1834 to 1860). After being vacant for many years, it was razed in the 1990s. (Courtesy of Jane Gallen.)

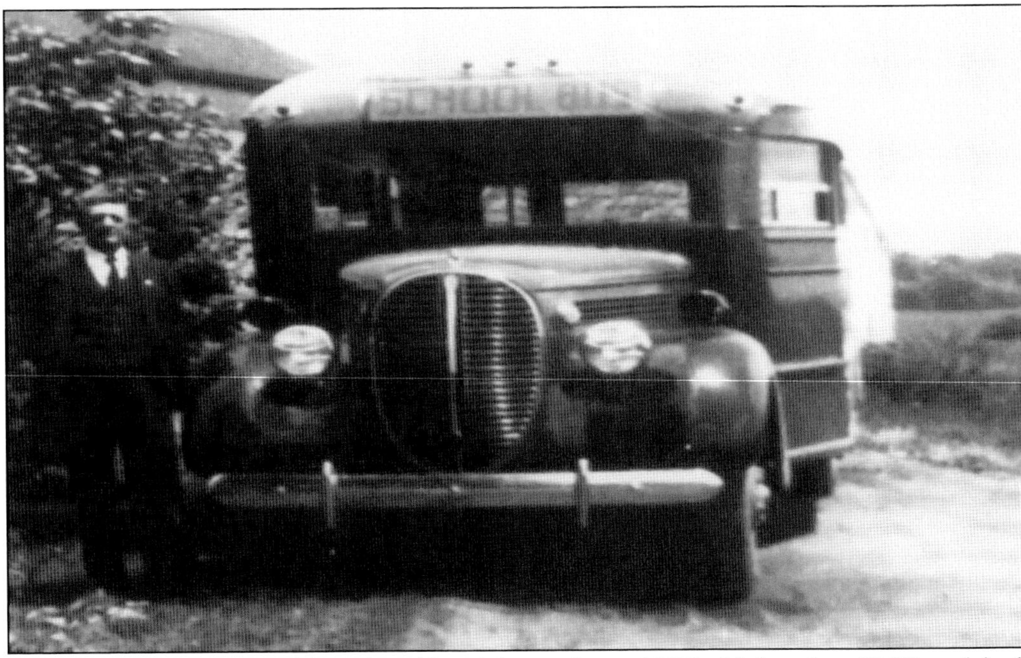

Eugene Kratz is pictured with his school/church bus in the mid-1930s. He bought a GMC truck body and had it equipped with windows and seats to transport children to the one-room schoolhouses. The bus was parked behind his home on Limekiln Pike, just opposite Woodland Avenue. (Courtesy of David Paterson.)

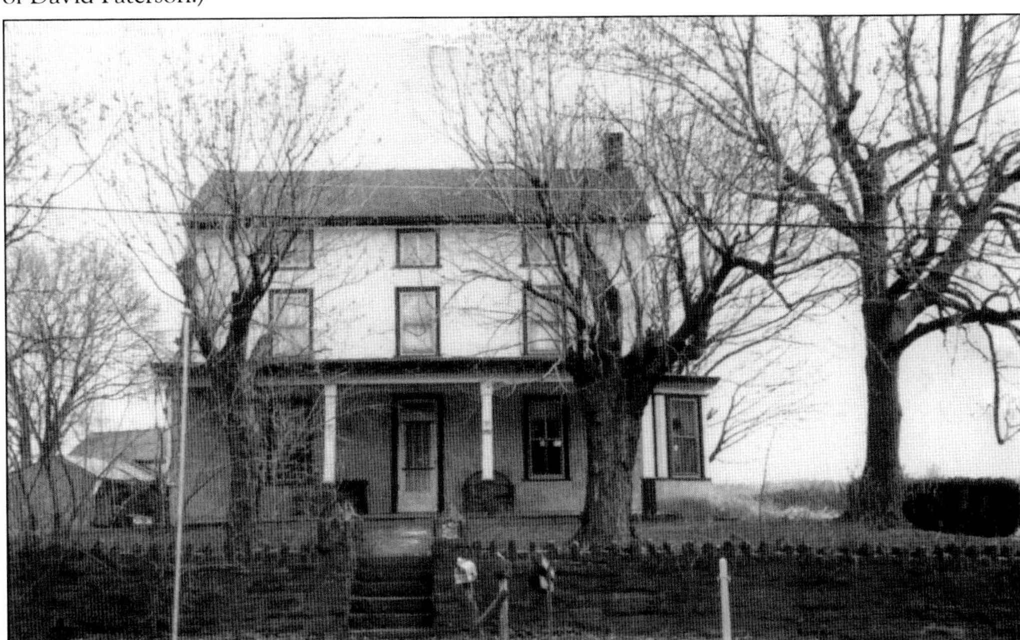

The Kratz house on Limekiln Pike, seen here in 1947, had an ornate stone retaining wall that ran the width of the front yard. In the middle of this wall, stone steps made a welcoming entrance to the house. G.W. Swartzlander owned this house and 34 acres in the late 1800s. The home was razed in 2010.

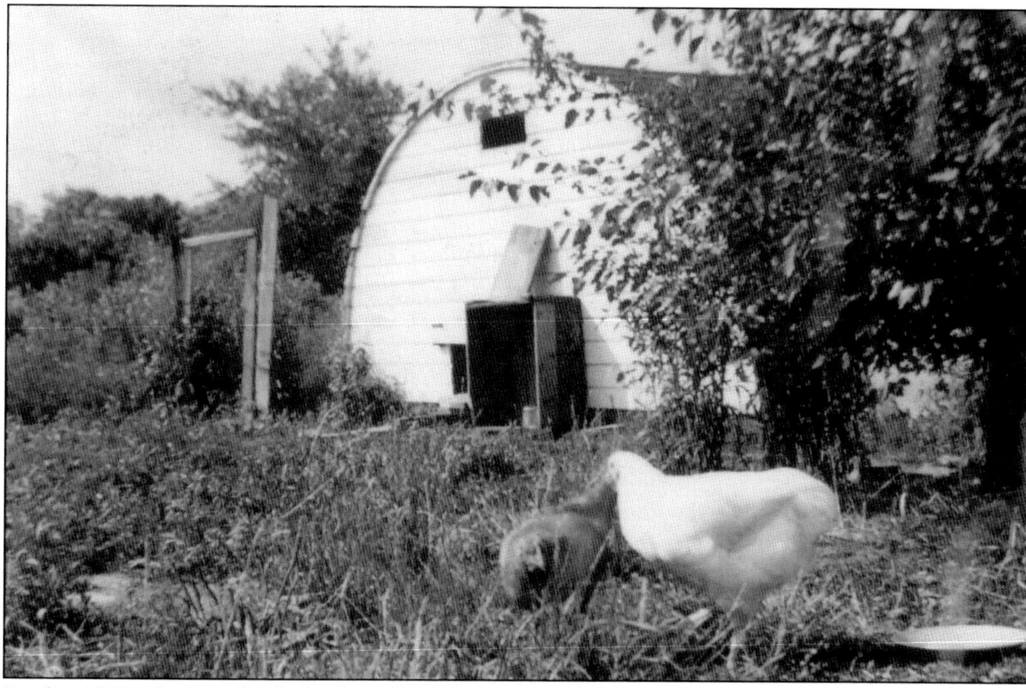

In the 1940s, houses built by Joseph Barness included chicken coops. Pictured here are the chicken coop and some chickens owned by the Doyle family, who resided on Barness Road. Joseph Barness felt that it was important to be able to provide for oneself by growing one's own food on a "miniature garden farm." (Courtesy of Janet Doyle.)

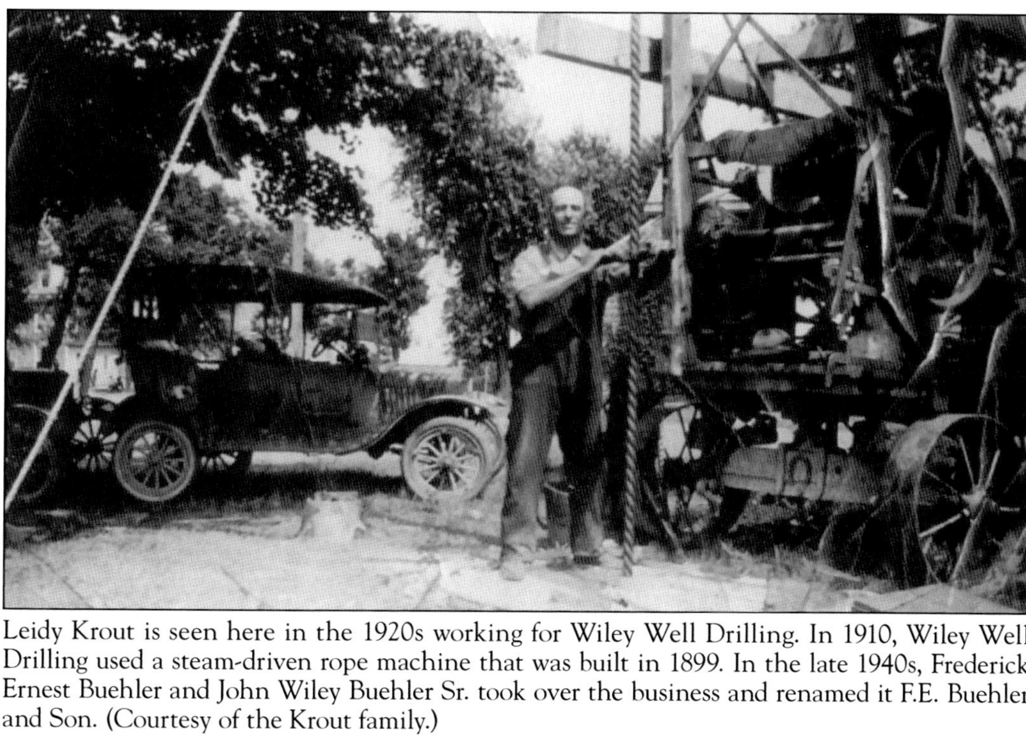

Leidy Krout is seen here in the 1920s working for Wiley Well Drilling. In 1910, Wiley Well Drilling used a steam-driven rope machine that was built in 1899. In the late 1940s, Frederick Ernest Buehler and John Wiley Buehler Sr. took over the business and renamed it F.E. Buehler and Son. (Courtesy of the Krout family.)

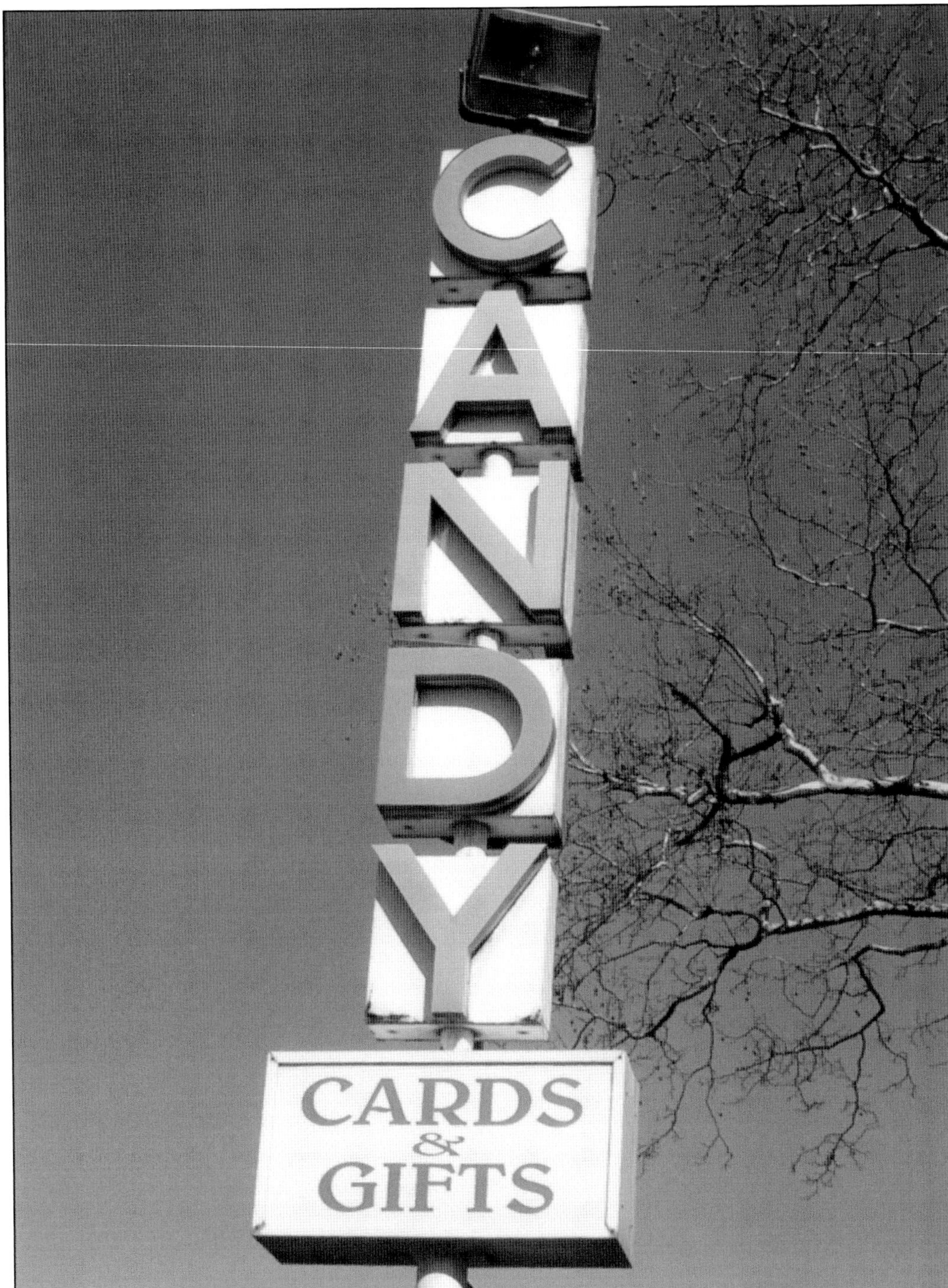

Up until 2013, this "Candy" sign at 1345 Easton Road lured in individuals with a sweet tooth. Stutz Candy Company has been located in Warrington for decades. Up until the mid-1980s, their shop stood on the same property but closer to the road. A fire at this location forced a new structure to be built.

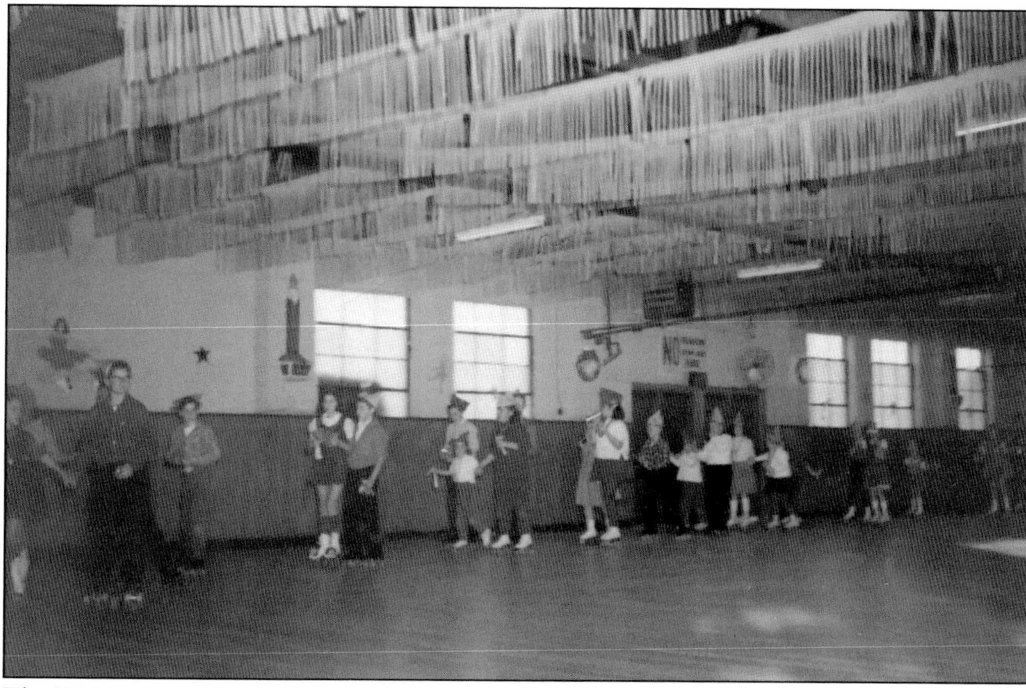

The Warrington Skating Rink, located at 925 Easton Road, was owned by George and Ann Mekosh beginning in 1955. It was a popular gathering site for all age groups. Youth and adult hockey leagues, public skating sessions, rink rental, and party packages were available. Ownership changed, and the rink remained open until the late 1990s. (Courtesy of the Lueckel family.)

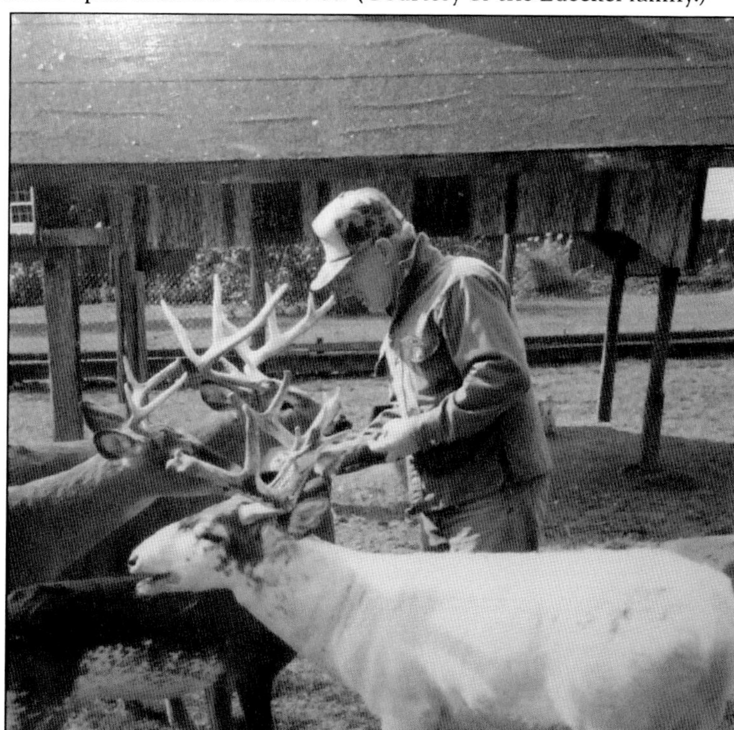

Across from the 611 Bar is where the Zaks family and many deer called home. Pictured here is Alexander Zaks. In the early 1950s, the family started to raise and sell deer as pets. The public could, at one time, pull off Easton Road to purchase produce at their stand and spend time with the deer and other animals on property. (Courtesy of Jeff Zaks Sr.)

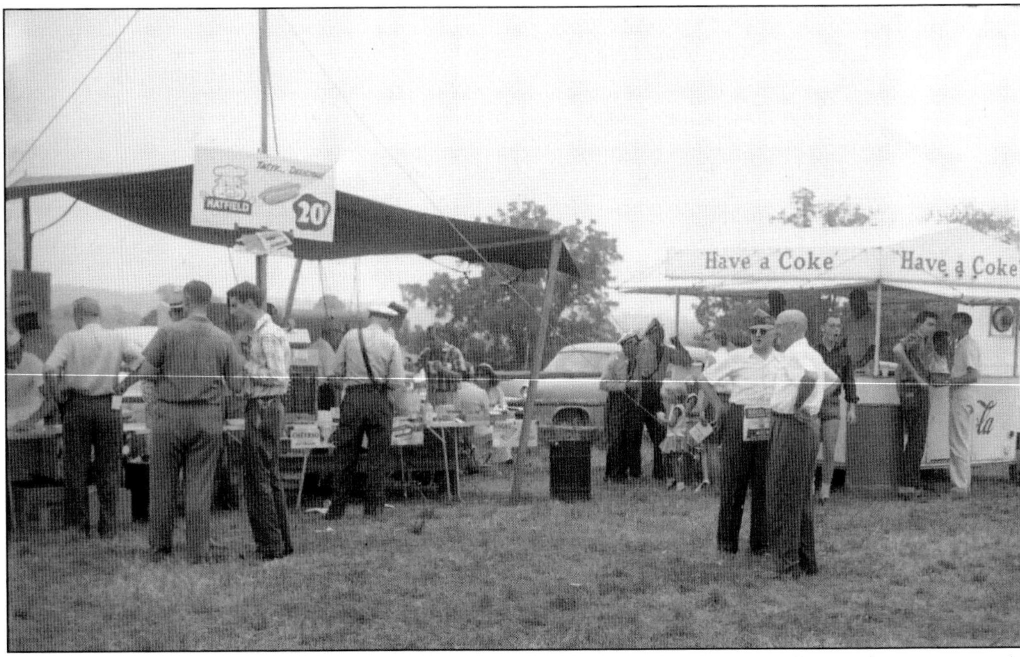

On December 28, 1954, Leonard H. Point was appointed to the position of township manager by the township supervisors. He assumed his duties on January 3, 1955. An official township office was set up in the basement of Point's home at 2080 Bristol Road. Point is seen here (right, with sunglasses) at the first Lions Club horse show in 1958, talking with Joseph Barness.

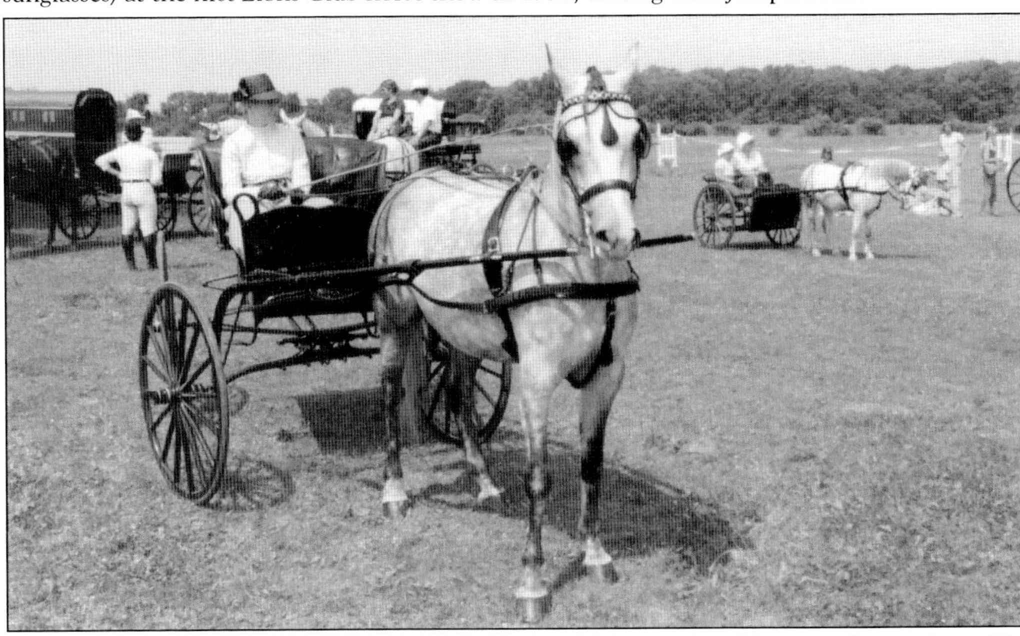

In August 1958, the Warrington Lions Club started holding an annual horse-and-pony show. The show grew steadily over more than 30 years, evolving from a one-day, one-ring, 32-horse event to a 400-horse competition over three days on multiple rings. Early shows benefited the Warrington Community Building, helping to pay mortgage and maintenance costs. Later, the shows would be held at John Rothrock's Redcoat Farm, located on Pickertown Road.

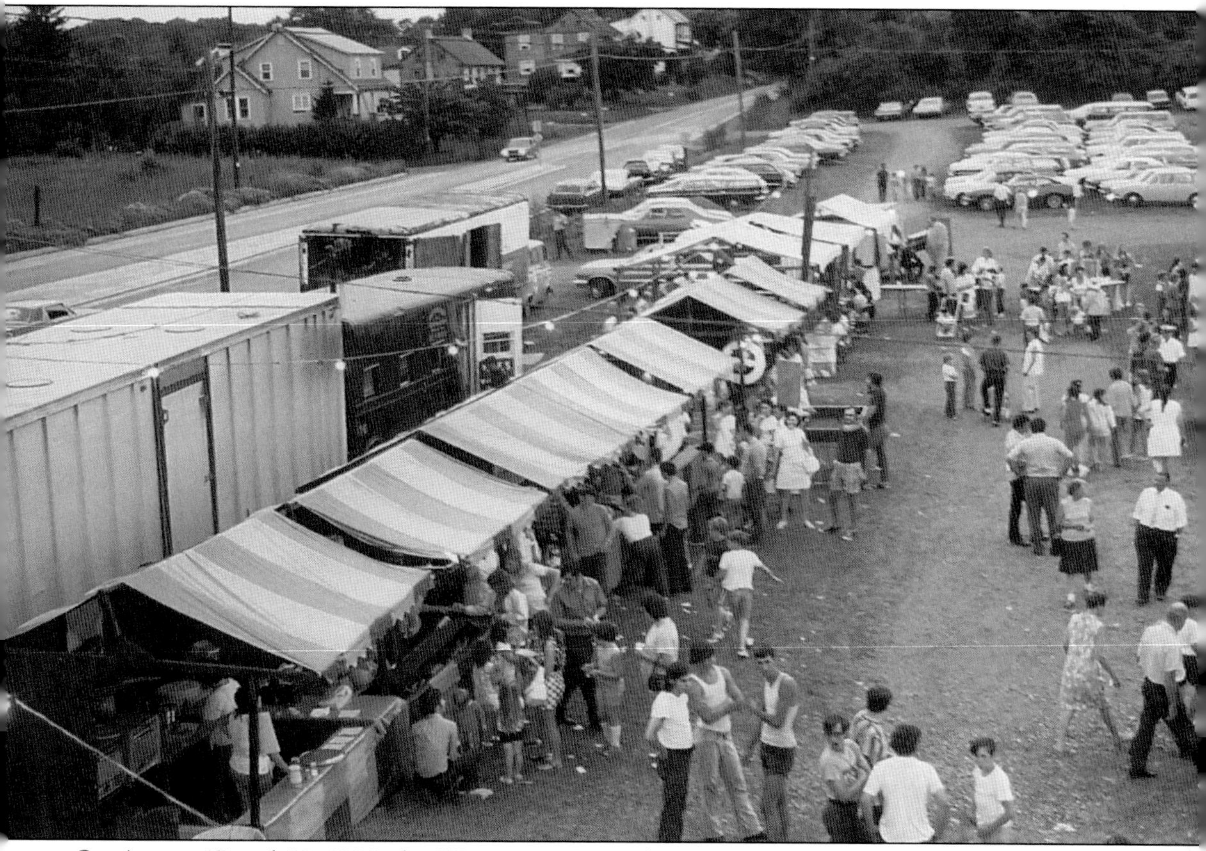

On August 27 and 28, 1926, the Warrington Township Fire Department held its first carnival to raise money for their building fund, which netted a profit of $286.42. On August 22 and 23, 1930, the carnival was held on land owned by the Kirsten family, located at the corner of Easton and Street Roads. This view shows the carnival's festivities in the early 1970s. (Courtesy of the Lueckel family.)

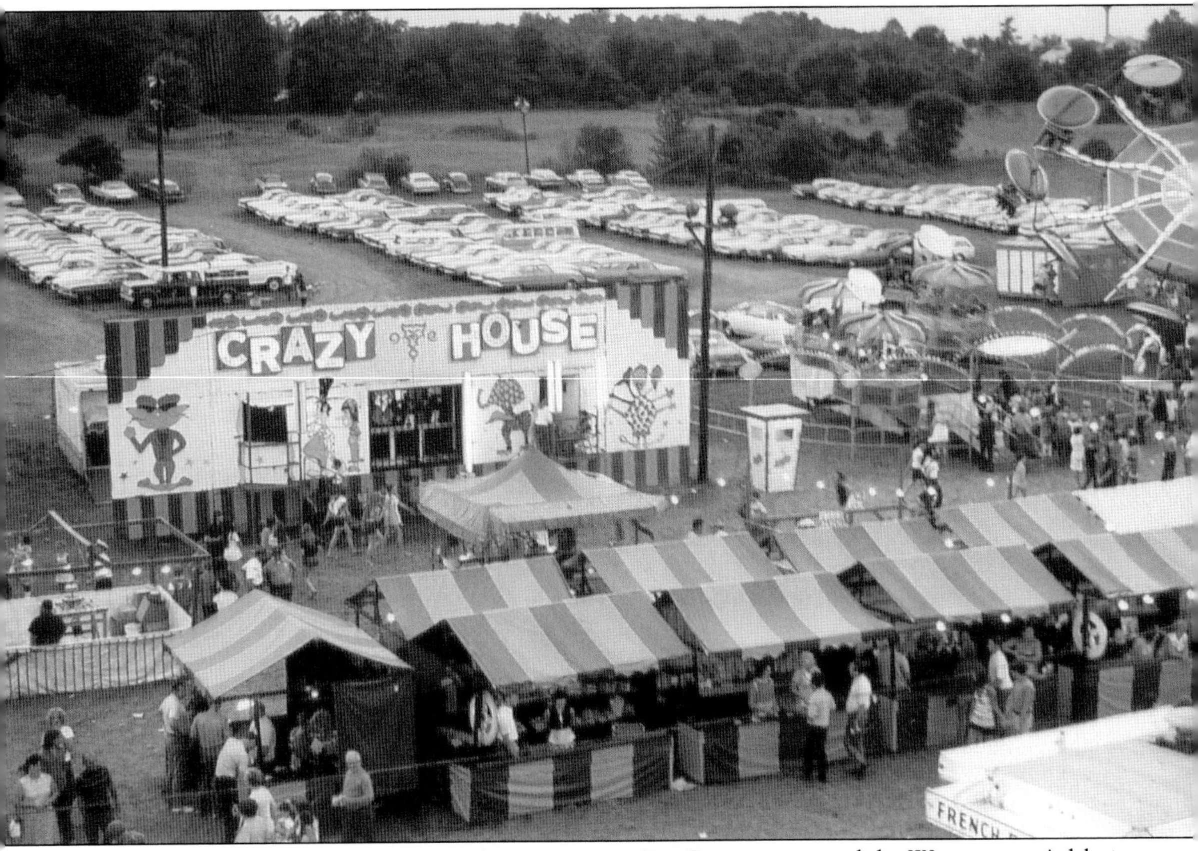

Later, these carnivals would benefit the Warrington Fire Department and the Warrington Athletic Association. The week of June 22, 1976, was the last time a carnival was held at this location. Shortly after it closed, bulldozers arrived, and the field was developed into the Warrington Plaza Shopping Center. Pictured here is another early-1970s view of the carnival's festivities. (Courtesy of the Lueckel family.)

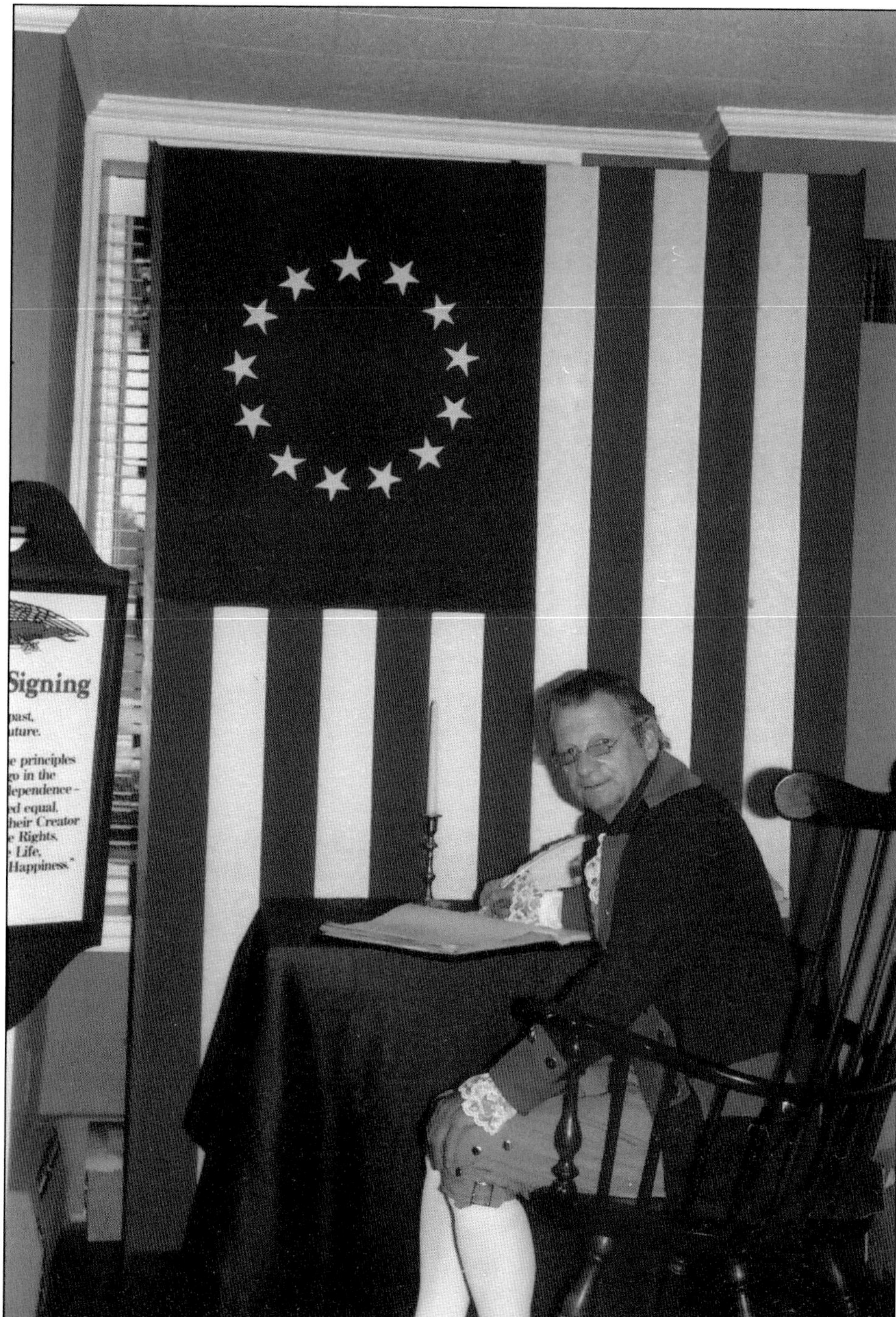

William Lueckel is seen here at the Hatboro Federal Savings Bank dressed in Colonial attire for Warrington's bicentennial. Lueckel served on the Warrington Township Board of Supervisors in 1973. In addition, he chaired many township commissions, including the one responsible for the celebration of the bicentennial in 1976. Lueckel also was a charter and life member of the Warrington Lions Club. (Courtesy of the Lueckel family.)

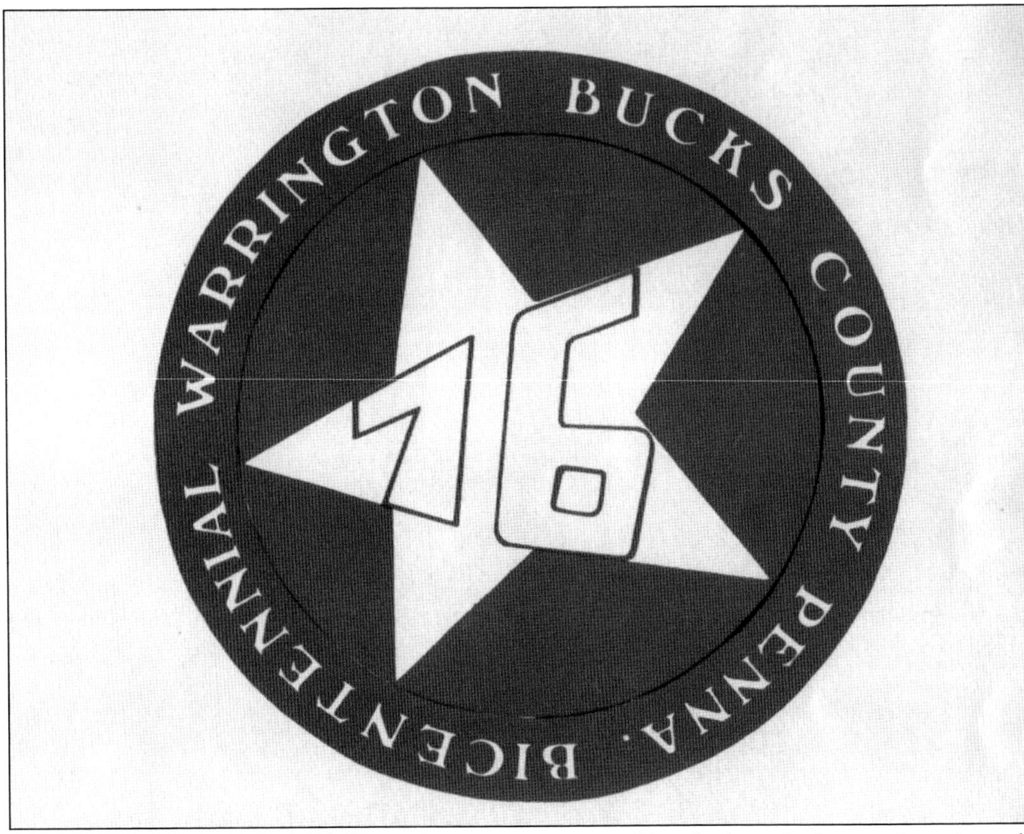

The Warrington Bicentennial Commission was appointed by the board of supervisors in early 1975. The members were Charles Card, Albert Dunbar, Nancy Gottshall, William Lahr, William Lueckel, Katy Scarborough, and Sally Steele. Shown is the Warrington Township seal designed by student Susan Sorace for the 1776–1976 bicentennial celebration. The seal was used on stationery and other official papers of the bicentennial commission.

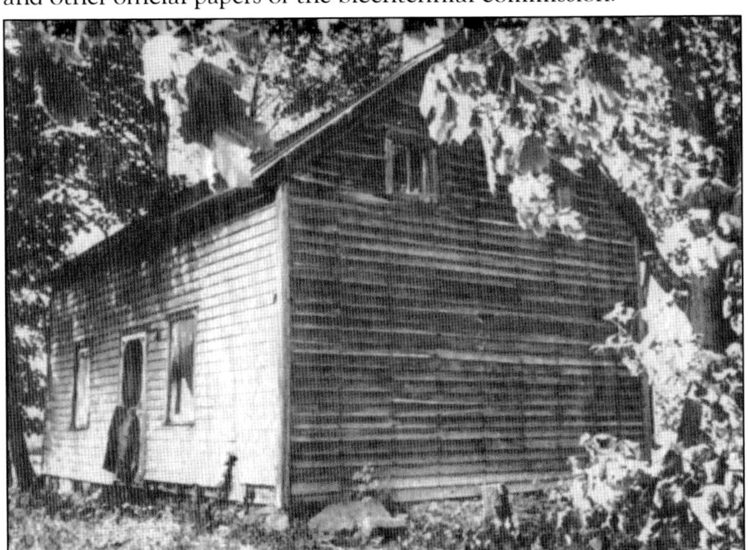

This log cabin, once located on Pickertown Road, was donated to the township by resident Margaret Kentopp. The structure was to be moved and restored as part of the bicentennial festivities. Although grants were applied for, and supervisor chairman Alvin Cohen asked for each adult to donated $1 to the cause, the cabin was never moved or restored and was razed in the 1980s.

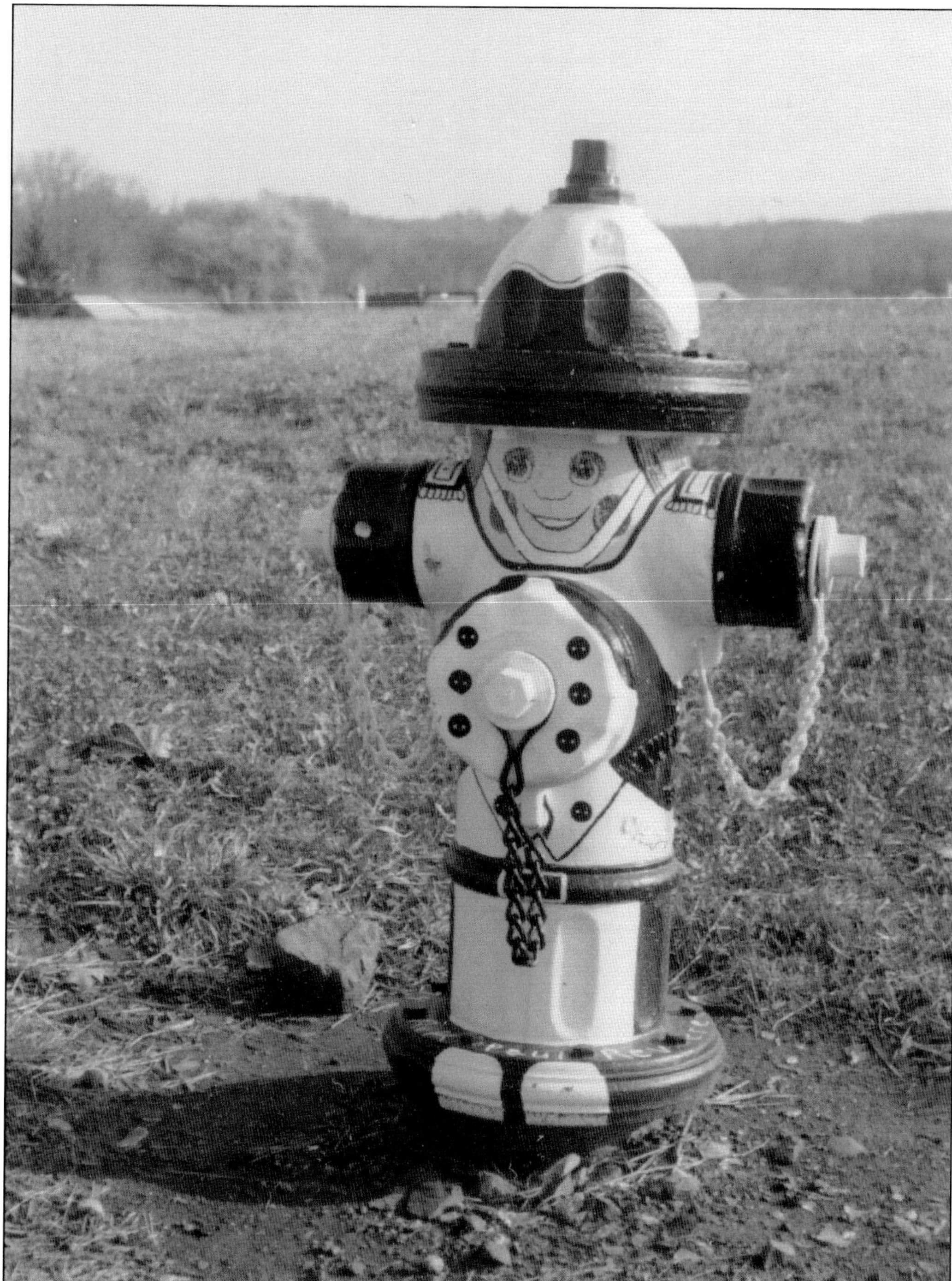

Fire hydrants throughout Warrington were painted as early as 1974 to resemble Colonial figures in preparation of the 1976 bicentennial celebration. Area school students were asked to design the figures. One of the benefits of the program was that residents were more proud of the hydrants, and township officials noted that while they were painted this way, grass was mowed, and snow was removed from the base of the hydrants without any delays.

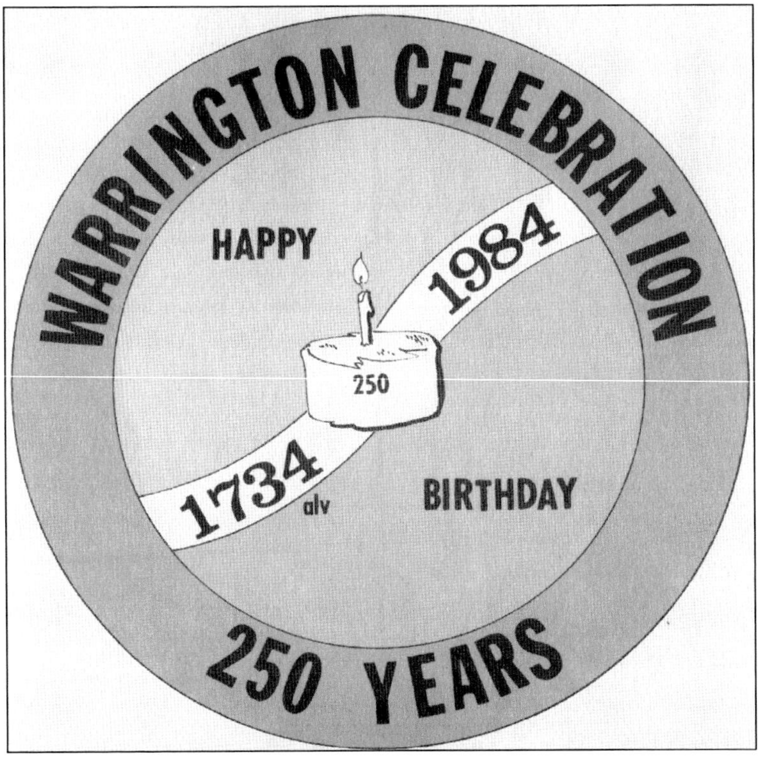

A history commission was formed to help celebrate the 250th anniversary of the township in 1984. The commission members were Amy Visco (chairman), Wesley Ahn, Susan Doerfler, Sally Engard, William Lueckel, Lois O'Donnell, and Laura Visco. The seal pictured here was created by Alice Visco. The commission created and printed a calendar for Warrington's anniversary that was made available to the residents.

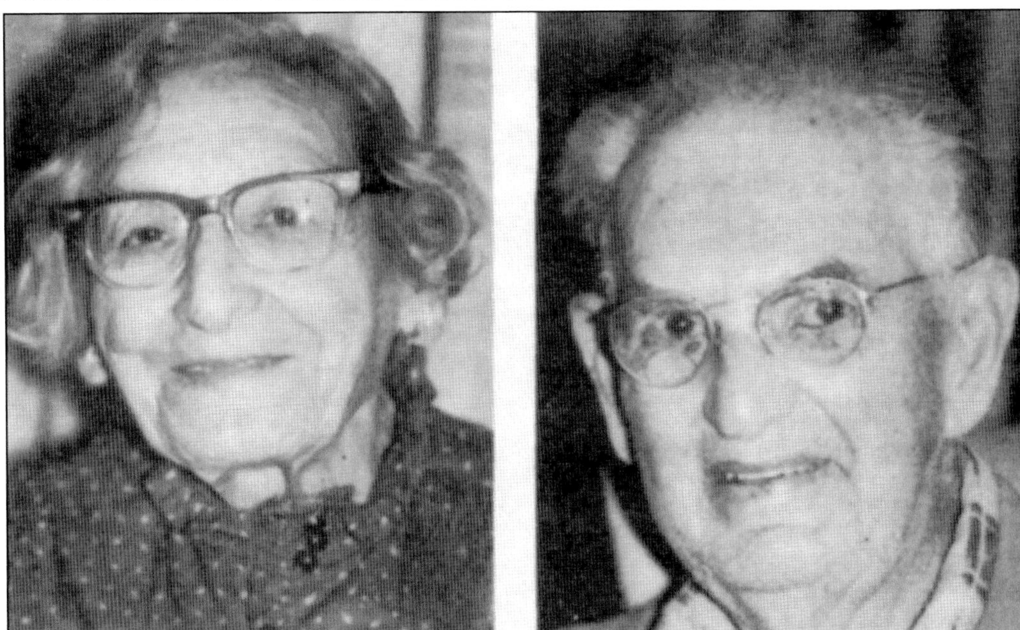

In 1984, as part of the 250th anniversary celebration, Anna Murray and Joseph Penrose were named Persons of the Year. Anna was selected for her years of service with the Women's Club and the Ladies Auxiliary for the fire department and as clerk of elections. Joseph was recognized for his years of service with the fire department, the school board, and his family's history within the township.

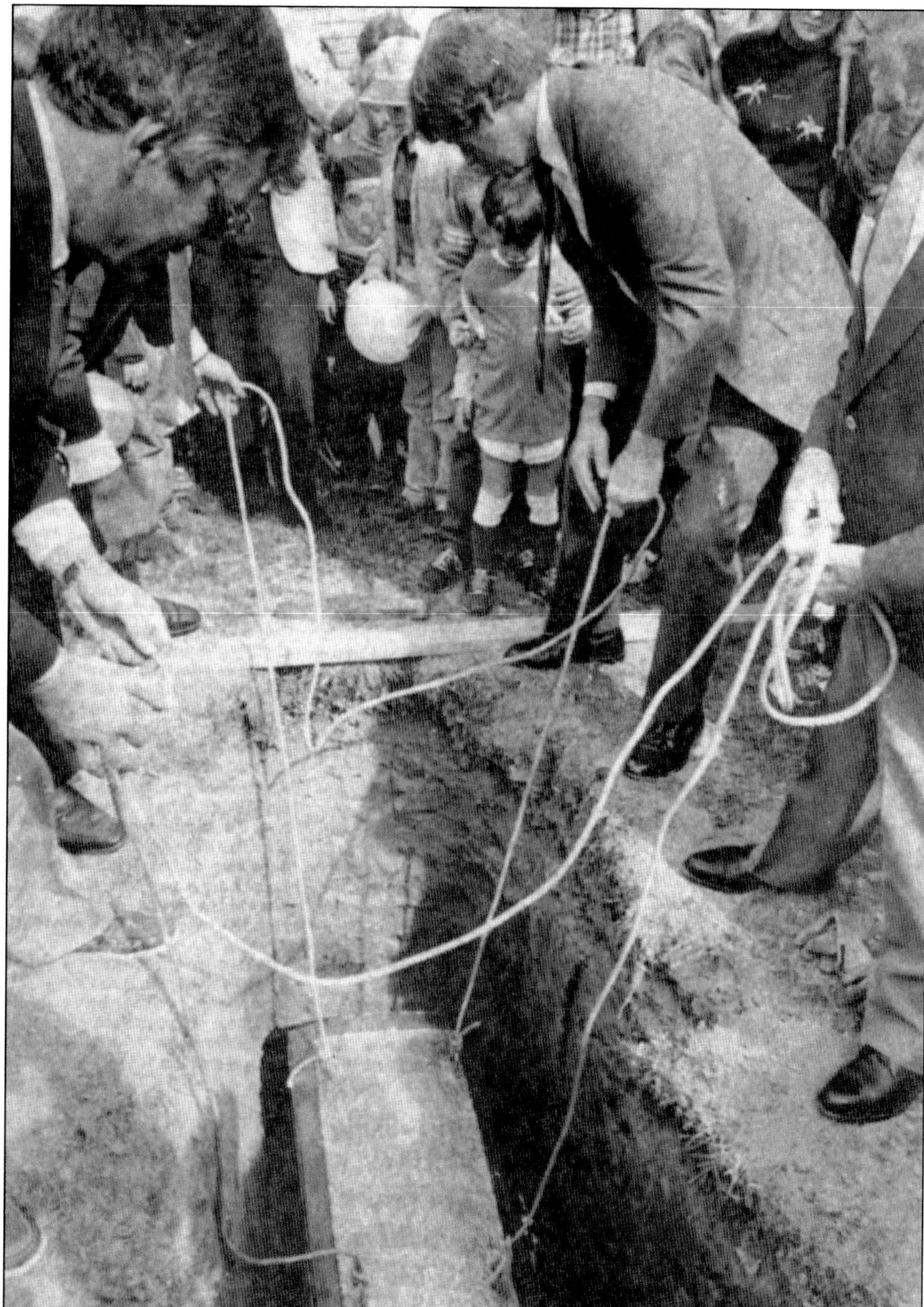

Surrounded by a curious crowd, Warrington Township supervisors, from left to right, James Molenari, John Meehan Jr., and Andrew Kaelin use ropes to lower the time capsule during the municipality's 250th anniversary celebration on October 7, 1984. The time capsule burial took place at the Warrington Fire Company building located on Easton Road and Freedoms Way. The time capsule is not to be opened until 2033, Warrington Township's 300th anniversary.

Bibliography

Battle, J.D. *The History of Bucks County*. Philadelphia, PA, 1887.

Capone, Delores Deabler. *From Wilderness to Bustling Community: A History of Warrington Township*. Warrington, PA, 1976.

Davis, William Watts Hart. *The History of Bucks County Pennsylvania*. 2nd ed. Doylestown, PA: Lewis Publishing Company, 1905.

Frackenthal Jr., Dr. B.F. *John Barclay-Biographical*. Riegelsville, PA: Bucks County Historical Society, 1938.

Hershey, S. *Business Directory and Gazetteer of Bucks County*, PA, 1871.

Pennsylvania Common School Register for the County Line School, Warrington Township, Warrington, PA: 1857–1858.

Penrose Sr., Joseph. Anne Miller, and Bertha Yowell. *Warrington Township Fire Department History 50th Anniversary*. Warrington, PA, 1974.

Proud, Robert. *Proud's History of Pennsylvania*. Philadelphia, 1797.

About the Organization

The Warrington Township Historic Commission was established by the board of supervisors on February 24, 1998. Five members were appointed, and the first meeting was held on October 5, 1999. Eventually, the commission added two additional appointments, bringing the total number of members to seven. The members of the Warrington Historic Commission formed the Warrington Historical Society in June 2007. The society was created to serve as an independent, tax-exempt organization to help with the solicitation of contributions and grants. The mission of the society is to locate, acquire, preserve, and exhibit any and all articles, documents, photographs, papers, artifacts, and other items of historical, cultural, or educational value that pertain to Warrington Township; develop educational materials for use with schools/the public and promote recognition of the history and development of Warrington Township; and restore and maintain 10 Folly Road/ County Line Road School House for use as headquarters/a museum/storage site of the society.

Anyone possessing an interest in preserving the history of Warrington Township and supporting the mission of the society may become a member. Please visit our web page at warringtonhistoricalsociety.org. The society can be contacted at PO Box 706, Warrington, PA 18976 or by email at warringtonhistoricalsociety@gmail.com.

Consistent with our mission to preserve history on a local level, this book was printed in South Carolina on American-made paper and manufactured entirely in the United States. Products carrying the accredited Forest Stewardship Council (FSC) label are printed on 100 percent FSC-certified paper.

MADE IN THE USA